LETTERS
FROM THE
DUST BOWL

LETTERS
FROM THE
DUST BOWL

BY CAROLINE HENDERSON

EDITED BY ALVIN O. TURNER

UNIVERSITY OF OKLAHOMA PRESS : NORMAN

Library of Congress Cataloging-in-Publication Data

Henderson, Caroline A. (Caroline Agnes) 1877–1966
  Letters from the Dust Bowl / by Caroline Henderson ; edited by Alvin O. Turner
    p. cm.
  Includes bibliographical references (p.) and index.
  ISBN 0–8061–3350–3 (alk. paper)
    1. Henderson, Caroline A. (Caroline Agnes), 1877–1966 2. Henderson, Caroline A. (Caroline Agnes), 1877–196 —Correspondence. 3. Women pioneers—Oklahoma—Oklahoma Panhandle—Biography. 4. Women pioneers—Oklahoma—Oklahoma Panhandle—Correspondence. 5. Dust storms—Oklahoma—Oklahoma Panhandle—History—20th century. 6. Droughts—Oklahoma—Oklahoma Panhandle—History—20th century. 7. Frontier and pioneer life—Oklahoma—Oklahoma Panhandle. 8. Oklahoma Panhandle (Okla.)—Biography. 9. Oklahoma Panhandle (Okla.)—History—20th century. 10. Oklahoma Panhandle (Okla.)— Rural conditions. I. Turner, Alvin O. (Alvin O'Dell), 1943– II. Title.

F702.N6 H46 2001
976.6'13053'092—dc21
  [B]   2001027569

The paper in this book meets the guidelines for permanence and durability of the Committee on Production Guidelines for Book Longevity of the Council on Library Resources, Inc. ♾

Text design by Ellen Beeler

1 2 3 4 5 6 7 8 9 10

For Mama and Carmelita

Henderson Homestead, 2000

The last person lived there
thirty-five years past, where
the barn roof is three-quarters gone
and folding.
The house—once the finest for miles—
now stands empty, forlorn,
bereft
of family and dreams.

They told her, too many times,
hollyhocks and such
did not belong here,
but her "brave flowers" endured
as long as she did, while
the lilac she brought from her Iowa home—
untended now three decades and more—
still flowers each spring
drawing on roots, deep in the land
she loved.

ALVIN O. TURNER

Contents

List of Illustrations   ix

Preface   xi

Introduction   3

1. Beginnings, 1908–1914   31

2. Hopeful Years, 1914–1928   63

3. Clouded Horizons, 1929–1934   93

4. Dust to Eat, 1935–1937   137

5. Slow and Partial Recovery, 1938–1951   167

6. When Hope Has Gone, 1952–1966   205

Epilogue   241

Notes   245

Bibliography   261

Index   269

Illustrations

Figures

(following page 125)
Caroline Boa and her sister, Susan, ca. 1885
Caroline and Will at the time of their wedding, 1908
Caroline and her sister, Susan, ca. 1936
Will and Caroline at a community gathering, 1964
The Henderson home, ca. 1908
Will and Eleanor outside their home, ca. 1911
Children gathering at Center school, where Caroline first taught,
    ca. 1914
Caroline and Will, July 1958
Henderson homestead covered by snow, ca. 1911
Caroline with one of her pets, ca. 1930
The Henderson home, ca. 1930
Construction of the Henderson barn, ca. 1925
An Oklahoma dust storm, September 8, 1937
Abandoned farmstead, Texas County, Oklahoma, 1937
A Panhandle orchard covered by dust, ca. 1936
Eleanor with Will harvesting broomcorn, 1911
Drifting dust reaches a barn roof in western Oklahoma, April 1935
Dust storm approaching Hooker, Oklahoma, June 4, 1937
Residents of Guymon, Oklahoma, watch as "roller" nears, 1937
Dust storm approaching Knowles, Oklahoma, 1935

Maps

Eva, Oklahoma, and environs   6
The Dust Bowl, 1933–1939   139

Preface

For the most part, working with Caroline Henderson's writings was an editor's dream. Her writing was nearly always well-organized, focused, and coherent, and she rarely misspelled words or made other grammatical errors. Even the variant spellings she employed, such as "plough" for "plow" and "drouth" for "drought," were used consistently and can be readily recognized by most readers. Moreover, a significant quantity of the material herein had been edited previously for publication. Together, these qualities permitted most of her writing to be published here as I found it. There were, of course, some exceptions, as well as certain editorial decisions that require explanation.

First, all of her writing that had been published previously has been reproduced herein as originally published. This was necessary because there are no known pre-publication drafts for any of her published writings. But it was also preferable—the published versions allow today's reader to experience her writing as did her original readers.

Within the chapters that follow, Henderson's published work is interspersed with her unpublished letters. Aligning the two types of material required organizing the published work either by the date of publication or by an estimate of when the pieces might have been written originally. I chose to date and organize the previously published writings by the date of publication rather than the estimated date of composition, recognizing that this could occasionally blur the chronology. The same problem presented itself in a slightly different guise in cases where personal correspondence was written at a date that would have required insertion within a body of published materials to maintain strict chronology. As that was clearly unacceptable, I chose to print such personal correspondence at the conclusion of the previously published material.

The conditions Caroline often encountered as she wrote presented another problem. She often wrote while working—while tending chickens, awaiting the birth of a calf, or churning butter—and she penned her letters by candlelight, in dust storms, or with temperatures below freezing. In later years, her deteriorating eyesight and handwriting compounded these already trying circumstances. Consequently, her intent regarding the placement of apostrophes for possessives and other fine points of punctuation is often unclear. In all such instances, I gave her writing the benefit of the doubt and followed the standards she usually employed.

There were four other areas where her usual practices required editorial decisions. First, she never wanted to waste paper and became even more careful about such matters in the last decades of her life. Her efforts to conserve paper meant that she often used very slight, if any, indentation for paragraphs, so it is possible that some of the paragraph structure herein is mine rather than what she intended.

Similarly, she did not always follow formal systems for quoting poetry, particularly in the less formal letters to her daughter. Sometimes she underscored lines and copied them in verse form; in other instances she quoted them with diagonals or dashes separating the verses. When she did follow more formal conventions, she either used quote marks or underlining to set the poetry apart. As there seemed to be no good reason to replicate these variations, I italicized longer poetry extracts and set them in verse and put shorter quotations in quote marks, run-in with the rest of the text.

Third, her closing salutations often ran into the body of her letters, which sometimes flowed from the back of printed pages or greeting cards she had adapted, to the fronts and around the edges. Even if it were possible to replicate that practice, neither it nor the appearance of her run-on closings would contribute that much to the reader's understanding. Again, I followed conventional forms in every instance.

Finally, in order to save space for material that might contribute to the reader's understanding or appreciation, I chose not to copy her closing signature. She signed "Caroline" to her friend Rose Alden, "Caroline Henderson" or "The Hendersons" to Eli Jaffe, and "Mother" to Eleanor with no major variations.

Other editorial decisions arose from the need to condense the large volume of her available writing. I chose to include most of her published writing except for much that she wrote for *The Practical Farmer* and *Ladies' World*. In the case of the former, her discussions of the merits of turkey raising and similar concerns seemed to offer little of note. Of the material from *Ladies' World*, I included only enough to give a flavor of her writing for that publication. That meant cutting a great deal of material that exemplifies Caroline's writing style or that could very well contribute to a discussion of the content of women's magazines in the early twentieth century. However, the inclusion of that material would have forced cuts from other bodies of material that I regarded as most representative of her life and contributions. I also chose selectively from the many letters she wrote to Eleanor in the last two decades of her life, the sheer volume of which virtually required sampling from that time period.

I always denoted the omission of material within the body of a publication or letter by ellipses, as neither Caroline nor her editors ever used that device. Conversely, Caroline often used dashes, so I refrained from their use. However, in some of the letters that Rose Alden condensed, she may have used dashes as I did ellipses—to denote omission. As the originals are not available, it is impossible to determine if the dashes in those letters are Alden's or Caroline's.

Bracketed interpolations are always mine and are intended to clarify abbreviations or other devices Caroline employed. End notes are intended to clarify her meaning, or, more often, to identify literary references or particular individuals she mentioned.

The experience of bringing this book together has reminded me why the author of Ecclesiastes lamented that "the writing of many books is endless." Endless too are the debts accumulated in the process of researching and writing. This book would never have been completed if not for the contributions of dozens of individuals. I hope that acknowledging the following people will demonstrate my recognition of the diverse contributions of those who have spurred, facilitated, and enriched my efforts.

My accumulation of debts began when I read Eli Jaffe's *Oklahoma Odyssey*. Jaffe's account of his meeting with Caroline Henderson shed new light on the woman I recognized only for her writings on the dust bowl. In turn, that perspective led to the beginnings of a dream to produce a small book using Henderson's writings to document her life on the plains. Jaffe's willingness to share the letters Henderson had written to him was the first step toward fulfillment of that goal. The second step came with the discovery of a collection of Henderson's letters in the archives at Mount Holyoke College, South Hadley, Massachusetts. The Henderson Collection at Mount Holyoke was compiled between 1908 and 1957 by Rose Alden, Henderson's girlhood friend and college classmate, who had retained many of the letters she and her mother had received from Henderson. Alden's letters added still more to my growing appreciation of Henderson as pioneer, woman, and writer and virtually assured a valid portrayal of her life through the dust bowl years. Patricia Albright and the Mount Holyoke archives staff proved most helpful at this stage, as they would for the remainder of the project.

The picture grew sharper and more complete when I encountered Dr. Eleanor Grandstaff, Henderson's only child. Grandstaff, who was among the first women graduates from the University of Kansas medical school, obviously inherited a fair share of her mother's abilities and embodied many of her personal qualities as well. The latter included a frugality that explains her retention of hundreds of the letters her mother wrote during the last two decades of her life, plus hitherto undocumented publications with *Ladies' World* and other magazines. Dr. Grandstaff's generosity with those resources, as well as with her photographs and her memories, enriched my life as well as my research.

By that time, the small book I had envisioned initially had grown to its present proportions. In the meantime, encouraging words from assorted friends and colleagues including Davis Joyce, Brad Luckinbill, Tom Cowger, Ken Brown, and Wayne Morgan spurred me onward as my debts accumulated. Annette Sneller found and mailed me the notes I had lost at the international crossing from Detroit into Canada after a crucial visit with Grandstaff. That visit was facilitated by Dolores Slowinski and her husband, Bob D'Aoust. Diana Turpen shared results of her research on Evelyn Harris, and John Winteringer helped to fill in the gaps on Henderson's family history. I also benefited from Stan Pollard's ready photographic expertise and the cartographic efforts of Serena Aldrich. Likewise, a host of Oklahoma Panhandle resources contributed their memories of the Hendersons and otherwise helped my research. Even a partial list must include the contributions of Jo Patton, Mr. and Mrs. Lee Johnson, and Maureen Minns.

This book was also made possible through the efforts of a number of people who worked directly on its publication. Randolph Lewis, the first editor I worked with at the University of Oklahoma Press, both encouraged and provided direction for my efforts, a pattern that continued in subsequent work with Jean Hurtado and her assistant, Susan Garrett, project editor Jo Ann Reece, and copy editor Patricia Heinicke.

Despite all that help, I am certain this book would still be on another of my many "back burners" if not for the continuing contributions of my secretaries, Janet Alexander and Sarah Garcia. Besides making my job manageable, each also provided invaluable assistance in varied aspects of the book's compilation. Sarah's efforts were especially helpful. Her ability to follow my editing notes and to accurately cut and move materials ultimately ensured that I was able to maintain some sense of order among an assortment of hundreds of letters and related sources.

Finally, my wife, Carmelita, graces every project I undertake. Although she does not particularly value the making of books, she is a perceptive critic who always manages to enjoy hours or even days in varied locations—from the Oklahoma Panhandle to abandoned courthouses or assorted archives. In short, she remains the silver answer to my every question.

LETTERS
FROM THE
DUST BOWL

Introduction

The life and writings of Caroline Henderson offer one of the more compelling stories of the American experience. A graduate of one of the leading liberal arts schools of her time, Caroline began homesteading in the Oklahoma Panhandle in 1907. She and her husband, Will, continued to pioneer in that harsh environment until shortly before her death in 1966, struggling against recurring droughts, dust storms, and similar disasters. Raising her daughter, laboring in the fields as well as in her home, she also found the time to attract a national following as a writer at two different points in her life and to complete a Master's degree in literature from the University of Kansas at the age of fifty-eight.

Caroline Henderson has been recognized for more than fifty years for the quality of her depictions of life on the Great Plains. A number of articles published between 1931 and 1937 in *Atlantic Monthly* and elsewhere drew national attention to the farmer's plight during the Depression and dust bowl era. The importance of those articles, especially the one entitled "Letters from the Dust Bowl," has been acknowledged by virtually every significant witness or chronicler of that dramatic era in American history.[1] In May 1936, Secretary of Agriculture Henry A. Wallace wrote to her, praising her contribution to American "understanding of some of our farm problems and the courage with which farmers are meeting them." Similarly, Vance Johnson's seminal study, *Heaven's Tableland*, along with a 1959 CBS television documentary, Donald Worster's *Dust Bowl,* and numerous other works on the era all recognize the importance of her firsthand accounts of the struggle for survival during one of the great environmental disasters of the twentieth century.[2]

Although the value of "Letters From The Dust Bowl" has been recognized for a generation, the full potential of Caroline's articles has been obscured by the narrow focus of both historical and literary treatments of the dust bowl. Most accounts create an impression of a "dust bowl moment,"[3] focusing on either the scope of that environmental disaster as portrayed in the many memorable photographs of the era, or on the resultant migration of "Okies" to California as depicted in John Steinbeck's *Grapes of Wrath.* In contrast, Caroline provided a portrait of those who stayed to face the stark conditions, which reduced living conditions on the Great Plains to a ceaseless struggle for survival. In doing so, she produced "a vital chronicle of one of the most pathetic and most heroic chapters in American history."[4]

Caroline's real significance extends far beyond the legacy of a series of articles she wrote about a single significant event. As Wallace recognized, she called the attention of an increasingly urban, industrialized America to the "changing, and in many ways diminishing place of agriculture in the American economy and vision."[5] In effect, those changes mirrored the destruction of the Jeffersonian promise, the nineteenth-century version of the American dream that portrayed the agrarian frontier as the foundation of American civilization.[6] The record of her life as a twentieth-century pioneer adds to our understanding of these fundamental shifts in American life. It also offers unique insights into the history of the Great Plains, where pioneering conditions, environmental threats, and relative isolation persisted through much of the twentieth century.

At the same time, Caroline's letters and published writings reveal a remarkable woman whose qualities far exceeded those seen in her analyses of the dust bowl era. True to the liberal arts tradition in which she had been educated, Caroline's vision always extended well beyond her isolated home on the high plains of Oklahoma to the larger world of culture and politics. Yet her interests were always rooted in her love of the land and nature. These values were also seen in her attention to the issues and people she encountered through her reading and correspondence. She wrote to dozens of individuals, ranging from childhood and college friends to an assortment of Unitarian ministers, former neighbors, authors whose books she enjoyed, and those who had written her in response to one of her articles. She treated letter writing as a literary effort but also used it to find comfort amid the struggles that threatened her dreams and her happiness.

Caroline Henderson was at first glance an unlikely chronicler of crucial chapters in frontier history. Born Caroline Agnes Boa in 1877, she was the oldest child in a prosperous farm family. Her father, Robert Boa, had immigrated from Canada to Wisconsin and then to a home near Clinton, Iowa, where Caroline spent her first seven years before her family moved across the state to Kingsley. At Kingsley, Boa established a successful farming operation that allowed him to provide an education for his children and a comfortable retirement for himself. Caroline attended Mount Holyoke College, which was then establishing itself as a leader in the teaching of the liberal arts, where she completed a degree in language and literature in 1901. Caroline then began teaching English and Latin in the Des Moines public schools. Her younger sister, Susan (Susie), chose business rather than academic preparation, which led to a successful career and prosperous life and marriage.[7]

In 1907, Caroline nearly died of diphtheria. Sometime during a prolonged recovery, she briefly rejoined her parents who had moved to Ponca City, Oklahoma, where Susie was employed. Caroline's physical illness produced an emotional crisis that led to her decision to abandon teaching to pursue a girlhood dream. That dream had been defined in the 1901 Mount Holyoke class prophecy, which portrayed her future "somewhere on a western ranch."[8] In a larger sense, her vision reflected her lifetime commitment to the Jeffersonian vision of a society based on prosperous, middle-class farmers.[9] By her early years, Caroline's commitment had been linked to a hope for advancing the frontier culturally as well as geographically. For Caroline personally, it also meant being able to achieve for herself the quality of life she had experienced in her girlhood home while providing a better life for her offspring, as her father had done for her.

Within months of her move to Oklahoma, Caroline determined to begin homesteading in the Oklahoma Panhandle. She secured a job at Center school near a settlement now known as Eva, establishing a claim on a quarter section of land across the road from the school. She resided at that location for all except the last few months of her life. She met Wilhelmine Eugene (Will) Henderson, her future husband, while he was a member of a crew she hired to dig a well on her claim. They courted for the next few months and then journeyed thirty miles by wagon to the county seat town of Guymon to be married on May 7, 1908.[10]

Caroline later wrote to her childhood friend and college classmate, Rose Alden, of that event as "the day of creation of our new world . . . one of the most perfect days I have ever seen." She remembered their return journey to the homestead as a "treasure" to carry through both life and eternity. Will would later comment, to her apparent dismay, that the well he had dug on her homestead was "the

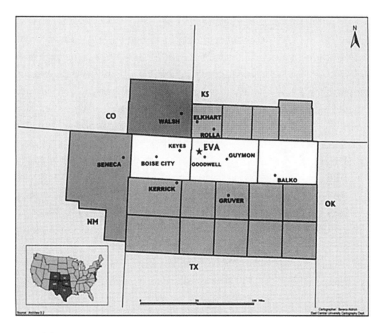

Eva, Oklahoma, and environs

best he had ever dug" so he "decided to keep it and the school teacher who went with it."[11]

Will and Caroline shared 1877 as their birth years, and at first glance that appeared to be one of the few things they held in common. He was born in or near Mulvane, Kansas, and probably acquired fewer than three years of schooling. He left home at the age of fifteen to spend the next half of his life as an itinerant cowboy and well digger. He was almost six feet tall but probably never weighed more than 150 pounds. His skin was darkened by life on the prairie, and Caroline once noted that she could not call him handsome, but she complimented his gentleness, optimistic spirit, and straightforward manner. Better yet, he liked books and shared her commitment to the land.

Will's love for books and his regard for learning, probably nurtured during the many lonely hours he had spent during his wanderings, were strengthened and refined throughout his marriage to Caroline. In turn, she was delighted to discover that he had carried a Bible with him on his wanderings and read from it regularly. He also encouraged her reading, insisting that her workday should stop when his did. The corollary to that rule was that he was as willing to help with her tasks as she was with his. He regularly assisted with household chores in the evenings and would do the dishes alone on the rare occasions when she had guests.

Will was also a versatile handyman. Except for the original claim shack, he built their home and most, if not all, of the barns and sheds. The house was considered one of the finer homes in the area, even years after it was built. Likewise, he did all of his own plumbing and most of the mechanical work on their automobiles and farm equipment, drawing on professionals only when he did not have the tools required for major rebuilding efforts. He spent many evenings engaged in hooking rugs, making cabinets, and similar projects to improve their home.

Besides cooking and house work, Caroline's workday consisted primarily of caring for their poultry and livestock, gardening, and a myriad of related tasks. She was proud of her ability to feed the family from the fruits of her garden and the farm. She managed to satisfy at least 75 percent of the family's needs until their last years on the farm. Her pursuit of self-sufficiency also required that she take on many laborious tasks, including grinding her own wheat for cereal and flour for bread and canning produce from her garden.[12]

Profits from the turkeys she raised were one of the family's most important sources of cash in the early years. Likewise, she reported as late as 1951 that "egg money," the profits from her chickens, netted more than two times their annual expenses for groceries.[13] The poultry she raised was also a major source of meat along with that obtained from butchering an occasional pig. For the most part, the Hendersons and their neighbors did not eat much beef. Cattle were too important as a source of cash to be eaten in the financially strapped households of Panhandle farmers.

Caroline also helped with any other tasks that needed to be done on the farm and was solely responsible for all duties anytime her husband was absent. She regularly assisted at harvests, herded cattle, and attended the birth of calves. One illustration of the range of her activities is her college paper "The Day When the Well Runs Dry," which describes her work helping Will pull the pump from their well.[14] Even in her last years on the farm, Caroline was still active, feeding livestock, shoveling grain, helping Will repair farm equipment, and regularly adding hours to her workday by cultivating a wide variety of flowers.

There were comparable demands on Will's time, and so the Hendersons was not always able to keep the rule about setting aside the evenings for reading. When they were able to honor their shared commitment, either they would read individually or Caroline would read aloud from the Bible or the few books she had retained from her teaching and college years. They added to the family library as the years passed, although financial constraints prevented them from purchasing more than an occasional book, especially in the early years. Much of their need for reading material was filled by family and friends. Rose Alden was their primary donor in the early years, a role later filled by their daughter and by regional library services.

Though Will was later especially devoted to westerns, he seemed to enjoy listening as Caroline read aloud from the variety of materials she enjoyed. They maintained that tradition as a family, often following a time of reading with related discussions. In the early years, her basic reading started with the Bible, regional and local newspapers, and varied farm journals and magazines such as *Practical Farmer*, *Mothers' Magazine*, *Everybody's*, *Success*, and the *American*. Subsequently, she added *Atlantic Monthly*, *Harper's*, *Time*, and *Arizona Highways* as her interests changed or as her earlier favorites ceased publication. At some point in their first decade on the farm, she began introducing to the mix assorted Unitarian publications, especially the *Christian Register.*

Caroline also read extensively in the classics, contemporary literature, and nonfiction, consciously selecting diverse materials. In 1911, for example, she read two histories, four contemporary novels, and two classics. A number of monographs on different topics and some of Charles Lamb's essays completed the mix. She lamented her neglect of poetry that year but had read two volumes of verse plus frequent selections from poetry anthologies she owned.[15] She probably supplemented her poetry reading by drawing on her remarkable gift for memorizing poetry, still evident as late as 1952. For example, in 1952 she requested a copy of "The Chambered Nautilus" from her daughter but then reported she had reconstructed most of it from memory during the ensuing weeks.[16]

The Land

The Hendersons' mutual commitment to the land was often tested but never broken. Caroline and Will discussed alternatives to keeping their farm, particularly during their early struggles, but they always determined to hold onto what they were building. In her Master's thesis, "The Love of the Soil as a Motivating Force in Literature Relating to the Early Development of the Middle West," Caroline explained the feeling that underlay their persistence. She defined the love of the soil as an appreciation of "the natural loveliness of unspoiled earth" and as a deep "inner response to ploughed ground," which drew people to the land and supported "one element of an eager, vitalizing love of liberty."[17] Ironically, she completed her thesis for the University of Kansas in 1935, a peak year for the dust storms that would destroy many of her hopes but not her love of the land.

Every element of Caroline's life affirmed her attention and devotion to that love and the corresponding values contained in the Jeffersonian vision. For example, she wrote of their farm, alluding to her Mount Holyoke class prophecy, "Our 'ranch' however, is a quarter section of Uncle Sam's land which will some day be my own if we keep our part of the contract. . . . Though we have the disadvantages as well as the inspiration of being so near the beginning of things, our pioneer life has for me an interest and a fascination that no other experience has equaled." She went on to note the "fullness of life" she experienced on her claim. And by her values, one of the most complimentary things she ever wrote about Will was in dedicating her Master's thesis to him as "a lover of the soil."[18]

Their shared love of the soil does much to explain the Hendersons' persistence through almost sixty years on their homestead. They found inner joy, a sense of purpose, and even beauty on Oklahoma's high plains. Thus, they stayed and worked when others abandoned their claims; they persisted through the dark years of the dust bowl; and they continued to work long after their energies and hopes had vanished with their youth and dreams of success.

The Hendersons' location on the southern plains assured that their land would require all they had to give in each of their six decades on their farm. Those who would enjoy the land's stark beauty and profit from its fertile soils must be prepared to face regular challenges from an environment that often seems hostile to every effort for human advance, if not to human survival itself. Droughts and floods, blizzards and scorching heat, and the ever present winds, which spawn dust storms nearly every spring, still regularly ruin crops and threaten the quality of life for residents of the plains. During almost sixty years, Caroline reported fewer than ten bumper crops. In every other year, adverse weather assured that the land would produce less than its potential and fall far short of the Henderson's investment in capital and labor.

That experience explained her defense of the historian, Walter Prescott Webb, in response to an article he wrote for *Harper's* in 1957. Webb's assertion that aridity was the primary determinant of Great Plains development triggered a storm of criticism from across the West. In contrast, Caroline wrote to her daughter, Eleanor, that she did not see any basis for disagreeing with that judgment. She went on to argue specifically that her experience supported Webb's estimate that Great Plains farmers would suffer crop failures at least one year out of four.[19]

Such harsh conditions help to explain why the southern plains generally and the Oklahoma Panhandle in particular were one of the last settled regions in the continental United States. Historic factors and perceptions also contributed to that result. The earliest explorers, as well as later visitors, were often disoriented by the relative lack of trees in the land. The Spanish, who claimed the region for more than two hundred fifty years, utilized it primarily as a buffer zone to protect lands they valued more.

Americans did little more in the first fifty years after acquiring a claim to the region in the Louisiana Purchase of 1803. Sixteen years later, the American explorer Stephen Long described the region as the "Great American Desert." Long's unfortunate choice of words accounted for much of the subsequent American reluctance to occupy the southern plains, although two generations after he encountered the blowing dust and blazing heat of western Oklahoma, Americans had yet to acquire the technology and techniques that would make farming possible there.

In the meantime, ranchers moved vast herds of cattle into the region, finally exploiting its potential as grazing land in the years following the Civil War. The farmers' frontier advanced haltingly, often retreating, in the face of periodic droughts or other weather-related problems. Nevertheless, favorable homestead laws and other government actions and the extension of the railroads enabled farmers to supplant ranchers on most of the southern plains by 1890. Isolated pockets remained, however, where the railroads were yet too distant or where other factors discouraged farmers from settlement. One such enclave was a region about 35 miles wide and 167 miles long located between the Texas Panhandle and the southern border of Kansas. This was the area that would subsequently become the Panhandle of Oklahoma and home to the Hendersons.

This area was identified as "No Man's Land" on the maps of the era—a name that described its legal status as well as the impressions of many who had encountered it. Although ranching interests claimed most of the region during the 1880s, it had never been attached to the jurisdiction of any state or territory. That situation changed in 1890 when Congress passed the Organic Act, which provided government for Oklahoma Territory and made No Man's Land the seventh county in the new territory. Officially designated as Beaver County, it soon became known as the Panhandle because of its peculiar shape.

Territorial status and the continued movement of the railroad, which reached nearby Liberal, Kansas, in 1887, encouraged the first movement of homesteaders into old No Man's Land, but only the hardiest ventured there, and many of those found it too great a challenge. As a result, the Panhandle grew slowly, attaining populations of only 2,674 people in 1890 and 3,051 a decade later. The greatest land boom in the region's history took place in the next seven years as land promoters and a generation of land hungry farmers focused on one of the last large areas of free land in the public domain.[20]

The pace of settlement accelerated as Oklahoma statehood approached. More than thirty-two thousand new settlers had moved into Beaver County by 1907 when Oklahoma was admitted to the union, among them Caroline Boa and Will Henderson. The Oklahoma Constitutional Convention then divided the Panhandle into three counties of comparable size. The central county, where Caroline had settled, was designated Texas County. Its population at statehood was 16,448, the largest number of people to occupy its 2,040 square miles until that bench mark was reached once more in the last decade of the twentieth century.

The population decline began immediately thereafter, and more than two thousand Texas County residents had already left by the 1910 census.[21] A dry year in 1908 broke many of the hopeful farmers. More were driven out by the inherent problems they encountered in trying to build lives and farms, often with limited resources, far from supplies or markets. Railroads did not reach the Hendersons' immediate area until 1916. Thus, even when their fields were productive, their profits were reduced by transportation costs.

The Homestead Lady

The Hendersons surmounted the first tests of their loyalty to the land as they would later ones. Living in primitive conditions far removed from medical help or other needs, Caroline gave birth to her first and only child, Sarah Eleanor, in 1910. The family continued to break new

ground, and they survived a second major drought that year by relying on the proceeds from a previous good year of crops, income from
the turkeys Caroline raised, and the occasional work Will was able to
secure from neighboring farms and ranches. Caroline weathered every
adversity, relishing her time with her baby and even the toil in the
fields, reflecting cheerfully on both her dreams and struggles.

Events beginning in the fall of 1912 shattered her confidence. A
prolonged dry spell began that September, and there was virtually no
snow the following winter. Great Plains agriculture is always threatened by moisture shortages, with average precipitation in the region
barely above the seventeen inches required for most regional crops. An
equally important variable, however, is the timing of the precipitation,
as the winter snows are the most dependable source of water for primary crops such as wheat. The Panhandle region received less than
one inch total precipitation in the ten months prior to July 1913.[22]

With no hope for a harvest that year, Caroline was desperate. On
July 16, she wrote a letter to the Ways and Means editor of *Ladies'
World* magazine, requesting suggestions for ways to help supplement
her income. The editor responded two weeks later with what she
acknowledged was a most unusual reply for one in her position. She
suggested that Caroline might try writing for the magazine. Caroline
responded quickly and in October received the welcome word that her
submission had been accepted. The editor enclosed a check plus some
books to "fill a niche on your book shelves."[23]

The phenomenal response to Caroline's article about her first years
on the homestead soon justified the editor's confidence. She reported
an outpouring of mail that exceeded anything in the magazine's history. That response led to a new identity for Caroline. She became
Ladies' World's "Homestead Lady," a role she continued until the magazine ceased publication in early 1918.

Caroline's initial letter to the editor did not hint that she had any
hope of writing for the magazine. Although she may have had exactly
that idea in mind, she was always ambivalent about writing for publication or income and evidently felt some embarrassment about her
plea for assistance. She never acknowledged writing for *Ladies' World*
to Rose Alden or other correspondents, although she mentioned every
prior and subsequent publication in her letters. Similarly, she used a
pseudonym when writing for *Ladies' World*, signing her contributions
as "Mrs. H.A.C.," and she used only the first letters of town names she
referred to.

The notion that Caroline could write for profit may have been encouraged by prior successes she had writing short pieces for the *Practical Farmer* in 1912 and 1913. One of these described the Hendersons' broomcorn farming, and others focused on her successes raising turkeys.[24] For those submissions, she had earned one to two dollars each, a significant amount in the cash-strapped Henderson household. As she once noted ruefully, the money she had received from the article on broomcorn ultimately represented most of their profit from that effort. Nevertheless, *Practical Farmer's* content and format limited the potential for any regular income from that publication. In contrast, *Ladies' World* paid much better, and it promised a wider audience and offered the writer the opportunity to explore a broader range of topics.[25]

Caroline followed her initial submission with a series of letters that were published irregularly during 1914, addressing subjects from letter writing to relaxation. In April 1915, she began writing a monthly column, eventually becoming the most popular columnist the magazine ever employed. She used two different formats during the next three years. Her columns, written primarily for women, generally mirrored the content and emphases considered appropriate at the time. For example, her thoughts on the First World War were unabashedly patriotic, dealing mostly with the contributions women could make to the war effort by sewing, conserving foods, and raising victory gardens.

Aside from these conventional themes, Caroline's regional orientation and the critical qualities that would define her later writing were often evident in her columns for *Ladies' World*. She wrote frankly about her own impatience, her tendencies toward depression, and other problems. She criticized those who thought of education as something one completed in school and those whose religiosity was ruled solely by hope of heaven. Some of her critical remarks could easily have offended some of her readers. But such comments and her frequent reflections on the importance of nature to her own sense of well-being reveal her early thought about issues that shaped her life.[26]

Given her continuing popularity with readers, Caroline probably could have continued writing for *Ladies' World* indefinitely. By the time of the magazine's demise, though, she was pleased to be able to abandon that occupation. By then, she was increasingly occupied teaching her daughter, an activity that had earlier led her to abandon turkey farming. She also needed the income less than she had five years earlier. Crop prices increased throughout the war, and the arrival of the railroad in 1916 increased access to markets and the corresponding income from their crops.

Cultural Pioneer

By 1918, the Hendersons seemed settled and secure, and they began a decade that would become the golden years on their farm. Increased prosperity permitted the family to quadruple their land holdings to six hundred forty acres and to begin purchasing mechanized equipment for many of their farming operations. The railroad and improved finances also permitted them access to products and services that had been inaccessible previously. They acquired a telephone, which they kept until the telephone company went out of business a few years later, and in 1928 they even took their first vacation.

Caroline was particularly pleased by Will's completion of their house during this period. He had originally doubled the size of the original fourteen-by-sixteen-foot claim shack in 1911 by adding a lean-to kitchen and another small room, adding insulation at the same time. By 1928, he completed a new house with a full basement, five rooms on the first floor, and a large undivided but finished area on the second. The primary living area included a bay window in the parlor, pocket doors between many rooms, and a completely furnished bathroom, though they would not obtain running water until 1946.[27]

Even the weather cooperated throughout most of the period. Caroline still wrote of blizzards, hail storms, and other typical problems, but the Hendersons faced no prolonged droughts. And the occasional lean years during the decade were more than offset by bumper crops in others. The Hendersons long remembered and cherished the year of 1926, when the Panhandle produced its greatest bumper crop to that point and for many years to come. The overexpansion of wheat production stimulated by such developments would soon exact a great price from Panhandle farmers, but that was still some time away.

Despite broad improvements in their way of life, the Hendersons' full enjoyment of their new status was partly offset by growing isolation from their neighbors. Population declines from the early years had left only three families, totaling twenty-four people, within the six square miles that surrounded their farm. More importantly, social distances increased even more sharply because of their separation from the only church in the area. Even more resentment arose after the Hendersons removed Eleanor from the neighborhood school so that

Caroline could teach her at home. The Hendersons sustained lifelong friendships with some early settlers, extending relationships to the second generation of some families such as the Grables, Ramseys, Wards, and Harts. But by the end of their second decade on their land, the Henderson family had become increasingly secluded, identified by others as the neighbors who did not really fit in the community.[28]

Caroline indicated growing discontent with the style and content of frontier religion as early as 1918. She was offended by the quality of preaching in area churches, where the sermons of unlearned preachers often stood in sharp contrast to the literate qualities she found in Unitarian publications. She also sought a connection between faith and broader concerns, which she did not find in the neighborhood church. For her such a connection meant a union between the "dynamic power of personal religious conviction . . . [and] a desire for the social betterment of the 'least of these my brethren.'"[29]

During the next decade Caroline clarified her doctrinal disagreements with the neighborhood United Brethren church they attended and began to identify herself as a Unitarian. That decision led to heated debates between her and her aging and devoutly Presbyterian mother. In contrast, both the Hendersons and their neighbors initially seemed to accept the stated differences between them, working together for varied church programs. Others, though, proved less receptive when the Hendersons invited Unitarian ministers to speak in their home. Finally, Caroline's stated disbelief in teachings about hell led to a crucial encounter at a revival meeting in 1927. An evangelist conducting a meeting at the neighborhood church sought to prove the truth of that doctrine by burning Caroline's finger. That confrontation led to the Hendersons' final withdrawal from the church and her only publication of the decade, a letter to the *Christian Register* describing the event.[30]

The second and probably more divisive conflict with neighbors arose from arrangements for Eleanor's education. Eleanor proved responsive to Caroline's teaching and was ready for a high school curriculum by age nine. Home instruction, which included German and Latin as well as deep grounding in literature and language generally, had clearly separated her from her peers. Some parents resented Eleanor's advancement and the family's subsequent decision to withhold her from area schools after she was about eleven years old. Still more neighbors complained about the action the Hendersons took in 1925, arranging for Eleanor to complete high school at Rolla, Kansas, about thirty miles from Eva.

In order to make this step possible, Caroline moved to Rolla and resumed teaching for the next three years. She and Will agreed that Eleanor's education was their primary goal even though it meant the family was separated for weeks at a time and Caroline had to leave the farm to return to teaching. However, that investment soon proved to be one of the best they would ever make. Eleanor was accepted into the University of Kansas as a sophomore in 1929, completing her medical degree there in 1935. Her acceptance and arrangements for a scholarship probably were facilitated by Francis Peabody, a minister and one of Caroline's correspondents.[31]

In effect, the Hendersons' social distancing from their neighbors reflected larger cultural changes that had taken place in the region in previous decades. Although females generally and female college graduates in particular were a rarity among homesteaders, Caroline's education and values stood out less in 1907 than they would twenty years later. America's frontier migrations had always included educated people who were drawn to the opportunities and challenges presented by unsettled lands. The conditions they encountered in the Panhandle, however, soon defeated most or convinced them that their opportunities lay elsewhere. The departure of educated people, including a number of physicians and attorneys who had homesteaded for speculative purposes, effectively reduced the number of people in the region who might have identified with Caroline's interests. One such person was Dagny Grevstad, a 1903 Mount Holyoke graduate. She was married to a land promoter and resided near the Hendersons at Guymon, Oklahoma. Caroline was able to visit with her on one occasion in 1910, and the following year, Grevstad visited Caroline at her homestead. However, Grevstad soon left the region as her husband's interests led him to new ventures in the Texas Panhandle.[32]

Even had these relatively cultured neighbors remained in the area, Caroline would not have fit in with them entirely. In fact, Caroline's love of the soil had always separated her from the more educated settlers. Thus, she stayed on the land even when it did not produce the economic gains she had hoped for and long after people such as Grevstad had left. Similarly, her differences with other neighbors arose from her devotion to her religious values and the kind of education she had received at Mount Holyoke. For Caroline, education was an essential ingredient in a meaningful life, despite her occasional questions about whether it had prepared her for pioneering.[33] In contrast, her neighbors were increasingly likely to think of education in terms of practical goals, such as acquiring the skills needed to improve their farms.[34] If they sought further education, it was as a means to escape the frustrations and drudgery of farming. The regional tendency toward limited education was exacerbated by both economic and demographic characteristics that worked against the establishment of high-quality schools.

The hallmark of Caroline's commitment to education for its own sake was her decision to begin work on a Master's degree in literature while living with Eleanor at the University of Kansas in Lawrence. She originally moved to Lawrence to accompany Eleanor at Will's insistence, as he regarded it unacceptable for his daughter to be unchaperoned in such an environment. Caroline and Eleanor cleaned rooms for their room and board to offset the costs of the move. Then Caroline undertook a rigorous and relatively expensive program of study for herself. Risking ridicule by beginning a Master's degree at fifty-two, she remained true to her educational ideals by focusing on personal enrichment rather than practical goals.[35]

Dust to Eat

Caroline's studies at the University of Kansas from 1930 to 1931 led directly to her recognition as a significant regional writer. She would not produce as many articles as she had with *Ladies' World*, but now she wrote under her own name while penning an enduring contribution to Great Plains literature. Her first step in that direction was linked directly to the encouragement she received from the literature faculty at the University of Kansas.

Despite her own fears about resuming her formal education, she immediately found many of the faculty supportive of her writing efforts. Both Dr. J. H. Nelson and Professor R. D. O'Leary were especially encouraging, later serving on her thesis committee and urging her to submit her writing for publication.[36] "Bringing in the Sheaves," her first publication for *Atlantic Monthly*, may have been written originally in fulfillment of a class assignment. Although primarily a description of the Henderson family's 1931 wheat harvest, the article also reflects Caroline's growing awareness of the increasing weight of the Great Depression on farm prices and farmers' diminishing prospects for the future.[37]

That article led directly to Caroline's correspondence with Evelyn Harris, a Maryland widow and farmer. Harris had already published a number of articles on local farm problems when she contacted Caroline in 1932, proposing an effort to publish an exchange of letters between the two. Caroline, at first reluctant to participate in the project, finally consented. Even though skeptical about her prospects, Caroline had once more begun to seek income from her writing as she had from 1913 to 1918. *Atlantic Monthly* accepted the letters immediately, publishing them serially in August and September 1933. The *Atlantic's* earlier experience with Caroline's work and the growing national sense of urgency about the Depression may have encouraged the *Atlantic* editors.[38]

The women differed significantly in both writing style and in their analyses of the conditions they faced. Harris frequently complained about changing government responses to the farm crisis, while Caroline tended to either favor such innovations or reserve judgment. Similarly, she was both more literary and more analytical, describing the farm crisis in larger contexts. However, both women were in strong agreement about the unfairness of agricultural pricing. Together their letters affirmed that the farm crisis affected all regions of the country and that it had severe consequences for farming communities as well as individual farmers. Those messages were important for government policy makers and the public, who often assumed that farmers were weathering the Depression with only minimal hardships.

At the same time, Caroline's letters clearly demonstrated the different degree of hardships faced by Great Plains farmers. While Harris's dependence on truck gardens and produce operations left her with a sharply reduced standard of living, the Hendersons and their neighbors were already dipping into reserves and questioning their prospects for survival. These letters, together with those Caroline wrote to Rose Alden during this period, also point toward a larger future disaster. Although Caroline could not know it at the time, the drought conditions she wrote of in 1932 would soon lead to the dust bowl. The year produced 17.82 inches of moisture, but the vast majority of it had fallen by the spring. In the period 1933–1937, the region received an average annual rainfall of 12.97 inches.[39]

Even more ominously, Caroline's letters from 1933 described some of the worst dust storms she had yet seen. This time, the storms would not stop with the change of season as in the past. This time a unique combination of successive dry years, seasonal winds, intense heat, and inadequate grass or other ground cover converged to produce dust storms of unprecedented severity and duration. Each new storm destroyed still more ground cover, leading to still more and worse storms. In 1932 the southern plains, with Texas County near the center, had produced fourteen storms, creating conditions that reduced visibility to less than one mile. From 1933 to 1938, there were at least 301 more such storms, many of which lasted for days. Another 64 disrupted life in the region from 1939 to 1941, as a decade of environmental chaos drew to a close.[40]

Every person who survived that decade would retain vivid memories of the great "rollers"—when dust clouds reached as high as eight thousand feet into the sky, often carrying dust as far as the Atlantic Ocean. Others talked of seemingly endless days of dust-driving wind that blew so hard it blasted the paint from every coated surface, eating into the wood itself. Destruction of feed crops forced many farmers to give up their cattle. Others adapted by grinding tumbleweeds and yucca to sustain their remaining livestock. In many years, the farmers planted seed, only to find the following spring that the seed had not even sprouted because of inadequate moisture. And if a few heads of grain did manage to triumph over the drought, they were likely to be smothered by dust. Even fences were often covered by the dust, permitting livestock to wander from the fields. Occasionally livestock or even people would be trapped and killed by the storms, while countless others suffered from dust pneumonia.

For Caroline, the era meant "dust to eat,"[41] as the very qualities of life she enjoyed were destroyed by the dust. The dust compounded her labors while assuring that she could not enjoy a clean house or even dust-free dishes, while she grieved over the loss of trees from the wind breaks and the obliteration of the flower gardens she loved. She lamented the suffering of the livestock and wildlife, even a helpless, wind-beaten jack rabbit.[42] She especially mourned for the people who were broken physically or had to give up their farms because of the storms. Texas County shrank to 9,896 people by the end of the decade.[43] Many residents who stayed moved to towns, leaving their farms behind and increasing the isolation for those who stayed.

Above all, Caroline witnessed the destruction of her own hopes and dreams. As early as 1932, she claimed that hardships forced by the Depression had robbed her of her self-respect.[44] The privations she faced during the next eight years of environmental destruction reduced her sense of dignity still further. She simply could not maintain the dreams that had preserved her in the early years. She was living in the future she had dreamed of in 1908, but it had become a nightmare.

She recognized she would not be able to establish the quality of life she knew as a child and could see no fulfillment of the Jeffersonian promise in the life she had built. Yet she persevered on the land and on the paths she had chosen there. The volume of writing she completed during the peak years of the dust bowl offers one measure of her strength of character. It also points to the crucial role that her writing played in her life, both during that time and subsequently. She completed her Master's thesis in 1935, wrote her best known publication, "Letters from the Dust Bowl," in 1936, and ended her writing career with two publications the next year.[45] Each of her works reveals her struggles against the elements and her growing sense of loss. Her Master's thesis, however, offers the greatest insight into her most personal thoughts.

Caroline must have recognized that both autobiographical and ironic elements were in play as she wrote about "The Love of the Soil as a Motivating Force in Literature Relating to the Early Development of the Middle West" even while the dust storms raged. She never abandoned that love, but now she called for a different understanding of pioneer and rural life than the idealized view she believed had been perpetuated in the popular culture. Her study examines seven writers on pioneering in the Midwest who had published their primary works after 1913. These were Willa Cather, Ole Rölvaag, Elmer T. Peterson, Elizabeth Madox Roberts, Hamlin Garland, Herbert Quick, and Martha Ostenso. The study also drew upon the works of other writers including Carl Sandburg, Pearl Buck, Louis Bromfield, and the historians Frederic Paxson and Frederick Jackson Turner.

As suggested by her title, the thesis was unified by a consideration of the importance of the love of the soil. She described this love as motivation for settlement, defined its basic characteristics, identified challenges to its survival, and described the compensations it offered to those who adhered to it. A final chapter discusses the special contributions of women to the conquest of the frontier. The novels she chose for her study all portrayed characters who seemed to fail despite the courage they demonstrated in the face of adversity—often fighting against the Indians, always opposed by the elements. At the same time, the protagonists came to love the land that they had won, sometimes if for no other reason than that "the hard won things are the most precious."[46] However, loving the land did not ensure that it would produce the quality of life dreamed of by the pioneers or even their descendants.

Caroline argued that droughts, blizzards, plagues of grasshoppers, and prairie fires ultimately were less significant than smaller details in destroying much of the enjoyment of life, especially for women, even after initial stages of settlement were long completed. Among such details were "a daily struggle for fundamental comforts—water, fuel, light, means of cleanliness or communication."[47] Caroline herself particularly hated burning cow chips for fuel, a practice she and Will resumed during the decade she wrote her thesis. The accumulative impact of such smaller deficiencies was compounded by lack of access to skilled care in illness or child bearing, plus the inherent isolation of the prairies and plains.

Caroline offered one faint note of hope in her study, but it was one she could not claim for herself. That promise is found in her answer to the question posed in her introduction, asking whether the settlers who had abandoned a deserted Colorado village had failed. She argued they had not, that they had been "pathfinders" who prepared the way for those who would follow and, perhaps, would succeed at some later time.[48] At the time she completed her thesis, Caroline may have retained a dim hope that her life could have comparable meaning, but she still faced five more years of dust. Besides, she had not set out to do the ground work for others, but to build something that would endure. She was not inclined to acknowledge her accomplishments, even under the best of circumstances. To redefine her dreams and focus on a distant future meant she would have to face the possibility of a defeat—even worse than the loss of her dream. That would mean abandoning her farm, leaving behind what she had built, and accepting a future apart from the land she loved. Her profound ambivalence about those choices marked virtually every aspect of the remaining years of her life.

Disappointment amidst Achievement

Caroline's decision to stay and work through the challenges she encountered, whether those presented by the elements or those that arose from her own sense of failure, is all the more remarkable because she had begun to face another hard reality at the same time. Even after the dust storms ceased and agricultural prices stabilized, she could no longer draw upon the strengths she had as a young woman. When she wrote to Rose Alden in December 1936, she had become increasingly aware of her age, and she looked ahead with uneasiness to the future challenges a hostile environment created for a couple fifty-nine years old. As she had written of the pioneers:

"Along with youth goes naturally the ability to live in one's dreams, to find stimulus to effort in one's vision of an alluring future."[49] That option was no longer available to her. She retained pleasant memories of pioneering but feared the years ahead.

If Caroline's concern about aging at first represented only a momentary lapse of courage, during the next few years she would find abundant evidence to justify her fears. She and Will both began to suffer regular illnesses and injuries stemming from their reduced vitality. Correspondingly, they found their myriad chores increasingly burdensome. The equipment they had bought during the good years deteriorated markedly as each year passed. Crop failures and low prices during the thirties effectively discouraged the replacement of tractors, combines, and even trucks. When prices finally stabilized at the end of the decade, wartime constraints prevented the purchase of new equipment that could have alleviated their burdens.

There were, of course, moments to celebrate even during the "dirty thirties." Caroline was especially proud of Eleanor's accomplishments: the completion of her medical degree in 1935, her marriage the same year, subsequent research on an experimental anesthetic, and the establishment of her private practice. She must have seen those achievements as some measure of return on her own investment, but they did not relieve her sense of failure. Neither did growing evidence of her status as a writer.

The acceptance of Caroline's articles by varied journals and the acknowledgment she received from Secretary of Agriculture Wallace and numerous other sources all confirmed her growing literary reputation. The *Wichita Eagle* identified her as a "noted woman writer . . . recognized as one of the nation's best descriptive artists with the English language."[50] Caroline appreciated the hundreds of letters she received in response to her articles and made every effort to answer each. She particularly valued letters from people within the region and maintained correspondence with at least one local reader until her death.

One admiring letter led to a 1938 visit from one of her readers who would also prove to be among the more unique people she encountered in her lifetime. The visitor was Eli Jaffe, a Lithuanian Jew from New York City and a self-identified Communist. Jaffe initially wrote Caroline expressing his admiration for her writing and his interest in seeing the dust bowl first hand. He hoped to write a novel about the difficulties encountered by families like the Hendersons. Caroline and Will both agreed to the visit and prepared to welcome him.[51]

In the meantime, Jaffe stopped for a few months at Claremore, Oklahoma, where he was severely beaten and barely escaped arrest for his organizational efforts on behalf of the Communist Party. He then spent two months with the Hendersons.[52] Caroline admired his idealism but by this time had become increasingly suspicious of the "Russian experiment." Though she had earlier expressed some openness toward it and remained open to political and social experimentation, she recognized the Communist threat to democratic values. Nevertheless, both the Hendersons and Jaffe enjoyed the time they spent together, maintaining friendship and correspondence even later, when Jaffe spent time in prison for his party efforts.

Following his Panhandle sojourn, Jaffe went to Oklahoma City to work in the state party organization, write for affiliated newspapers, and work in a Communist bookstore. On August 17, 1940, he and three co-workers were arrested and jailed for violation of an Oklahoma statute prohibiting "criminal syndicalism." Each was in turn convicted; Jaffe was the last to be tried, whereupon he was sentenced to ten years in prison and a five thousand dollar fine. The convictions were overturned in February 1943 by the Oklahoma Court of Criminal Appeals. Caroline had written to that court assuring the judges that Jaffe was an idealist who posed no threat of violence, but her letter probably did not affect that outcome. Jaffe then entered the military, serving until the end of the war before returning to New York and a career in public relations.[53]

Although she enjoyed the new relationships that arose from her writing, Caroline found little solace in that achievement because it was not the one she had sought. Moreover, she never enjoyed writing for publication and may have associated it with the economic pressures that had triggered both of her ventures into that activity. Such ambivalence would help to explain her subsequent refusal to be interviewed for a 1959 CBS documentary on the Depression and the dust bowl. By this time she was also concerned about her appearance, describing herself as resembling "an owl with colic."[54] In any case, "Spring in the Dust Bowl," which *Atlantic Monthly* published in 1937, was her last article.

The Western Gate

By now, Caroline had begun writing letters on an almost daily basis to her daughter, Eleanor. That correspondence established a new avenue for Caroline's writing that proved especially important to her as she grappled with her sense of loss and the conviction that she had failed. The improved conditions that prevailed during the decades after the dust bowl era would seem promising for a restoration of hope, but nothing could change her conviction that she had spent her life in vain.

The period from 1939 to 1949 rivaled any comparable period the Hendersons had experienced for good weather and relative prosperity. By the beginning of that time, dust bowl conditions had abated in response to the reformed farming practices implemented in prior years. The dust bowl era ended decisively in 1941, when the region received the heaviest precipitation recorded in the twentieth century, 33.25 inches of moisture. Every other year in the next ten, except 1943 and 1945, produced precipitation above regional averages, while American entry into the war and a postwar boom ensured even better prices for regional crops.

In 1948, the Hendersons reported their best year ever, showing net profits of more than six thousand dollars, even while withholding some grain from the market.[55] Yet, growing economic security, bumper crops in 1948 that rivaled those of 1926, the birth of a grandson, and other happy events were not enough to offset Caroline's fears. She had faced too many blizzards and hot summers, too many crops ruined by drought or flood, too many dust storms. She now dreaded each new year, anticipating fresh disasters, which all too often arrived on time.

And the disaster she feared was nearing. The Hendersons lost most of their wheat to army worms in 1950. Despite 22.03 inches of rain the next year, Panhandle wheat production was so sparse that many combining crews and other migratory workers bypassed the region. A prolonged drought began in 1952 and lasted until 1956.

The conditions the Hendersons faced during that five-year period can be summarized in the following details: From 1952 to 1956, the Panhandle and surrounding areas received 13.33, 17.29, 12.04, 14.81, and 11.61 inches of moisture. The prolonged drought and seasonal winds soon led to the return of near dust bowl conditions. In June 1952, Caroline broke down and cried as the region suffered from the eleventh straight day of extreme heat and winds.[56] The agricultural practices adopted during the 1930s ultimately prevented dust bowl extremes, but relief was not ensured until the rains finally returned in 1957, washing out many of the Hendersons' crops. In the same year their original well caved in. The prolonged illness of their son-in-law and his early death in 1958 compounded the trials and tribulations of this time.

Even before the accumulated woes of the 1950s, Caroline seemed to be searching for a graceful exit. In July 1950, she wrote that she hoped it was "not too far to the western gate," one of her standard allusions to death, and subsequent letters frequently echo that sentiment.[57] Sadly, she seemed to have forgotten the very lessons she had written of in years past, lessons that might have abated her fears and frustration. In her columns for *Ladies' World*, for example, she had written of the importance of remembering that one was not "responsible for averting a blizzard" and that an individual's attainments are not nearly as "important as our own determination to be unconquered."[58] But for the last decades of her life, Caroline forgot the limits of her abilities and seemed to assume that she was solely accountable for every mistake, for the results of each year, and for the meaning of a lifetime of work. For his part, Will seemed untroubled by such burdens, adding to Caroline's aggravation. Interestingly, in her first letter from Oklahoma to Rose Alden, Caroline had recognized that there might be a time when she would see Will's optimism and refusal to worry as a burden, rather than a strength. And so it was that now, as she assumed the burden of worry she had so often advised against, she complained all the while about Will's apparent unconcern about such matters.

Will did not seem to share all of her worries and certainly had not experienced the sense of loss she felt. In contrast to her dreams, he had surely attained more than he had experienced as a child. However, he was not as oblivious to her concerns as she supposed. He wrote occasional letters to his daughter urging her to try and persuade Caroline to spend some time in Eleanor's Arizona home, where she could relax and leave her burdens behind.[59]

Caroline's deep anguish about the problems she perceived was rivaled only by her ambivalence about the possible escape offered by retirement. She fretted regularly about Will's obstinate refusal to consider that action, but she may have been more reluctant to embrace the decision than he was. She did not want to leave her home and could not stand the thought of the two of them confined to a small room in a rest home, as some of their neighbors were. She rejected any idea of turning their property over to managers because they had "worked too hard and too long to appreciate having any small return . . . doled out . . . by strangers of some far away money gathering corporation with no possible interest in this small bit of the 'good earth.'"[60] Thus, less than a year prior to her death, Caroline's call for retirement was modified by the word "possibly."[61]

Will's and Caroline's advancing age did make the prospect of future hardships more daunting, but some of Caroline's concerns were much greater than their circumstances warranted. By 1952, she and Will were well positioned to maintain a moderate standard of living after their gains in the preceding decade. The Hendersons had no debt, limited investments, and about five thousand dollars in savings. Their security increased further with occasional infusions of lease money for oil or gas rights on their property and the beginning of Social Security payments after they worked through a series of bureaucratic snarls in 1957. In addition, Caroline received $1,920 in annual income from the Iowa farm she had inherited from her parents. By the time of Will's death in 1966, his estate was valued at almost thirty thousand dollars. When Caroline died later that year, her estate totaled more than one hundred thousand dollars above the amount she had inherited from him.[62]

Her continuing sense of loss even during relative prosperity stemmed from her memories of the Depression and dust bowl, linked together with her commitment to the goal she believed might still make her life of sacrifice worthwhile. To salvage the meaning of her life, she hoped to leave something substantive to Eleanor and her grandson. Caroline's fear that the family's investment in land and capital would erode in retirement led her to insist that they meet their annual expenses with income produced by their farming operations. Unfortunately, that decision reduced their likelihood of either increasing or enjoying their investments. It meant they could not afford to expand their landholdings to increase annual income potential. Certainly, further land investments might not have made sense in light of their advanced ages, but a corresponding decision to continue relying on the equipment they had bought in the 1920s added to their labors and to Caroline's sense of failure.

Her frustration deepened as she intensified her efforts to economize whenever and however she could. She continued to make their underwear and made mittens for Will from remnants of her father's robe. When electrical service reached their home in 1952, she worried about the additional expense, anxiously watching the electric meter and timing her use of the few labor saving appliances she permitted herself. Despite complaints about the "infernal heat" in summer, she also refused to bear the expense of a fan. By 1955, she was so concerned about finances that she even attempted writing again, but this time to no avail.[63]

Despite Caroline's evident overreaction to their financial status, her responses were not entirely inconsistent with her circumstances. Clearly, the future offered no more promise of the life she had dreamed of than did the years she had left behind. The Hendersons were even more isolated in the last years of their life than they had been in their first decades on the farm, whether because of the death or retirement of friends from the early days or regional demographic patterns. Texas County populations remained at the levels reached in 1940, but many families within the county were moving from farms to small towns. This trend was particularly evident in the western half of the county where the Hendersons resided. Those patterns largely explain the late arrival of both rural electrification and phone service, either of which would have done much to ease the solitude of life on the Henderson homestead.

Because of the Hendersons' advancing age and Will's deteriorating driving skills, Caroline could spend weeks without seeing another person. At times, these circumstances threatened their physical as well as their emotional well-being. For example, in the great blizzard of 1957, they were stranded without access to supplies for three weeks, having only one contact with another person in that time, a neighbor who came via tractor to check up on them.

In the early years, Caroline's regular reading of the Bible and Unitarian literature seemed to be adequate for her spiritual needs. In contrast, the letters she wrote in the last years of her life indicate that the comfort she had found in these sources had vanished with the loss of her dreams. This was particularly evident as she faced the prospect of her death. She never stopped reading Unitarian materials completely and sent annual contributions to the Unitarian-Universalist Service Committee, while maintaining correspondence with Jack Mendohlson, a leader in that denomination. Otherwise, though, she was gradually breaking those religious ties. This break reflected both the increasing distance between her own continuing theistic beliefs and changing Unitarian thought and her concern that the denomination had become "too smug" in its liberalism. And she was not able to accept the assurances offered by the religious doctrines she had left behind. The dust bowl era apparently had broken the remnants of that faith, and she increasingly rejected the idea of a benign providence.

She acknowledged that she might find some solace in the assurance of a better afterlife but could not accept that hope for herself.[64]

Amid such circumstances and struggling against her own sense of loss, Caroline still managed to retain her perspective on most matters other than the family's finances. She remained an astute observer of literature, current events, and her surroundings, and she undoubtedly found hours of enjoyment in her reading. She retained a wry sense of humor, hoping "Papa Truman" would not mind their naming a calf "Margaret," making small jokes about Hadacol, a popular tonic of the era, and regularly ridiculing rain-making efforts. Writing of a two thousand dollar loss on stock in Selected Investments, she commented that in any case, it had not been as great as the losses they had suffered in the six years they tried to make a wheat crop.[65]

Caroline's continued sympathy for the needy and oppressed was manifest in her giving as well as her words. Regular donations to numerous causes, from Easter Seals to Navajo Missions, Cal Farley's Boys Ranch, and the Mount Holyoke Alumni Association are especially noteworthy in light of the financial pressures she perceived. She also demonstrated sympathy for the plight of minorities, in her writing as well as her giving. She wrote to Jaffe condemning the "silly" fences that had been installed at the University of Oklahoma to separate black students from whites as the university began integration under court order. Her attitude toward Native Americans was probably best summarized in her opinion that American "treatment of Indians has been one of the darker stains upon our record."[66]

Above all, Caroline supported her family. She frequently complained about—and probably at—Will, but she stayed up nights in advance of their fiftieth wedding anniversary sewing fancy stitching on a night shirt for him. More importantly, she also affirmed that she could not leave their place as long as he wanted to stay. The contrast between these actions and her regular complaints about him can be understood in the light of her isolation. Will became the focus of her frustrations because he was the only person with whom she had regular personal contact. At the same time, she was using her letters to Eleanor to vent her fears and frustrations.

Caroline wrote at least three letters, plus three to five postcards, to Eleanor each week for the last three decades of her life. Written on scraps of paper, on the backs of letters or used cards, and on an occasional piece of stationery, the letters typically ran to five pages or more. Besides reflecting her interests and commitments to family, her letters to Eleanor became what she described as "her actual life" as well as the means she used to address her own continuing frustrations.[67]

She would frequently shift abruptly from writing of some painful topic to a discussion of her flowers. Similarly, she seemed to use her discussion of area wildlife, family pets, and even the livestock to remind herself of the things she still enjoyed. These were the themes she returned to in her final letter to her daughter in December 1965. That letter had to be among the most painful she ever wrote. Weakened by age and facing the complications of an abdominal tumor, she wrote to confirm arrangements pertaining to her and Will's move to Arizona where they would live with Eleanor. Despite her obvious stress and the difficulty of writing, Caroline left instructions for the care of the family dog and wrote of her "long beloved home." She and Will would return for one last visit the following March to take care of business. Will died three days after their return on March 17, 1966; Caroline died on August 4.[68]

Chapter 1

Beginnings, 1908–1914

The first part of Caroline Henderson's story is told through her correspondence and publications from 1908 to 1914. In those years she began homesteading, married Will Henderson, and gave birth to her daughter, Eleanor. Although she relished the challenges of pioneering and establishing a family on the Oklahoma plains, chronic cash shortages forced her to seek new income sources. In 1911, she began publishing small pieces in *Practical Farmer*, earning one to two dollars per submission. Her topics ranged from the Hendersons' experiments with broomcorn cultivation to her successes in turkey farming.[1]

Most of Caroline's submissions to the *Practical Farmer* offer information of interest only to specialists in agricultural history; however, one article from her early efforts reveals more about her life on the plains. "What I Read Last Year," which was published in May 1912, is included herein because it reflects the qualitative concerns that guided her reading. The other article reproduced in this chapter, "Our Homestead," gives an account of her first five years on the homestead. The article was published by *Ladies' World* in February 1914 along with the letter Caroline had originally written to the editor of the magazine to ask for her advice about how to supplement her income (see Caroline's letter of July 16, 1913). The editor suggested that Caroline write about her experiences, which work was then published as "Our Homestead." This initial publication produced such a deluge of responses that her editor encouraged additional submissions, which led to four years of writing for that magazine.[2]

The remainder of this chapter consists of letters to Caroline's lifelong friend, Rose Alden, and her mother, identified only as Mrs. Alden. Rose and Caroline both graduated from Mount Holyoke in 1901 to begin careers in teaching. Unlike Caroline, Alden found teaching a rewarding occupation. She was employed as an English teacher in New Jersey, Vermont, and Virginia public schools until her retirement in 1942; she died in 1961. Never married, Alden was active in numerous clubs as well as school-related activities. She wanted to write for publication but did not have any known success. Instead, she shared her efforts with a women's pen club. At least two of her submissions to the club were based on her contact with Caroline: The first of these was an interpretation of Caroline's first years on the homestead and the second was based on Alden's visit to the Henderson farm in 1940.[3]

Though Alden was a less successful writer than Caroline, she did recognize the historical quality of the letters she received through the years from Oklahoma, retaining many, including those originally sent to her mother. She continued compiling letters from Caroline until about 1940, when she arranged for their donation to the Mount Holyoke College Archives. At first reluctant to make her correspondence available to the public, Caroline was persuaded to approve the donation when she visited with Victor Murdock, an editor for the *Wichita Eagle*, who convinced her that her letters would be valuable as a resource for social history. Her subsequent reading of Bernard Devoto's *Year of Decision* reinforced that conclusion.[4]

Caroline's letters to the Aldens are the only personal letters from her first thirty years on the farm that are known to have survived, and most are included in this or subsequent chapters. Those that duplicate content found in Caroline's published writings have been omitted,[5] and when Caroline wrote on the same topics to both Rose and Mrs. Alden, Rose's letter rather than her mother's was selected for inclusion herein.

⤙⤚

APRIL 28, 1908

MY DEAR LITTLE ROSE:

Your letter reached me by round about ways and I felt truly grateful for your forbearance, for I remembered, though you did not mention it, that the letter of a year before had not yet been answered. It would take longer time than I have now at my command, and longer I presume than you could spend to listen if I were even to try to tell you of all that has filled my days since last I wrote to you. But I want your friendship still if I may have it, I will try to suggest a mere "table of contents," and let you fill in the rest.

First there was a winter of rather poor health when work was too much of an effort and too little joy, then new spirits and strength with the spring, then a diphtheria germ and its consequences which lasted for long. I was very, very sick. They gave the anti-toxin, repeatedly, five times altogether, and at last stayed the advance of the wretched disease. In a sense my recovery was rapid, but nervously I was all shaken to pieces. The delirium of the fever was too awful and it was months before I could do anything that required any concentration of mind. This is one reason for the long silence, because letter writing was of all things the most impossible. I would sit down and cry over a little note of appreciation for kindness received because I was so weak, and I couldn't write as I wanted and sometimes I would have to try two or three times on just a short letter. So after a little I gave it up until I should be better able for it.

A return to the old routine seemed intolerable. I hungered and thirsted for something away from it all and for the out-of-doors. So here I am, away out in that narrow strip of Oklahoma between Kansas and the Panhandle of Texas, "holding down" one of the prettiest claims in the Beaver County strip. I wish you could see this wide, free western country, with its great stretches of almost level prairie, covered with the thick, short buffalo grass, the marvelous glory of its sunrises and sunsets, the brilliancy of its star lit sky at night . . . [and] much more has made the last six months a delight in spite of hardships and exposure that I could never advise anyone to encounter. There was a three-months' term of school in the school house across the way, a two months' siege of well-drilling and boarding the men, at least getting meals for them, and so the time has gone, busily and happily. And now this part of the story is almost finished, for, little Rose, out here in this wilderness has come to me the very greatest and sweetest and most hopeful happiness of all my life.

The seventh of May I am to be married to Mr. W.E. Henderson. We have not known each other long for he found me here, yet we do not doubt that our whole lives have been preparing us for a new life together. Someday we may go together to fulfill my part of the prophecy up on Mount Holyoke in 1901, for that located me on a western ranch. And Mr. Henderson had been planning to go to Texas or Old Mexico this spring and get cheap land for stock raising. But I could not leave my claim now without losing it, so we shall remain here for the present and wish to raise a crop this summer which is our reason for seeming to be in such immoderate haste.

You may wonder what sort of man you will meet when you come to visit your old friend some day on a western ranch. I know he will not seem the same to you as he does to me, but I think you will know that he is plain and simple and direct, that (unless he is teasing) his "yes" means yes and his "no" means no. I believe you will see too that he is <u>clean</u> and gentle as any woman, though he has a strong man's energy and resourcefulness. And you could not help but realize that he is an optimist of the sincerest sort, ready to do all his part to <u>make</u> things come right, with a faith above and beyond his own effort. I think sometimes it will worry me because he simply <u>won't</u> worry over anything, but that is a pretty good failing after all. Personally he is tall and brown for he has lived on these plains for years now. He was here long ago before there were any inhabitants but great herds of cattle and the antelopes and prairie dogs. He is rather homely, I think, to most people, but you will see the kindness in his gray blue eyes and won't mind, I am sure.

So busy I have been this spring, Rose, with my chickens, for I am getting a pretty good start now, with my big garden of an acre and a quarter, and with all these extra preparations for the seventh of May. I have wanted to write to you much sooner, but the day's work has hurried me on each day. And this day I am letting everything go that should be done and writing anyway. I have no machine so the very simple and not numerous preparations have been made by hand. They are helping me at home too, by getting some things ready. Susie will come out then, as it seemed impossible for me to leave here just now to go home as they wished, and Mother and Father will come later—perhaps in watermelon time. . . .

Please remember me most kindly to your friends at home. And

may life bring to them and to you all good and gracious gifts. I hope to see you some time. Till then even if sometimes life's burdens make me silent, won't you try to believe me, Ever loyally your friend,

⌒⌒⌒

AUG. 17, 1908

MY DEAR ROSE

I do thank you very truly for both your letters and the friendship they have meant to me. So often during these happy summer days, I have wished you might know how much I have appreciated your good wishes and the pretty gift—different altogether from anything I had—which so often reminds me of you and Susan.

You were quite right in suspecting that it has been a busy summer for me. In a short letter or even a long one I could scarcely suggest the variety of employments that have fallen to my lot. But Rose, dear little girl, I have been so happy. It has been such a revelation to me of what life may mean under the most absolutely common place conditions. For I realize that it is all commonplace enough when I imagine myself as a third party—but it hasn't seemed so. It is as new and full of blessing to me at least, as if all this had never happened before.

The day of the creation of our new world, May seventh, was one of the most perfect days I have ever seen. We had driven the thirty miles to Guymon on the preceding day going in a prairie schooner in real western style, not for the sake of the style, however, but as a protection against the wind which that day was very strong and cold. One of Mr. Henderson's five sisters (they have but one brother) had stayed to care for the chicks and look after things generally. At Guymon (our railroad town) we met my sister who had leave of absence from her office work just long enough to witness the ceremony and return by the first train. She brought <u>the dress</u> from home; they had made it themselves of some soft-thin white stuff, very simply but daintily with much fine hand work. I treasure it for all the loving thoughts that I know went into it.

After we had watched Susie's train out of sight, it remained for us to load our schooner and start for home. It was toward evening before we got away but I shall always be glad it was just as it was, for the memory of that perfect night of moon light and starlight when we seemed to have the world to ourselves is a treasure to carry with me through life, and I believe through all eternity.

Since then such busy days! Besides the house-keeping which seems like a new thing under these different conditions there have been for a regular thing the care of a half acre garden which I assumed for this summer, though Mr. Henderson helped whenever his regular farm work would permit and also the chickens—an unfailing source of interest, pleasure and work. We have as yet limited accommodations for chickens so are not going into the business yet on a large scale. But I have about a hundred young ones with several more "setters" yet to hatch so I hope for a fair start for another year.

For extras there have been service as chief assistant at fencing a forty acre pasture, some carpentering and building, erecting and painting a windmill, and the thousand little things not big enough to remember but which all have to do with making a <u>home</u> on the prairie. We have also first and last had a good deal of company. Mr. Henderson's mother was here for nine days and one of his sisters for three weeks, so altogether it has been very much as you said—scarcely time enough to sleep.

On the whole so far as farming is concerned it has been a rather discouraging season. Not foreseeing what was to befall me I had rented the old ground for this year so we had to depend on sod crops. The rains were very late and the ground too dry for breaking until after the rain came June 6. So it made the planting extremely late and we have not had as much rain as we hoped for since. However there is time yet to make a feed crop if we have rains later on and it is a constant inspiration to be with one who really believes that even if we fail of any success whatever in that way still for some reason it is all right and we may nevertheless be unworried and content.

I wish you could see our beautiful little colt and our new tiny mule. I can not call him beautiful but he is as cunning and smart as a little mule can be. Last night I went away down in the pasture to make sure that the horses were alright. The baby mule has a real mule's curiosity and though he is very wild yet, I sat down on the grass to see what he would do, pretending not to notice him. He kept approaching in smaller and smaller circles till his nose touched my shoe. The slightest movement sent him flying to his mother—head and tail high in the air and the tips of his toes barely touching the ground. He and the colt have the grandest frolics. I never tire of watching them.

All our varied occupations give us little time for reading. I have feared sometimes that I might forget how in the deepest sense. We do try, however, to keep up with one or two magazines that they send us from home. Lately I have been picking up "Romala" in odd moments of time—too short for much of anything else, inspired to another re-reading of it by a card from Helen Bowerman in Florence with a picture of one of the old public buildings—"Palazzo Vecchio"—frequently referred to in "Romala."[6] How sorrowful such a story is but how true it may be! And nights we read the Bible—are going straight through. I never did it before. In Mr. Henderson's old days on the range that was often his only companion and he read it for interest and companionship as other people read story books—through and through—over and over. He has the same little Bible yet that went with him all those lonely days—a present—when he was a little boy from his old German grandfather. . . .

I hope the summer has given you the change and rest that you need before entering upon another year of your unselfish work. Please tell me about it for it will now have for me even more of the interest of a work so different from my own. May it be a happy and satisfying year for you, a year of successful effort and realized desires. Do write again as of old and in spite of the long breaks in our correspondence, please believe me still, Heartily your friend.

◀━▶

AUGUST 17, 1909

DEAR ROSE:

I am reminded that vacation will soon be over and that if my letter is to reach you before your return to work it must be sent soon. . . .

The thought of snow and cool spring rains and the sweet arbutus which came with your letter is refreshing now in these days of almost unendurable heat. And I must thank you for the hyacinths and their message. As I grow older I realize more and more the truth that "man cannot live by bread alone." And now when even the matter of <u>bread</u> seems a problem, I am thankful, indeed, that other things than material comfort do enter in to make life worth while after all.

If it were not for those "unseen verities" of which Dr. Young spoke to us in chapel one morning, such a summer as the present would have been almost too much to bear. We worked so hard, both of us, early and late, putting in the crop, gardening etc. and did it all so hopefully and so happily. And our hopes seemed to have been justified. Through June there was plenty of rain. Everything grew wonderfully. Corn, cane, broom corn, millet, maize, and kaffir corn, all promised an abundant return for our labor.[7] One of our particular pleasures at that time was the Sunday morning walk through our fields, noticing the growth of each separate planting, our hearts full of thankfulness for the hope of it and for everything.

And now there is nothing left—except the invisible blessings I spoke of. During the latter part of June, and all of July and August so far, we have had no rain. The heat has been the most intense I ever experienced and has been accompanied day after day by "hot winds," scorching withering blasts which seem to come from a furnace seven times heated.

You cannot imagine in the midst of any desert a drier more desolate spot than those fields which promised us so generous a harvest. There is literally nothing—not enough on the whole farm to feed one of our pretty pigeons for the winter. The problem is really a serious one for we are far from wealthy and truly needed something of a crop. The other day we were wondering about books for the reading we had wanted to do together this winter. Mr. H. suggested going without supper Saturday and Sunday evenings. My thoughts returned at once to the hyacinths you sent, and I thought his suggestion excellent until I reflected that judging from the ordinary state of our appetites, the Sunday and Monday breakfast would probably leave a very small cash balance to be turned over to the book fund. . . .

At present, Mr. Henderson is working at pulling broom corn about twenty miles from here, where they had more rain and fair crops. . . . We had a short but very pleasant visit from Grisell McLaren[8] in June. Her father died in the spring and on her way to visit relatives on the Pacific coast she stopped over at Guymon and come out for a few days. She is to return to Turkey this fall, though I believe she is not to enter the active missionary work at once but will be studying the Turkish language as they expect gradually to be able to extend their work among the Turks. . . .

She told me Alice Browne's[9] sad story. I have often thought of it since as one of the most pitiful things I have known. She spoke also of the very remarkable success of her work in China. . . .

I should like to tell you about the little improvements we have been able to make during the summer but must not dwell long upon them. Perhaps the greatest has been the adding of a bedroom and kitchen to our little cabin and the painting of it, also of the barn and chicken houses. Our house is a tiny place yet but such an improvement over the one room for everything.

I had fair success with my chicken raising and have something over a hundred young ones—more than we shall be able to get feed for.

However we shall use a good many of them before winter. We have nine young turkeys also which are the most [amusing] pets we have unless it is the two colts. They shake hands very prettily and never get enough petting.

I hope the summer has brought new strength and inspiration for your work. I always look forward to your letters and hope you will tell me of all that interests you. With remembrance to all the family and sincere good wishes for a happy year for yourself I am still, Your friend,

FEB. 22, 1911

MY DEAR ROSE:

You and Mabel[10] have both been so generous about writing that it is hard for me to realize that it must be nearly if not quite a year since either of you has heard anything from [here]. I presume hard luck stories are just as tiresome to read as they are to write so now I am thinking that while we are feeling unusually rich and prosperous will be a good time to write some very long-delayed letters. There are two reasons for our feeling unwonted prosperity first and principally because Baby is now quite well again and full of fun as ever after an illness which for a few days seemed pretty serious and second because the country is now buried in snow from several inches to as many feet in depth, after six months without either rain or snow. A drift nearly as high as the chicken house kept Mr. Henderson shoveling for an hour before he could open the door and there are other drifts waist high around all the buildings so we know there will be a little moisture in the ground anyway for the opening of spring.

Last year was quite a little more favorable for farming here than the two "lean years" before it. The price of broom corn, our only money crop, has been too low to do much toward a bank account but we raised plenty of feed and have been able to live more comfortably than before. We now have a fair start in the turkey business for the coming year besides having sold enough to buy material to ceil the living-room over head and at the sides. It was previously just one thin layer of boards papered over and was almost impossible to heat in really cold weather. We think the turkeys are here more profitable than chickens. Our hens have laid well this winter but with January eggs at ten cents per dozen we preferred to use them ourselves. Our cow made us a day-after-Christmas present of a pretty red calf and we have since then had plenty of milk and cream and butter. Butter too has brought only ten cents a pound since soon after the new year so it isn't worth while to be too stingy with ourselves for the sake of selling it. In fact I haven't sold any for less than [$].15 which seems little enough.

We had a good garden last summer but it kept me busy for Mr. Henderson had in about all the crops he could care for so the garden fell to me. I used to take Eleanor out in tub or clothes basket and she played while I worked. I even had cabbage enough to make some sauer kraut and I surprised myself by liking it pretty well. I also raised about three bushels of peanuts in part of the garden. They are nice clean plants with neat little yellow blooms. I should like to raise more of them but the jackrabbits are so thick that it is labor and good peanuts wasted to plant them anywhere except within a rabbit-proof fence. We like to eat them fresh even better than roasted.

The fall was a strenuous time for me. The value of the crop didn't warrant our hiring more help than was absolutely necessary. We did all we could by ourselves. We began cutting our millet hay Aug. 23 with a rented machine and I took my first lesson in running a mowing machine. From then until away along in November when we finished heading maize I worked out of doors at all sorts of work just as much as the care of the baby and the absolutely necessary housework and cooking would permit. Often we took Eleanor along and she grew as brown and rosy as a little gypsy. We couldn't spend $25 for a corn binder so Mr. Henderson made a sled which, however, required two hands to operate one to drive one to care for the cane and maize, corn and Arabian corn which we cut with it. So day after day as soon as Baby was awake in the morning we started out, Mr. Henderson tending the feed, I driving the team and Eleanor riding in a special little chariot which trailed on behind. And at night there were the whole days dishes to wash, house to put in order, often churning and all such tasks besides a sleepy baby to wash and feed and put to bed.

. . . But in spite of trying in every way to lighten work you will not wonder that much was neglected—sewing and mending especially. I still have some few things to mend which were laid away at that time though I have been gradually trying to catch up ever since. Then came the broom corn pulling—such a long tedious task. I didn't do very much at that, though went out and helped whenever it was possible or else tried to do work about the barn so that Mr. Henderson could put in longer days. . . .

You asked about little Eleanor. I wish you could see her. We think she is a dear little baby. "Father" is holding her now and she is holding her cloth kitty and chattering first to me and [then to it]. . . . She is the happiest little thing, full of play and cunning little tricks as long as she is awake. She is so loving too. At times of special household stress the multitude of her kisses sometimes grows embarrassing though too precious to be refused even if they are pretty moist sometimes.

I shall not soon forget the night when she grew so sick and Mr. Henderson decided to go for the doctor. It was a wild, dark, windy night. Everything shook and rattled and banged. Baby had a high fever. Her little face burned like a glowing coal. When her father at last returned, the poor little thing roused from her uneasy sleep and the first thing she did quite of her own thought was to "pat cakes" for Father. They are the greatest chums. He is never too busy or too tired to romp with her or give her any necessary attention. . . .

It is such a vainly impossible dream that I like to think sometimes that I did go to the reunion at South Hadley to recall old memories, to renew old associations, to see the trees and hills and most of all a few of you who I feel sure would still be the same friends in spite of my make shift clothes and seamy hands. But I shall not be there and as Mabel said she could not go either I shall hope to hear something about it from you.

We have appreciated very much the magazines you have sent. I had meant to ask you something about the history and maintenance of your school but the magazines have answered part of my questions. It does us good to read such things—so different from our own work which in a way seems at times pretty selfish—just working to gain a foothold and make a living. You will not mind I am [sure that after] reading them ourselves I pass them on to others who may find them interesting. . . .

With all good wishes and sincere thanks for the magazines from both of us, I am still your friend

⁓

JAN. 20, 1912

DEAR ROSE:

When I promised a New Years letter I little knew what a struggle was in store for us before that time. The sleet storm which was in progress the day I sent my card, during the night turned into the heaviest snow storm we have ever seen here. It will be five weeks tomorrow and the ground is only just beginning to show in sheltered places while there is snow in the fields to last a couple of weeks yet and plenty of drifts about the buildings shoulder high. For all the week before Christmas there was no mail going or coming and we were busy trying to keep ourselves from freezing and also to provide entertainment for some travelers on their way to Arkansas. They drifted along the night the storm began, a man and his wife, two turkeys, five horses, five mules and sixteen canary birds. They were with us six days—until the morning of Christmas day—we really couldn't decently turn them out into the drifts any sooner. But with our limited accommodations for man or beast it was an experience one wouldn't choose to repeat. I am sure they felt the same way about it, especially as our little coal supply was fast nearing the vanishing point. I had to do the cooking on the tiny heating stove in the living room. The top measures just 11 x 26 inches and stands 18 inches high from the floor. So you can imagine that we had "plain living" if not high thinking. It was too outrageously cold and shivery with too many wet overshoes, mufflers, felt boots and mittens piled around the one little point of warmth for one's thoughts to be greatly exalted, while trying to keep things on the table from freezing and on the stove from burning all at once.

Just at the time I wasn't well, had a very painful gathering in the breast and when it was all over, I collapsed temporarily and went to bed to try to keep the poultices adjusted. So you can perhaps with this introduction realize a little of how much pleasure the Christmas mail brought to us when Mr. Henderson reached home late in the afternoon with half a grain sack full of letters, cards, papers and packages. I thank you heartily for the dainty handkerchief and if you could see little Eleanor with the pussy cat book I am sure you would believe in her sincere appreciation. . . .

Last year was rather disappointing to us in some ways. Our farming here often reminds me of the man who when asked to embark upon some rather doubtful business venture replied that if he wanted to gamble he would prefer roulette, I believe, where the chances were only 32 to 1 against him. We had our full share of the hot day weather that seemed to be so general. The rains never seemed to come when we thought they would do the most good and hail did considerable damage. Broom corn and grain were light crops, potatoes a failure, and the garden only moderately successful. We thought we had an abundance of fodder, mostly cane, but the heavy snow and continued

cold weather with the consequent necessity of keeping up all the cattle and feeding heavily, is making the pile look small. However we sat
out on the cave door[11] one moonlight night, when things were looking the worst, and possibly we were moonstruck. At any rate as we discussed the situation we decided to stay here and be ready to welcome
prosperity if it ever comes this way instead of joining the procession of
those who have left and are still leaving to go in pursuit of it. They
may be doing the wiser thing. I do not know. But at any rate we so
decided and recently have proceeded to anchor ourselves down more
securely by purchasing another quarter-section one mile from our
homestead. It is not all paid for yet, and I don't like being in debt, but
we are hoping that the years to come may prove that our faith in the
future of our big lonely country was not mistaken.

Our greatest success the past season was with turkeys. I had 125 to
sell for the Thanksgiving market—two big wagon loads. They weighed
out very well and if we could have received city prices I should have felt
quite prosperous. Even at the comparatively low price of 10 cents for
hens and 11 for gobblers, they brought quite a nice little sum; I never
felt quite so much satisfaction from any money I ever earned before. I
don't know how I shall succeed next year but want to try it again. . . .

Your long delightful letter in June furnished me material for a
number of pleasant dreams and I have attended several reunions since
then. At the last you were devoting yourself to the care and entertainment of little Miriam Schutt.[12] I was owing Mabel a letter so didn't
receive her usual Christmas letter, though she sent a postcard picture
of the little folks and a brief note saying that the little boy had been
seriously sick, but was gaining again.

Do you remember Dagny Grevstad of 1903,[13] Mount Holyoke? Her
home is now in our trading town of Guymon 30 miles from here. Her
husband is a lawyer, though now dealing in real estate and acting as
father to a colony of Scandinavians down in the Texas Panhandle. . . .
They now have three babies and are doing well in business and building a good new house. . . . He said he was going to bring them all out
to see us some day. I really hope he will for I am often lonely and
though I did not know his wife at Mount Holyoke, except as I
remember her face, it would seem pleasant to renew with someone
who had been there, memories of what still seems one of the most
beautiful places in the world.

. . . Please remember me kindly to your father and mother. I hope
that all goes well with them and that the hens are generous with eggs
at $.50 a dozen.

With thanks and every good wish for a happy and successful year I am ever sincerely your friend.

~

MAY 4, 1912

"WHAT I READ LAST YEAR," *THE PRACTICAL FARMER*

When we set out in life together, the head of the house (I like that old-fashioned expression) proceeded to lay down the law that his day's work and mine should end together; in other words, that my evening should, in general, be leisure time for reading, writing, studying or resting, as I pleased, instead of being devoted to left-overs from the day's tasks, or the inevitable mending basket. I assented, though with a mental reservation that time would prove the plan an utterly unattainable idea. To my surprise, as the years have passed, we have found this ideal more nearly attainable than I then supposed. It has required planning and real co-operation, working together, yet it has seemed worth while. As I look back over the years of struggle to transform our "claim" into a farm, our homestead into a home, in the face of every difficulty, it seems that I could never have endured the strain and stress of it all, had it not been for the relaxation of the evenings, when sometimes separately, more often together, we have striven to forget temporarily our own small affairs and enter into the larger life of the world.

Crushing physical weariness has often been forgotten as our minds traveled away from our storm-swept or drought-stricken or hail-beaten prairie into other scenes and engaged in struggles far greater than our own, or felt the inspiration of noble, conquering lives.

We soon established the custom of keeping the family birthdays by the gift of a book of permanent value. So year by year our little library grows and to me, at least, these books, for which we have sometimes sacrificed other desirable things, seem particularly precious. The birthdays of last year brought us Prescott's "Conquest of Mexico," Parkman's "Conspiracy of Pontiac," and an ABC book. We were deeply interested in the histories with their records of deeds of courage and self-sacrifice, as well as the civilization of the Aztecs and character of our own Indian tribes.

In the line of fiction I read "Aunt Jane of Kentucky," whose humor and homely good sense are most refreshing; "The Shepherd of the Hills," "The Calling of Dan Matthews," "New Chronicles of Rebecca," "The Mill on the Floss," "The Magic Story," a very little book which leaves a very big impression, and "The Days of Auld Lang Syne."

Of miscellaneous reading, besides several farm bulletins of special interest in our work, there were Herbert Spencer's "Education," "The Song of Our Syrian Guest"—a most helpful interpretation of the 23rd Psalm; the suggestive little essay, "What Is Worth While?" "A Little Journey to the Home of Thoreau;" some of [Charles] Lamb's essays, and "Stories in Stone from the Roman Forum."

Poetry has been too much neglected, just a bit now and then from the authors we have, as I felt inclined. I thoroughly enjoyed a re-reading of Stevenson's "Child's Garden of Verses," which Christmas brought to little Eleanor; also "Pictures of Memory," a compilation of poems of childhood.[14]

Of periodicals we receive *The Practical Farmer,* the *Farm Journal* and the *Oklahoma Farmer,* besides one eastern and one western weekly newspaper, and lastly, the *Mothers' Magazine,* which well deserves the good words our editor has written in its behalf. Through the kindness of "the folks back home" we receive a second-hand reading of *Everybody's, Success,* and the *American Magazine.*[15] These periodicals have all been read more or less exhaustively, according to the interest and value, from our point of view, the articles contained in the farm papers probably receive the most careful attention. It is our custom to close the day with a reading from the Bible. Often when we have indeed seemed heavy-laden, we have found in its words new life and courage. Here on our lonely prairie we have felt a sense of nearness to Him who "giveth power to the faint," and have realized anew that "to them that hath no might He increaseth strength."[16] However it may be for others, I feel that no homesteaders equipment would be complete without this book of books.

Situated as we are, in a very sparsely settled community thirty miles from a railroad, and at least a hundred, probably more, from a library, my choice of reading is necessarily limited. Under different circumstances I might read more methodically, perhaps more profitably; yet I doubt whether with much greater inward refreshment than has come from the little reading of 1911.

AUG. 11, 1912

DEAR ROSE:

It was kind of you to write when you heard from Mabel of my Father's death. Though I cannot here realize his absence as keenly as Mother and Susie do there at home where there is so much to keep them constantly reminded of him, yet the summer has been lonely, we have seemed farther away than ever, and I have welcomed eagerly the companionship of letters.

I tried hard to get away for a time in the early spring thinking that it might do us good to be together for a time, but the storms and hardships of our furious winter lasted so late that it was impossible for me to get away in time for any satisfactory visit at all. So I again postponed it. . . .

On the whole this has been the most favorable season we have seen here. We have had some hot weather but at no time have deeply-rooted, well-cultivated crops really suffered for moisture, though I have had to do a good deal of irrigating to keep the garden going. It wouldn't do, however, for everything to be a success for us. A cold wet spell in May just after we had planted our big peanut patch under apparently ideal conditions caused them all to rot in the ground. (A neighbor told us we planted them when the moon was in the wrong "sign," if you know just what that mysterious statement means). So that had to be put into cow peas for which the "sign" seems to have been favorable and they have flourished accordingly and we had to content ourselves with a small plot of peanuts planted with purchased seed.

Then I very unwisely took the middle of June, when every minute was needed for weed killing, for a sick spell which lasted a couple of weeks and caused Mr. Henderson to lose so much time from the field that we have more weeds than we like to see. And the grass hoppers have been a real pest this summer, somewhat as in the old days of Kansas. They destroyed all our later planted broom corn and even though the turkeys take revenge upon grass-hoppers and we eat and sell the turkeys, I fear we shall scarcely come out even. Still the turkeys are doing well—132 young ones—the Kafir corn and early broom corn are good, maize fair and cane promises an exceptionally heavy crop. Millet is ready for cutting and the busy harvesting time will begin this week with little interruption from the time we begin on the millet hay through the care of the corn crop—the broom corn pulling, and gathering of maize and Kafir corn, at least we hope for all this. There is of course always a possible hailstorm to do our cutting for us.

Our garden has been more than usually satisfactory. We have had or have good prospect of having over twenty different products not counting distinct varieties, as for example string beans and Mexican beans. With the cow and eggs and chickens, "garden truck" and maize to grind for bread or breakfast food we begin to feel quite independent as far as food is concerned. I dried a good many peas this year, drying them in the pod just when the pods began to be well filled. We think they are good and I am hoping the weevils will not get them. . . .

I appreciated the magazines which you sent and enjoyed particularly the Dickens articles which made me want to read some of his books over again—also to read some which I have never read. Last night came the little magazine from your Father. I feel grateful to be so remembered, glad too, to know that some are working unselfishly to put into practice their ideas for human progress. For it is "here a little and there a little" that the old world does go forward.

Recently I read Thoreau's "Walden." I was just getting over the illness I spoke of which was brought on by a very foolish and really needless bit of overwork so was in a mood to sympathize with his view of life. I realize of course, that simplicity for some would mean more of the world's goods (as when the clothes-pins run out on wash day) for others far less than they now struggle along with. But on the whole I was both charmed and helped by the spirit of the book and by the beauty of its closing words—"There is more day to dawn. Our sun is but a morning star."

. . . It is nearly a year now since I have heard from Mabel with the exception of a line or two with a picture of the children at Christmas time, but I have an idea that two little folks can keep one pretty busy and I haven't any idea how one gets along alone as so many do, with a houseful. Our nearest neighbors had four when the oldest was 5½ and the second one not 3, and yet Mrs. M . . . works in the field with a team and pulled broom corn all last fall, and the children all wear starched embroidery ruffles on their sunbonnets. I shouldn't know how to do it as perhaps the "higher education" in which I suppose we shared, really does [not fit] one for domestic life. But those were happier days than we knew then and I am glad we had them and that you were there. . . .

Last time you said all would be voting for Taft. Is it Taft again this time or T.R. [Theodore Roosevelt], or your own New Jersey man [Woodrow Wilson], I wonder.

Your letters are most welcome as you would be yourself. . . . With love,

---

DEC. 22, 1912

DEAR ROSE:

We are still plodding on in the same old tracks but as the [post] office at Shelton has been discontinued for lack of a postmaster we now receive our mail at the absurd address given above [Eva, Oklahoma]. Not withstanding the change, your letter, the magazines and Baby's dear little book have all reached us safely, and I have been sincerely grateful for all. I sent the pages from the *Outlook* on to Mrs. Dagny Grevstad Mordt in Guymon thinking that she would also be interested.[17] She and the children with a young friend from Chicago came out one Sunday afternoon this fall and we had a pleasant visit, though it was a little hard to realize that the mother of three with hair beginning to gray like my own—was the girl I remembered at Mount Holyoke. Mr. Mordt was away up in Iowa searching for home-seekers for his Texas colony. . . .

We have all found much to enjoy in the Centuries, though as you said of yourself we have postponed the reading of some parts until the fall work was nearer to completion.[18] Eleanor has enjoyed the pictures greatly. . . . I know she will be delighted with the "garden" which is different from anything she has. She will not see it till Christmas but I have been repeating some of the verses in place of some of the stories for which there is an almost incessant demand. . . .

When I wrote last I think we were wishing for rain for the broom corn. It didn't come, at least not in time to do any good, though we had the very unusual experience of a September rain which hindered to some extent the gathering of the crop and damaged the quality somewhat. Rain in the gathering time causes the brush to turn red instead of keeping the light green color desired. However our crop was fair . . . the country over was unusually heavy so the corn is worth almost nothing, from $20 to $40 per ton. (A ton will make 1200 brooms, according to govt. bulletins) So ours has not been sold, indeed it has not yet been thrashed, thought we expect to have it done Thursday and I laugh at Mr. Henderson a little about the profits of his crop, telling him that all we have made from it was the $2.00 which the "Practical" [*The Practical Farmer*] generously paid us for telling how the crop is handled here. Fortunately the turkeys did fairly well though they were later than last year and not quite as heavy. We have kept twenty hens for next year so you know about how my summer will be spent again.

All through the fall we were greatly worried about Eleanor. An overlooked "sticker" in a finger, though poulticed and removed as soon as noticed, led to a case of blood poisoning in a sort of local form. It affected the glands of the lymphatic system of her whole arm and for a time looked very bad. We are so far from any reliable help that I felt exceedingly anxious and for some time tried to keep things in readiness for going away with her if it seemed absolutely necessary. But gradually she improved and about Thanksgiving time we began to feel that she was out of danger. And ever since the relaxing of the long strain, I have found myself a very useless person.

We threshed maize, Kafir corn and cane seed Thanksgiving day, not because we chose so to celebrate the day but because the outfit happened to have advanced so far on the day before and didn't want to lose a day. Then we began hauling in and stacking cane and Kafir corn fodder. We have had extra help for this work and I have found myself very busy, not so much because of the work as the way in which it has to be done. When you go to ranching if you will take some advice based on experience, you will choose your habitation some where within reach of a more satisfactory fuel than cow chips.[19] It takes just about a third of one's time to carry in chips, poke the fire and carry out ashes but with coal from $7.50 to $9.00 a ton at the railroad 30 miles away we are glad to do almost anything to reduce fuel expenses.

We are hearing a good deal about a new railroad coming this way. They say that the work is actually advanced now within 38 miles and that it will come within 18 miles. That is far enough but still one could make the round trip in a day which is not possible as we are now located and we should be very thankful for the change. I have not been to any town for three years—just three years yesterday since I reached home with Eleanor. I did make a few inexpensive Christmas plans this year but didn't get much beyond the planning. I had a bit of a gift planned for Rose which involved the purchase of a scrap of ribbon and to avoid all mistakes I sent a sample. . . . Mr. Henderson took length for breadth and bought home 2½ yards of half inch ribbon instead of the one yard of 2½ in ribbon which I had sent for. He brought home soup plates for cereal dishes and for our small family two vegetable dishes that hold about a gallon apiece. Once I sent for white cheese cloth for dusters and because they didn't have any except cream color he thought it wouldn't do and didn't bring any. So instead of the more ornamental gift I planned for, I will send you a mud pie apron for next summer, made of the fragments from something else. . . .

I am deeply disappointed for Mother's and Sister's sake even more than for my own that I could not take [Eleanor] home for Christmas. It will be a lonely season for them both and I hoped that a baby in the house might help to brighten things up for them.[20] But it seemed impossible and I had to give it up again.

With best wishes to you all for a happy Christmas time. I am Lovingly your friend.

⟨⟩

JULY 16, 1913

WAYS AND MEANS EDITOR, *LADIES' WORLD*
DEAR MADAM:

If, out of your experience and knowledge, you can suggest any way whatever in which I may help meet the needs of the situation which I will describe, you will confer a favor which will never be forgotten.

We are homesteading a claim here in old No Man's Land, what is usually called the "semi-arid" portion of Oklahoma. So far as our experience goes, the qualifying prefix is quite superfluous. Still, in spite of droughts and hot winds, blizzards, dirt storms, hail storms, grasshoppers, and in fact almost every form of discouragement, the fascination of being so near the beginning of things, of finding ourselves not quite mastered by various calamities, has held us. We have always felt that if we could hold out a few more years we should succeed; our homestead would really become a home.

Since September of 1912, ten months now, we have had less than one inch of rain, almost no snow. In spite of having done more extensive and also more careful work of preparation than ever before, we have nothing whatever on 160 acres of land which would support one pigeon.

It is not safe for me to remain here alone with the baby so that my husband could go away somewhere to work. Of course there is no work here.

We are fifteen miles from the railroad in a thinly settled community. In our township—36 square miles—there are barely a hundred people, a large portion of them babies. These people are most of them nearly, if not quite, as hard beset as we find ourselves. I cannot expect to wash or scrub or sew for them, persuade them to buy books, or subscribe for magazines, or have their lives insured. I cannot start a "tea room:" when, on an average, less than one person a day passes the house. Gardening is out of the question without at least a little rain. I have already done my utmost with poultry and have over 200 young chickens and about 160 turkeys. But they will not bring in anything for some time and our prices are always low, five or six cents a pound for chickens and ten or twelve for turkeys is the limit. Eggs bring 8 cents a dozen.

I have a good sewing-machine and could do any kind of plain sewing. I couldn't do embroidery or crocheting, at least not fast enough to make anything at it. I do not think summer boarders would find conditions here attractive.

I cannot think of one thing that I can do to earn a cent, and yet the need is so urgent that I feel as if I must be doing something and as soon as possible. Can you suggest anything not requiring over one dollar of capital at which I might hope to earn even a very little?

I feel that this is imposing a hard task upon a defenseless person whom "The Ladies' World" has generously placed at my mercy. So do not fear to hurt or greatly disappoint me if you also fail to think of any employment that fits into the conditions I have tried to suggest.

RESPECTFULLY YOURS, H. A. C.

OCTOBER 1913

"OUR HOMESTEAD," LADIES' WORLD

Our wedding journey was made in a prairie schooner. Our destination was the "claim" which was to be and still is our home, a tiny cabin in the heart of No Man's Land, and for us ever since the center of the world. No experience of life can ever efface for me the memory of that journey through the sweet fresh air of spring. How strong we felt! How hopefully we looked forward to all that life should bring! The night of our arrival a half-grown moon stayed up to light us home. . . .

My life had been of the quiet, uneventful indoor sort; Will's just the opposite—hunting, trapping, cow-boying. And here we were, "for richer, for poorer, for better, for worse, till death do us part," to live, to learn, to work, to overcome, to make a home, to do our little part toward making glad "the wilderness and the solitary place."

Work began the next day with unloading the plough, fence wire, wash boiler, iron bed, mattress, rocking chair and provisions. A cook stove, table, two chairs and a few dishes had already been brought to the little "box" house, which contained just one room, 14 x 16, without lath or plaster or ceiling overhead—just one thickness of boards roofed over and lined with red building paper. This was our castle.

It was now May and time that crops were planted, but as we had no ground broken, we had to depend on sod crops. It had been too dry all the spring to permit breaking sod, so we kept hoping for rain and meantime were busy every day fencing a forty-acre pasture, using cedar posts hauled by wagon from over the New Mexico line sixty-three miles away, building a house for my fourteen hens from packing boxes, and a little windbreak shelter for the horses. A real wind came along one day and picked up the last improvement and threw it down in a heap across the hog-yard fence, so we decided to postpone a stable till we could build more substantially.

The sixth of June brought a light rain, which enabled us to begin breaking sod. After that, work went on early and late until, by July 4, we had in five acres of cane and forty acres of silo maize, the principal feed crop of this southwest country. A heavy rain on June 15 soaked the soil thoroughly and gave great encouragement to my struggling garden. Though we had no other rain, our feed crop, late as it was, did fairly well, and in the fall we cut about one hundred shocks of well-headed maize. I smile to remember my efforts to help in the gathering. We had no corn harvester or money to buy one; a corn knife seemed heavy and awkward to me, and I cut down several acres of feed with the butcher knife while Will used the corn knife and did the shocking. He must have realized much sooner than I did that our crop was a slight preparation for the winter, but he said nothing to cause me anxiety and I thought we were doing pretty well. Still I knew there was no money in it and braced myself up to staying alone in the fall, while he went away well-drilling some twenty-five miles from home. We spent practically our last cent putting up a windmill, which would be a permanent improvement to the place and help me greatly about caring for the horses. The well was nearly two hundred feet deep and pumping by hand a difficult task.

By his work on this well and another nearer home, my husband earned enough to buy material for a stable, hauling the material from G[uymon], our railroad town, thirty miles away. This was built before winter, though not shingled. We thatched it temporarily with bundles of broom corn fodder, taken in part payment for one of the wells, and did not get the roof on till the next spring. . . .

Will got work on another well in the neighborhood, which made us feel quite prosperous, though much of the profit had to go into feed for the stock. During the winter we decided to use a little money, that was coming to me, for a sewing machine and an addition to the house. We built a "lean-to" divided into two rooms, a bedroom and a little 6 X 10 kitchen, which added greatly to the comfort of the house. We were full of plans for the coming year. . . .

The spring came on with frequent showers; my hens were doing well; we had purchased three turkeys, with which I hoped to make my fortune, and had fenced, chicken-proof, a large garden near the wind-mill, so that at least part of it could be a "watered garden." Maize, cane, Kafir corn and broom corn all came up well and grew fast. Every Sunday morning we used to walk through the crops, noting the luxu-riant growth and promise of an abundant harvest. I had never dreamed of being so happy.

Late in June, when our crop was a little over knee high, we had our last rain. This was succeeded by two or three weeks of extreme heat with the "hot winds" we used to hear about in the early days of Kansas, when it seemed as if the heat must come from a nearby prairie fire, so burning and blasting was its intensity. . . . Our fields, which had looked so rank and green, were burned to a crackling brown. We knew there was no hope of any harvest whatever.

Wishing to give all his attention to our farming and feeling confi-dent of his ultimate success, Will had sold the well drill, but for quite awhile he couldn't collect anything for it, and we didn't have a cent in the world. Even flour played out, though we still had a little meal and I could make corn bread. I couldn't get material for the little clothes I wanted to make and cut up old garments of my own and made other things from flour sacks. It seems to me now, if I hadn't had that to work for, I should have felt quite paralyzed with the disappointment, but one instinctively keeps struggling when there is something ahead.

Later in the summer we received payment for the well drill and there was a chance for Will to get work by going away, so it seemed best for me to go home for a while, as father and mother were anxious to have me do. In the fall Will drove across the State [to Ponca City] in time to welcome the little daughter, who came in November, a healthy, happy little thing who has brought us both the blessing of "forward-looking thoughts," even when the burdens of the present seemed heavy to bear.

We were not without our problems. After the doctor's bill was paid I remember we had just four dollars left and were three hundred miles from home, with winter approaching, and the necessity of being back on the claim as soon as possible to meet the requirements of the homestead law.

Will had work in an elevator for a time, but when little Eleanor was three weeks old he started on the long drive home, a lowering day which filled me with anxiety. . . . After three weeks I received the final message to meet him in G[uymon] on the day he expected to reach there. It looked like a big undertaking. I was utterly unused to the care of children and my strength was only just beginning to return, but it had to be done. . . .

At last we reached what seemed the end of the earth and alighted in the cheerless gray dawn to find the station quite deserted except for the telegraph operator. While he was vainly trying to learn whether the telegram I had sent on leaving home had been called for, according to our agreement, I saw a shadow on the frosted glass and, a moment later, we were a reunited family. I forgot my own difficulties when I saw how haggard Will looked after a journey of the utmost hardship and exposure.

Hotels were not within our means, but we went to the camp-house, where they had a good fire and I rested while Will prepared our breakfast over the camp-house stove.

About ten o'clock he had everything ready for our last start. It was cold and the roads were in terrible condition. Heavy snows had melted; the roads were cut up deeply and then frozen hard. The horses were gaunt with short feed and the exposure of their hard journey. One had slipped on the ice a day or two before and was quite lame. We could barely creep along with our heavy load, mile after mile over the frozen rutted roads.

It was the shortest day of the year by calendar, . . . and the sun set when we were still fifteen miles from home. There seemed nothing to do but to push on. The country was almost deserted after the failure in crops. At one or two places where we had thought we might stop to get warm, everything was desolate. It was moonlight again and I tried to warm myself with the thought of that other moonlight night when we had traveled the same road. The baby slept nearly all the way, waking only about the usual feeding times. . . .

The next day we tacked canvases over the walls of the bedroom and set up the "monkey" stove, a heater and cooker drum set transversely in the pipe, in which I learned after much tribulation to bake bread which would be neither raw on top nor burned black on the bottom. We were crowded in the small room, but it was better for the baby than attempting to warm the living-room, where all the heat seemed to go up among the rafters or out at the cracks between the boards. We really had a very comfortable and happy winter. . . .

In the spring we had our first experience with dirt storms. The failure of crops the preceding year had left the whole country bare and exposed to the pulverizing action of the frosts. When the March winds began in earnest, the dirt flew in clouds, so that often we could not see as far as the barn, and the dirt was almost as thick in the house as out of doors.

I remember one day in particular. I had put some pigeons on to cook, but at dinner time we couldn't think of setting the table in the sifting dirt. We sat up close by the "monkey" stove, slipped out our pieces of pigeon and disposed of them as quickly as possible. The worst day of all I covered the baby in her clothes-basket with the umbrella, and went to bed myself and covered my head to get out of the dirt. That evening when the wind went down, I shoveled up just from the small kitchen floor a large dish-pan full of pulverized soil.

However, we had had some snow, which had moistened the sub-soil, and later showers stopped the dirt from blowing and gave us a favorable seed time. I now had six turkey hens and in April we bought a cow on time, paying ten percent interest. This was our first venture into debt, but Eleanor needed extra milk and the cost of milk would more than pay the interest. We called our cow "Diana," because she proved so fond of the chase, that is, of being chased, but she is still a good cow and has brought us three calves, worth considerably more than she cost.

The summer brought alternately hope and fear. We really couldn't tell until almost harvest time whether we should have anything or not, but after two long periods of drought, showers came in time to save at least part of the crop. Broom corn pulling began in September. I did what I could to help . . . . [but] just as I was getting the art well learned, I had to resign and come in to cook for five men—a much less entertaining occupation.

After the corn was pulled and stacked, we began on cane, which was a heavy crop. We couldn't see our way to buying a harvester, so Will fixed up what he called a "corn sled"—a low platform on runners, with a scythe blade bolted slantingly across the middle of the front end and a place at each front corner to which to hitch a horse. It proved impossible for him to manage the team and care for the cane at the same time, so I "hired out" again.

Next came the maize-heading, and then the great day of our first broom-corn threshing. It was now late October. We had had some snow and cold weather, but that morning was like spring, with a delicious sweet dampness in the air, and the meadow-larks had come out of the "breaks" and were singing early on the garden fence.

After dinner Will took me down to see the corn. The twenty big greenish-yellow bales lay there in the October sunshine looking as solid as the boulders on a New England hillside. They had done a good smooth job of baling, and we felt much satisfaction in our first broom-corn crop. It was well we did, for that was nearly all we got out of it. Broom-corn was plentiful that year and the price very low.

Still, we had been learning all the time to reduce expenses. A small hand-mill, in which we could grind wheat, maize or Kafir corn for flour or breakfast food, had proved a wonderful help.

The fuel question was the big problem. We had a few tubfuls of wet chips all buried under the drifts, and possibly two hundred pounds of coal. No more was to be obtained within thirty miles; the roads were practically impassable and the storms continuing. Any track that was made was obliterated by the wind and drifting snow before the next day. So we hoarded our small supply as carefully as possible until about the middle of January, when the weather seemed to become settled and people in utmost need began to try the trip to town for fuel and supplies.

Will started on a Thursday morning which promised and proved to be a fine day with little wind. I dreaded the trip for him, but we simply had to have fuel, for the supply was now down to a few small lumps of coal and an armful of wood from broken fence-posts. The day passed slowly, and Friday came with a high-drifting haze of cloud, which made me anxious, though it seemed to grow no more threatening. . . .

While I was preparing Eleanor for her crib, all at once the doors and windows began to rattle savagely, and before I could get her to bed the snow was blowing in. I made haste to get out to gather up the little remaining fuel and, if possible, to give the stock more feed, lest the storm should be so bad that I couldn't get out in the morning. But it was already too bad. I could scarcely stand or get my breath or see the barn at all in the whirling drift, and didn't dare venture for fear of not getting back at all.

It had turned desperately cold; the wind was furious, and I knew that no living thing could follow a trail five minutes in such a storm. . . .

I didn't dare to sit up or keep a fire, for there was no knowing how long the storm would last and no way of getting help, whatever I might need. After tacking up blankets over the doors and windows and setting the lamp in the window toward the road, I went to bed and shivered all night with cold and anxiety. We had no thermometer, but a pan of hot water put into the hot oven at midnight was a solid block of ice before daylight.

The morning dawned clear, but I could find no comfort in it, thinking of all that might have happened during the night. . . . At dusk . . . I had given up hope. . . . And in almost utter exhaustion I fell asleep. A few minutes later I was wakened by Will's voice at the door.

He had had to abandon the wagon miles back on the road and tramp on through the drifts leading the team. He was pretty thoroughly chilled by his long tramp in the snow, but his supper was still warm in the oven, and after a night's rest he seemed none the worse for his trip, and I think does not understand yet why the thought of anyone's being out in a blizzard is to me absolute torture. But the fact that four other men, leaving G[uymon] in different directions about the same time, were found frozen to death, proved that my fears were not so groundless.

. . . We then moved the little stove into the kitchen, and there we lived till spring. In February the weather improved, and Will got work, running a well-drill for its owner, but it was near, so he could be home nights. He finished the well just the evening before the worst storm of the winter, on February 25th. After it was over, we took twenty bushels of packed snow out of the house and loads and loads from barn and chicken-house.

The unusual amount of snow had put the ground into better condition than ever before. Grass came early, which was fortunate for us, as the hard winter had taken all our feed. Thanks to the . . . snow . . . this was our best year.

We had a good garden and the crops were good. I dried peas and canned beans, put up sod peaches with lemon to make them sour, and pieplant with raisins to make it sweet, and made quantities of pie-melon butter with dried apricots to give flavor.[21] My chickens had done well, and we had raised one hundred and twenty-three turkeys. We now had two cows, and the young stock were doing nicely.

As it happened, Thanksgiving and our maize threshing came together. Nearly everything for our dinner was home grown, and I know our hearts were indeed thankful for the encouragement of a fair return for our hard work. During the winter a new railroad was built to our State line, with promise of continuation later. This cut down our distance from a railway to fifteen miles and held out the prospect of a nearer and possibly better market.

The comparatively few who had struggled on through these trying years, as we had done, and remained on their homesteads, began to look forward to better times and more comfortable conditions of life. A new spirit of hope and courage was in evidence everywhere. How fortunate that we could not look far into the future!

⌁

Oct. 5, 1913

My dear Mrs. Alden:

I have just been reading again your last letter and wondering why I have been so slow to answer, when it brought me so much cheer and inspiration. To tell the truth the year has been so difficult and disappointing that I have hated to write about it. We had very little snow last winter and practically no spring rain, just the lightest of local showers which never wet down more than an inch or two. Then we had a regular Egyptian experience with grasshoppers and blister beetles which destroyed things faster than they could be replanted. Extreme heat with "hot winds" through July and part of August destroyed all hope of even a late feed crop, which we tried to believe in as long as possible, so the sum total of our years farming operations amounts to just nothing at all. For a time I felt very rebellious and very unwilling to waste any more time or strength in trying to make this particular part of the desert rejoice.

At the same time I realize that we should have to sacrifice the little we have got together in order to make a change now and start over empty handed. So whether wisely or not I do not know, but we have decided to try our fortunes here one more year, hoping that by that time we shall feel more sure what is best. Even a garden failed us this year though I worked very hard in the early spring planting and watering and it has hardly seemed like home.

My 36 hens and the two cows, Diana and Mary Jane, have really provided the greater part of our living. Next year we should have three more cows, Topsy, Minnehaha, and Psyche, and I plan to keep 100 hens and pullets so . . . next year things may not look quite so doubtful as they do at present. We have been following the Sunday school lessons lately and I have felt a new sympathy with the Israelites, wandering in the wilderness. "Lord, for to-morrow and its needs I do not pray"[22] is easier to say than to feel altogether sincerely.

I had pretty good success with my chickens this year, raising some few over 200 besides 150 turkeys. My April pullets are now as large as the old hens and I am hoping they may begin laying yet this fall. My turkeys are lighter than usual as we have to be so saving of feed and I am afraid we have scrimped them a little too much.

Eleanor is my great helper in the poultry business. She simply never tires of doing anything she can for either chickens or turkeys. They are very tame with her and she usually has one or often two, carrying them around under her arm for company. She was greatly pleased with your letter to her and the picture of the pretty sheep. . . . In just a month more she will be four years old and it is hard to believe that the time is passing by so swiftly.

Mother has been so very anxious to see her before she loses her baby ways and I had hoped to go this fall but don't know whether it is going to be possible or not. I wanted the place "proved up" first so that there could be no possible chance for trouble in that respect, and we arranged for it in June, but when the notice was advertised, according to the requirements, the paper which was a new venture, failed after one publication, while five are required. So . . . it cannot be completed finally, until they get ready to have the notices published again, and there is no telling when that may be, for they usually take their own time for such proceedings.[23]

Mother and Susie have just recently returned from quite a trip to Mother's old home in New England with quite a bit of sight-seeing by the way in Washington, New York, Boston and Niagara, with visits on the way back at our old Iowa homes in Plymouth Co. and Des Moines. . . . Mother said she saw almost everyone of the old friends still living in that part of the country and I know it has been a wonderful satisfaction to her. Things are so very different here. The population is shifting all the time, and there is so little of common interests or neighborly feeling. Perhaps it is not strange when people are so scattered and so much engaged in getting on at all. Yesterday I was thinking about our neighborhood. In the nine sections or square miles of which this is the center there are just twenty-four people! Thirteen of those are in two families, so you see there is a good deal of vacant space. That is just about the way it is all over this country. And yet all we need is rain to make it productive and prosperous. . . .

I intended to write while Rose was having her vacation but let the time slip away. I wonder whether I cannot let this do for her too this time, if you can give or send it to her. I feel as if I ought not to stop without confessing that in one respect you are quite mistaken. I really am not brave at all and never expect to reach the place where I shall be able to "glory in tribulations"[24] which make me very wretched and uncomfortable. Letters like yours and things I read in other places and Mr. Henderson's unfailing faith in things working out for the best help to keep me braced up for the most part. . . .

I will slip in some pictures which may help to suggest why we feel like taking one more chance. Eleanor's little wagon has in it beets, melon, citron, pumpkin and pie plant and peanuts. There are others on the table with a few flowers, also from corn, cane, maize and kafir corn. . . . The blue prints show bits of the broom corn last year. The were all taken in 1912. The picture of Eleanor on "Fader's" shoulder was just exactly like her a year ago. . . . He is very nearly 6 feet tall, so you see the broom corn gets up pretty well. . . .

With best wishes to everyone as ever sincerely yours,

~~~

JAN. 16, 1914

DEAR ROSE:

Your letter was very welcome. It seemed long since I had heard from you directly. And I am looking forward with pleasure to reading the Christmas book of verses when we are home again. I am wondering whether it is "The Enchanted Island,"[25] a notice of which I read some time ago, slipped into a copy of "The Montessori Method" lent to me by one of the teachers here.[26] Whatever it is I shall enjoy it and appreciate your gift. Mr. Henderson wrote of having received it but did not mention the title.

I was interested in the variety of things you find time to enjoy in the way of reading. The library here is much like the creek on the Texan's farm—a fine place for one. That is—Brother Carnegie presented a roomy and attractive building, four fifths of which is absolutely empty space and the few shelves at one end are principally supplied with the passing fiction that doesn't make much difference. It is open only three hours a day at a time when I cannot go, so I have managed to miss one of the things I expected to enjoy here—poking around and looking into all sorts of books. Two books I have read lately, however, interested me, "Marie-Claire" and more especially "The Promised Land" by Mary Antin.[27] Doubtless in your work you see more or less of the wonderful transforming process which her story portrays so vividly, but it was quite a revelation to me. Something like a little experience here this winter.

Dr. Robertson in whose office I am working—writing just at present —is the Government doctor for the Ponca Reservation. Just before

Christmas he brought in an Indian boy, 21 years old, for an operation for appendicitis. He was here for nearly two weeks in one of the back rooms. He recovered so nicely that a trained nurse was not required after the first day or two, but he seemed to appreciate my very untrained attentions, and I became much interested in the boy and in all he told me about his people. His own family were here more or less, father, mother, and little sister, and now I feel rather ashamed of my surprise at finding them so very human. I have never seen greater tenderness than that Indian father showed toward the sick boy. The mother, born the same year I was, seemed old and feeble because of being almost entirely blind from cataracts, and I do not see how any white man could be more gentle toward his best-beloved than the Indian husband was in his care for her comfort.

The afternoon following the operation the boy suffered much pain and was very restless. He told me that during the preceding week when he was sick and couldn't sleep nights his father would always talk to him and tell him stories. He wanted me to go and have his father come to sit by him. The poor father who had taken the operation awfully hard, had gone to sleep in another room on a couch and I hated to rouse him, but he seemed glad to go and sat there by the boy's bed hour after hour, very evidently from his gestures, telling stories of days gone by, pausing only to wipe the perspiration from his son's face as it gathered from the pain. No woman could have been gentler, and the language which I had always supposed nasal and harsh was soft and soothing. I would give a good deal to know the story which seemed to quiet the boy so much more effectively than the hypodermic morphine had done.

We found both Mother and Aunt Susie very well. . . . I had heard of the satisfaction that grand parents take in the second generation but never realized how great it was until I brought my baby home for this visit. Yet though she has had such a good time here she says very decidedly that "Home is where Fader is—<u>away</u>, way out there," (pointing to the westward) and that she will go home pretty soon—about March 15—"to help Fader feed the little bossies. . . ."

Mr. Henderson writes that we certainly chose the right time to make our visit. We have had a beautiful open winter here, but at home it has been a succession of storms, rain, snow, sleet, fog, wind and everything disagreeable in the weather line. But we are grateful for the prospect of some moisture down in the subsoil and so do not complain of the discomfort of cold and mud and bad roads. . . .

The country around Ponca is developing into quite a productive oil field. We have been out around the south field twice now and it is quite a sight. They arrange to pump a dozen or more wells from one central pumping station by means of rods or cables some of them extending at least a quarter of a mile and then the oil is piped to a refinery here in town. I don't know how permanent a source of wealth the oil is likely to prove, but people who used to be "just like folks" are now receiving several hundred dollars a month in royalties and Ponca streets are full of "fine feathers."

I am glad you find your work pleasanter this year and hope you receive some returns of responsiveness and appreciation for all that I know you give. . . . Thanks again for the book of verses and the pretty Christmas card. Love and best wishes for the year. . . .

Chapter 2

Hopeful Years, 1914–1928

In 1913, the Hendersons renewed their commitment to stay on
their homestead. They affirmed that decision again the following year when they completed the requirements for homesteading
and gained full title to their farm. Events during most of the next
fifteen years seemed to confirm the wisdom of those decisions.
Caroline still wrote of blizzards, hail storms, and other problems
typical of their location, but these threats were more than offset by
her sense of accomplishment.

Caroline's life and thought from the first years of this happy
period were reflected in her continuing correspondence with the
Aldens and in the columns she wrote for *Ladies' World*. After her
initial publication, she employed three different formats in the
five years she wrote for that magazine. First, she wrote a series of
letters that were published irregularly during 1914. These addressed
topics ranging from letter writing and relaxation to meditations
on the celebration of Thanksgiving and on the closing of a year.
Second, from April 1915 until March 1916, she wrote a regular
monthly column entitled "Our Homestead Lady's Calendar of
Everyday Thoughts." This format required brief thoughts aligned
with selected days for each month. The feature proved to be the
most popular column the magazine had developed. Finally, she
maintained her audience after returning to a letter-writing format
in a column called, "The Homestead Lady's Scribbling Pad."[1]
This third format gave her greater flexibility and was most consistent with both her interests and her strengths as a writer. The
pcolumn consisted of reflective pieces on varied topics—from
children, education, and household and gardening tips to the
national response to the First World War.

Unfortunately, the demise of *Ladies' World* in 1918 and Rose
Alden's decision after the war to stop saving the letters she received

means that we have none of Caroline's letters or publications from that time until 1927. For the Hendersons, the decade was dominated by the family's growing prosperity, tensions with neighbors, Eleanor's education, and Caroline's three-year stint teaching at Rolla, Kansas. The gap in the record ends in 1928, when the *Christian Register* published a letter from Caroline (see letter of November 15, 1927). The letter described the problems in a local church that led her to break with that group in favor of her growing Unitarian convictions. Coincidentally, the following year, Rose Alden began again to excerpt the letters she received from Caroline. Subsequent letters to Alden discuss Caroline's resumption of her education at the University of Kansas.

Caroline's writings for *Ladies' World* are especially significant for what they reveal about her philosophy and values. Her love of nature, her social and religious beliefs, and similar concerns may be seen in many of her articles. Other references help to define the nature of her struggles against the depressive tendencies that would be more evident in later life. This chapter contains examples from each of the formats she employed while writing for *Ladies' World*. It also includes "The Woman Who Raised Her Hand," her 1927 publication in the *Christian Register*.

⟜⟞

"Greetings from 'Our Homestead Lady,'" *Ladies' World*

Recently there has come to me one of the very happy experiences of my life—an experience which, like "the old-time religion," has warmed my heart with a new feeling of human kinship, and has made me marvel anew at the mystery of the transference of thought and feeling through the medium of written language. Some time ago I sent out into the world a little account of our day-by-day life on a Western claim. I truly expected no return, except perhaps the return which does come to those who persistently try to whistle when they feel courage slipping away. *That* I was conscious of receiving. I think it is Walt Whitman who says, "The song is to the singer, and returns the most to him."[2] I know now what he meant. . . .

Then, one cloudy day, after my surprise at receiving a more tangible reward had somewhat faded away, and I was busy with new duties, there came to me as a free gift such an outpouring of friendliness and helpful sympathy as I could never have anticipated. In response to our little homestead story came a bundle of letters from the four corners of our great, beautiful country—and several places between—each with its word of encouragement, its practical suggestions, its reminder of the very real blessings which I know are ours, or its revelation of others struggling with their own hearts' pain.

It seemed a literal proof of Emerson's idea that the things our souls require do come to us. Truly, in the wireless telegraphy of spiritual things, the messages meant for us do not go astray if our hearts are in tune to receive them.

Since that gray-gold day I have been thinking of what letters may mean. Since we began life together on the homestead, so often it has happened, just when the way seemed especially dark, that a letter would come—perhaps from one of our mothers, perhaps from some friend—which would seem to turn for us the edge of the cloud. Conditions would be precisely as they had been before, but they wouldn't look the same, which really makes a world of difference. Once, in a time of special stress, the trip to the post-office yielded only a ridiculous printed circular: "Don't you want to make $300 a month organizing a mail-order business?" We both laughed and said, "No, thank you; that is more than we need," and with the laugh felt better. . . .

I have a friend who sends me no Christmas gift, but I can depend on a long letter from her every year at Christmas time, full of her dear, funny ways of looking at things, bright little sayings of the babies, glimpses of their happy home life. If all my other friends knew how much I love her for not sending me anything but that dear letter, I should probably never have another Christmas present as long as I live.

Then there are all those letters that we do *not* write. We are so busy. So many impulses toward special words or deeds of kindness we feel ourselves physically unable to carry out. And yet it is sad that buds should wither before they bloom. So much happiness has come into my life with those surprise letters, I am wishing it might be multiplied in the lives of others—that more often we might find time to send to some burdened heart an unlooked-for thought of cheer. . . .

⤛⤜

CA. SPRING, 1914

"RELAXATION," *LADIES' WORLD*

Last winter I read an old book, Dana's "Two Years Before the Mast." I enjoyed it all, as stories of the sea have always had a fascination for me, perhaps because of the entire unfamiliarity of their setting. Moreover, the vivid pictures of the California coast, eighty years ago, when California was a foreign land, suggested the hope that our own desolate region might make, in four-score years to come, some small fraction of the progress made by that once forbidding coast. But what impressed me most was a word-picture of a scene in the far south Atlantic:

"There being no breeze, the surface of the water was unbroken, but a long, heavy swell was rolling. And we saw the fellow, all white, directly ahead of us, asleep upon the waves, with his head under his wing; now rising on the top of one of the big billows, and then falling slowly until he was lost in the hollow between. He was undisturbed for some time, until the noise of our bows, gradually approaching, roused him; when, lifting his head, he stared upon us for a moment and then spread his wide wings and took his flight."[3]

The thought of the great bird there in all the tumult of the heaving waters, peacefully sleeping, unafraid, has become a beautiful memory to me. Over and over I had wondered what our lives might become, if only we in our hurried, striving days could at times attain the attitude toward life which came without effort to the albatross—surrendering ourselves freely, without fear, to the great forces of life, truly resting, even amid circumstances quite beyond our present understanding. . . .

To prepare the ground as well as we may, to sow our seeds, to cultivate and care for, that is our part. Yet how difficult it is for some of us to learn that the results we must leave to the great silent unseen forces of Nature, whether the crop be corn or character. How impatiently we often do our waiting! Having planted and watered, we are still eager to add the weight of our own efforts toward securing the increase. Many a time I have found myself tired out from having tried unconsciously and without success to bring the distant rain-clouds nearer, to water our thirsty fields. Often I have felt as if the responsibility for averting a blizzard or a hail-storm rested upon me, and I seemed actually to be struggling against some great overpowering weight. I am beginning to see how worse than useless is this exaggerated feeling of one's own responsibility; to understand a little the thought of someone who wrote long ago, "He that observeth the wind shall not sow, and he that regardeth the clouds shall not reap."[4]

To me one of the most beautiful portions of Doctor Montessori's book is the incident in which she brings before her pupils a sleeping baby. She had just been giving the children a lesson of silence, in which their little bodies were relaxed, their little minds refreshed through the mystic influence of the quiet, darkened room. Leaving the school-room, she met a mother with a tiny baby asleep in her arms. Taking the child, Doctor Montessori returned and told the children she had brought them a new teacher. All interest and eagerness, they crowded about, and as she called upon them for a new silence, she showed them how the sleeping baby surpassed their most earnest efforts to be quiet. The little group became hushed and seemed to feel, as so many of us have felt, the wonder of the sleeping child—so sweet, so warm, so full of life, yet so perfectly passive, a little quiet fountain of life, filled from the inexhaustible sources of the infinite life. To feel confidence in those invisible forces . . . is a difficult matter nowadays. So much there is to learn, so much to do and such a hurry about it all. . . .

Last summer, while the disappointment of a barren year seemed so hard to bear, I would often take my mending or a sack of carpet-rags and a book, and we would go to spend the afternoon under a little group of cottonwoods a mile from home. They were set out there by one of the earliest settlers in this section, around a little pool kept full of water by a windmill. The tiny box-house and the sod-barn are gone, the dug-out is nearly filled in, the settlers have drifted on, but the trees remain and, growing more deeply-rooted year by year, are a landmark for the country round. Baby would throw bits of wood into the little pool and squeal with joy as her dog splashed in after them; the meadowlarks and snowbirds would come to drink or bathe, and the bullbats would skim over the water quite near us, dipping to drink as they flew. The leaves of the cottonwoods never ceased their satiny rustling. And in some way the actual physical contact with the "brown old earth" would always seem to bring refreshment. I could forget for the time the anxieties of the present. I could feel once more the lure of this great, lonely land, waiting with its stores of fertility all untouched for those who shall one day learn to meet its demands, to give to it their patient thought and labor.

There are few who could not find as favorable a place for a vacation. From our own gardens, the whiteness of our Monday's washing against the green of trees or the blue of the summer sky, the drifting of cloud-shadows over a field of ripening wheat or the roofs of some great city, the hush of early morning broken by the first bird's song; the sympathy of friends, companionship of books; most universal of all, the heavens which do "declare the glory of God"—from these things and many more may we gather restful thoughts, may we learn the lesson: "In quietness and confidence shall be your strength."[5]

⌒⊜⌒

SEPTEMBER 1914

"BACKGROUNDS: ANOTHER LETTER FROM OUR HOMESTEAD LADY," *LADIES' WORLD*

. . . One of the best ways to cultivate a large-minded attitude toward life is through the habit of general reading. There are times when nothing brings quite so much mental refreshment as a well-written story, and much of the world's greatest literature is in the form of fiction. But to form standards of living, I feel that there is a special value in those things which are true in fact as well as in spirit.

In history we find portrayed the slow but ever onward development of nations, great groups of people like ourselves with their own hopes and upward strivings.

Biography gives us more personal knowledge of those who have lived victoriously. Carlyle tells us that "the great man is the living light-fountain which it is good and pleasant to be near."[6] A little "hero-worship" does us no harm. It is rather a sign that the spirit of youth remains with us and that some nobility in ourselves responds to that which we admire. Such books as "The Making of an American," "Up from Slavery" and "The Promised Land," while not formal biographies, belong to our own time and country. They are also self-revelations of a most inspiring character.[7]

Books of travel broaden our interests and prepare us for world citizenship, which is a larger patriotism. Stories of exploration and missionary enterprise record many deeds of great unselfish heroism. We all know how the heart of the world has been quickened by the courage and chivalry of those members of the Scott expedition who met death so bravely in the fierce Antarctic storms.

A little boy I once knew divided all stories into three groups, "true stories, made-up stories and Bible stories." And it would hardly be fair to leave the subject of reading with reference to forming standards for life without mentioning the Bible: "Wherefore do ye spend money for that which is not bread and your labor for that which satisfieth not?"[8] No book is a more eloquent protest against such failure to see things in proportion, such waste of energy upon the purely transitory. . . .

"OUR HOMESTEAD LADY," *LADIES' WORLD*

In the early fall, at the end of a long, hot day spent in the broom-corn field, there came to us an envelope bearing the stamp of the U. S. land-office. The document within proclaimed that, as we had fulfilled the required conditions, a certain designated portion of the United States had become our own, in the words of the patent, "to have and to hold forever." Since then I have thought many times not only of what this means to us, but what it has meant in times past to many who have gone forth to make homes in new and lonely places. I feel that we personally owe tribute to all who have ventured and toiled and endured, and in so doing have made the homestead way plainer to all who have followed them.

It seems true that the original settlers rarely become permanent. In our own township, after eight years of settlement, out of one hundred and thirty-six quarter-sections only eleven are now occupied by the original claimants. Approximately four-fifths are no longer occupied, but just lie waiting. Yet those first settlers were the road-breakers.

Now, in late October, as I write, it is about a year since we decided to give our homestead one more chance. Reaching a decision seemed all-important. Having made up our minds, we seemed to find the way becoming clear. Un-thought-of means of providing became apparent. Someone opened a bone-market at our new railroad town, thus enabling people to turn into some small profit the losses of the old ranching days. Baby gathered up in her little wagon all the little bones she could find "to help father." In the brakes there grows in great abundance a tropical-looking plant, a great cluster of long, needle-pointed leaves springing from the root and sending up in June a beautiful tall spire of creamy, bell-shaped flowers. Someone, experimenting with the tough fibre of this plant, found that it could be used for cushion-filling, mattings, rope and twine. Thus yucca, or "soapweed," became a commercial product at four dollars a ton, dried and delivered.

After the turkeys were sold, Eleanor and I went for a long-promised visit with her grandmother, some three hundred miles eastward. We enjoyed it all and missed a stormy winter with heavy storms of rain and snow. However, it seemed good to be home again and planning for spring work.

. . . Our reward is largely a new feeling of permanence. In planning for the future, we no longer say, "*If* we stay."

Feed crops of Mill maize, Kafir corn and cane are more than sufficient for winter feed. We had one of the most beautiful pieces of millet I have ever seen. Before the heads turned downward, heavy with their burden of seed, they just missed reaching my chin. Cow peas, with their profusion of wax-like cream or lavender blooms, were a lovely sight each morning, and yielded a heavy crop of hay. The unusual yield of broom-corn proved a doubtful blessing. We were quite unable to gather it all ourselves or to secure help, and part of it dried too soon. Smaller plots of peanuts, pumpkins and popcorn were wonderfully productive. Feterita, a new grain-sorghum crop, similar to maize, but earlier, more drought-resistant and with large heads of beautiful white grain, promises to become an important crop for this region.

We still have our first cow, Diana. During the summer her first heifer calf, Psyche, "found a red little bossy." Our mythology seemed already sufficiently mixed, so we called the newcomer Poppy, as a companion for the other new calves, Daisy and Marigold. A separator and the sale of cream have given larger returns from milk. Our little herd of ten cows and heifers should in a few years yield fair profit.

Wishing to make the most of our feed, we planned and started a pit silo. The pressure of fall work prevented its completion, but we shall have it ready for the next crop. A permanent chicken-house is to replace the present temporary building. The old material is to be used toward a granary. A plot of ground is fenced and ready for trees. These things, small as they seem, mean to us rooting down, greater comfort and economy.

For this country, which has grown to seem our own home-land, the past season has been one of great productiveness. The response of the fertile soil to the more abundant rains has shown us all that we must learn to store in the soil whatever moisture is given; that gradually we must prepare our fields to resist the times of drought. "Waste not, want not," must be applied to matters large and small. Here lies hope for the future.

To a stranger everything still seems crude and primitive. The great distance from railroads, the large proportion of abandoned land with its rank crop of Russian thistles[9] or its returning growth of buffalo grass, the need of better improvements and of work everywhere, all make the work of redemption seem most formidable. Yet evidences of progress are not lacking. One school district is preparing for a new building to replace the original dugout, and there is talk of a church and of a telephone system. While these things are not accomplished, the fact that they are considered at all, indicates progress. . . .

A few days ago I rode to the store for the mail. Coming home I passed through a deep draw already in the shadow of the coming night. But as I came up to higher ground again, I saw the whole country transformed in the sunset glow—all the brown prairie turned to gold. Little low buildings grouped about upward-reaching windmills made tiny specks upon a wide horizon, each telling of effort, sacrifice, aspiration. . . .

DEAR ROSE:

I have so many things to thank you for—your good letter, so much like a real visit, though all too short; and the beautiful book at Christmas time, with the pictures which Eleanor enjoyed so much; and then last night your New Year note, with the lovely thought you took the trouble to send on to me. I hadn't wanted you to send me anything for Christmas. Thank you so much.

I had read a few of David Grayson's Adventures several years ago when they were first published in the "American," enough to love them very much and wish I might read them all. . . . I shall keep it for a kind of missionary book. . . . I am anxious to have our "preacher lady" and some of our neighbors here enjoy it, and thank you sincerely for their pleasure in it and mine.

The little poem, "Souls," seems a very beautiful summing up of the lessons that life has been bringing, the beauty of that inner gleam which makes us each different, but each of some high worth if we only knew. My husband is one shining example. You have observed that penmanship is not one of his strong points. Neither is grammar. But he is "true blue."

And such a lovely thing happened to me at Christmas time. It seems to me I must have written to you last Christmas of the Indian boy who was so sick in Ponca [City], and his blind mother and his knightly father. Of course I thought of them as Christmas time came on and truly meant to send through the care of the agency thoughts of remembrance and perhaps lighten a little the mother's dark days. But just a few days before Christmas while my plans were yet incomplete, we were butchering, and with characteristic suddenness a regular "norther" came rolling over the prairie; Will had come in from the field in shirt sleeves but in half an hour the thermometer had dropped about 50 degrees and a fierce wind drove the cold right in. But we couldn't leave a job like that half done and before we were through I was so chilled and tired that I guess it brought on rheumatism or neuralgia in my head and neck and shoulders and right arm so that for several days I was useless, could scarcely turn in bed and even being turned was a painful process. So all my Christmas plans and many letters had to be postponed or given up. But among the Christmas mail came from that poor blind Indian woman, (by Dr. Robertson's help in addressing) a perfectly beautiful beaded hand bag of buckskin—with a small patch over a bullet hole in the back—all the real Indian work and designing, every one of those thousands and thousands of tiny beads, being strung on the finest sinews, sewed through the leather. And the worst of it was I hadn't been able to do a thing for her except to be sorry for her trouble and sincerely interested in all that in her darkness she seemed glad to tell of the recollections of her life.

You asked about gray hairs. You might have asked more precisely, if you had only known, whether I had any brown ones left, and then I might have answered, "Yes, a few." . . . The time does fly so fast. Do you remember that I spent my first vacation from Mount Holyoke with my father's people in Canada? . . . There was a little boy then in the old stone house. About three years old I suppose. . . . And not very long ago they wrote that [he] . . . was to go with the next body of troops from Canada. I can't make it seem possible at all that that baby boy is going, may have already gone forth to do his part in killing or being killed in this red madness of war. It is terrible even here to think of. It must be much harder for you where opinion as to responsibility and hope as to the out come must be so much divided. Susie sends the "American" and "Everybodys" and an occasional "Outlook." Another friend has been sending their "Independent" after they are through and we had the "Saturday Evening Post" as a Christmas gift. So we get a good many articles about the war but I know of course that all the reading and imagination in the world can't picture the horror of it.

It is hard to feel in such a time that the faithful doing of our own small task with such vision and sympathy as we possess is of any value to the suffering world. Yet I suppose that is the way the kingdom must come to one by one, in the hearts of all. But it seems so <u>slow</u>. . . .

It has been a full year for us, with more of encouragement for the future. Indeed when Mother was here in September and rather lamented the hardships that possibly we shall always have, I tried to convince her that according to statistics, we probably have something near our share of the world's wealth already. She said, "Well, the Lord pity the rest of them then."

Lots of things are hard yet. I have to do so much outside work that I can't keep things as well as I would like to indoors. And there is always the conflict between the quiet rather monotonous existence I seem to desire, and the unrest of the necessary long trips to town, the constant planning and effort to get things into shape so we can really <u>settle down</u> and the difficulty of getting anything I want when I want it. On Mr. Henderson's last trip to Elkhart [Kansas][10] I wrote down in his book—Iodine—just like that. I wanted it for a frost-bitten foot. When he returned he handed out with the air of duty faithfully performed a box of sardines! . . .

APRIL 1915

"OUR HOMESTEAD LADY'S CALENDAR OF EVERYDAY THOUGHTS," *LADIES' WORLD*

It is hard to be enthusiastic about a New Year in the short cold days of January. For myself, I like to remember that the old Roman year began in spring, when nature feels the stir of rushing sap and sprouting seeds. It seems a twisted desire for consistency which caused them later to put the New Year back to January, all due respect to Janus, their god of beginnings, notwithstanding.

April meant originally the time when the earth was opened anew to the sun and showers and scattered seed, all the influences for fruitfulness. And it occurred to me to-day, in the midst of a bit of housework, that while nature is busy cleaning and decorating out of doors, we may regard our work within as part of a great general process tending toward comfort and simplicity and beauty in living.

Most of us keep too many things. We might take a suggestion from the Japanese, who considered his room sufficiently furnished with a single beautiful vase. "Wilful waste makes woeful want," if not for the water, then for some unrecognized neighbor. I confess that the sight of crumbs thrown into the stove causes me an involuntary sense of discomfort. I am jealous for the needs of the little birds.

But there is a middle course between waste and letting things pile up to our own confusion and the destruction of simple living. To find this middle course, to put in places of real service things possibly useful to others if not to ourselves, to destroy things neither useful nor beautiful for anybody, is a very necessary part of house-cleaning.

And while we are about it, may it not be well also to examine our mental furnishings? We shall not wish to discard the established principles which serve us faithfully like good old solid furniture. But we may well open the doors and windows of our minds to currents of fresh thought which shall sweep away lurking germs of prejudice, trivial grudges, uncharitableness, or unreasoning discontent. . . .

⟨⟩

"Our Homestead Lady's Calendar of Everyday Thoughts,"
Ladies' World

Another year half gone. Real summer now, "the high tide of the year." Venus, the morning star, in all her wonderful beauty, proclaims each new day as a day of opportunity for all.

July 3—Time to prepare for the Fourth of July picnic. Better read your June magazine again.

July 4—Sunday and Independence Day. In this year of strife is it not a blessing to have a quiet time to think of what the day really means?

Read Edward Everett Hale's "Man Without a Country." It is in truth a story that "every child should know."

Lincoln's Gettysburg address will take scarcely two minutes, but how much it still means! Is not "a new birth of freedom" perpetually desirable?

. . . By the way, let us not regard our citizenship lightly. Whether we may or may not vote, whether we wish to or don't, we already have many opportunities for service and for being served.

In October, 1913, "Uncle Sam" asked 55,000 farm women how the government might better serve women and homes. Just 2,241 replies were received. Were all the rest not interested? . . .

⟨⟩

Sept. 19, 1915
Dear Rose:

It was surely kind of you to take the trouble to send me the roll of <u>Atlantic Monthly</u> stories. It is a pleasure when I have just a few minutes to pick up the little collection and feel sure that I shall enjoy any story that I may happen to pick out. They are all so good and some of them so unusual in setting or treatment, yet all that I have read so far deal after all with the simple common experiences of life which are the great things after all for most of us. I wonder whether you remember the little story "The Way of Life"—of the mother who had her dreams. I read it last Sunday. It was so very still here, for Eleanor had gone with her father to herd the cattle and I was quite alone. I read it while I was churning some cream that I just hadn't been able to get churned on Saturday. (The rush of the fall work began before the summer work was ended.) Now I am wondering which of my friends would most enjoy crying over the little story as I did. It is so wonderfully true and so simply told. Thanks so much.

Eleanor and I went to Elkhart on Friday to meet Mother. It was quite an adventure for us, for I rarely go far from home. Mother's train was two hours late so we had most of the journey home by moonlight. The sky was so lovely and I thought of how the sky and the lonely prairie had affected the man in one of your stories. I have never lived anywhere where the sky seemed so wonderful and so always new as it seems here.

Frost still holds off for which we are most thankful as early frost would catch much of the later planted feed, or even earlier crops which were held back so long by hail or "hoppers." We have also had fine fall rains which will do much good. . . .

Mother will be here about a month and Baby and I may go home with her for just a few days if we get on pretty well with the fall work. Love and thanks,

⌿⇒⌿

Feb. 1, 1916

Dear Rose,

Your promptness always shames my slowness. Nevertheless I enjoyed your after Christmas note with its pictures of your quiet at home surroundings. My own days have been full of cares which seem to keep running over into all the tomorrows, though just now things are by comparison peaceful enough. At Christmas time Mr. Henderson had succumbed to the wave of grip which has swept over all this country. He never gives up till the last point of endurance is reached so I always feel very anxious when he really admits that he isn't well. And then before he should have gone out at all Eleanor had something wrong with her. High fever and delirium which always frightens me I think and we had to have the doctor and for several days it was all day and all night. Then just as she began to be around, without a minute to straighten things out of the confusion which sickness seems to produce in a little poor place, came our long anticipated threshing. I really didn't think I could ever get through it alone, but managed some way, though their stay was prolonged by the necessity of stopping in the

midst of things and sending a man and team 30 miles for more appa-
ratus to Guymon.

And since then it has been storms and hauling both to Guymon
and the nearer town of Elkhart (a load of cane seed is ready to go
tomorrow) and I must care for all the outdoor family, which increases
creditably. Last week we had the pleasure for eyes, if not for feelings,
of a freezing fog storm which left everything coated an inch deep in
the loveliest of frost work. And in brief moments I have had time to
look over and enjoy and read or tell to Eleanor portions of the
Christmas book. It is really a treasure. I am very grateful for it, for
many of the old stories are worn so threadbare I can scarcely bear to
tell them again. I was glad to see some I had quite lost track of. Bayard
Taylor's story of the man and the wolf who spent the storming night
together, and the little poem, "Opportunity," the king's son who picked
up the broken sword and led them on to victory. Also, there are many
new ones which we shall all enjoy, so thank you for all of us.

Your mother's note will be answered some of these days. I am so
sorry for your aunt's accident. It is hard to be helpless. Mother and
Susie go on their quiet way in Wichita. "Doot" (my Canada Cousin
who is 19 and measuring 6 ft 2) is a Sergeant Major in France. His
poor mother is so glad he is not in the trenches. Suppose we might feel
the same if Doot were our own. Do you feel as if the world is growing
accustomed even to a thing so terrible as war? I must stop. I hope your
days are not too difficult but full of all good things.

⇝

MAY 18, 1916

DEAR MRS. ALDEN:

You have not been forgotten in all the long time that I have failed
to thank you for the Christmas message for Eleanor and myself and
later for the dainty Easter gifts which our young "Sky Pilot" brought
from the office as he came by on his motorcycle the evening before
Easter. Thank you very much for all these kind remembrances. That
was such a very attractive card you sent Eleanor at Christmas time—
just like a real photograph of old Santa and his prancing reindeer.

I could hardly tell of all the things that filled the winter days fuller
than they would hold. It wasn't simply "one thing after another" but
two or three at a time. A sick spell for both Mr. Henderson and

Eleanor at the holidays, gave me rather more of both work and anxiety than I felt able to bear. But of course I had to just the same. And then the care of the heavy crop of fodder, hauling and stacking, heading the Kafir from the shocks, two threshings, pulling out 3½ tons of broom corn brush, getting it threshed or rather seeded, and marketed, all these things gave us not one day of leisure the winter through.

We had no snow or rain through the winter and so, although last summer was wet and cool, the moisture now is all gone from the upper soil and that is really the reason why I have leisure to write today. I am sitting out in the field by a stack of rye straw, herding the cattle on a piece of fall-sown rye. We intended to save it for grain, but the dry weather has damaged it so much that we thought it would do more good for pasture than anything else. The buffalo grass on the prairie is just as dry and brown as November and fairly crackles under one's feet.

Of course if we could have plentiful rains even in a month from now, we could still raise a feed crop if the later season were favorable, so we try to hope still that the seed time will not altogether fail. We had about 40 A[cres] planted to Kafir corn, but as it was only sprouting to die, Mr. H. thought he might better stop planting and just keep working the ground to keep the weeds down, and be ready to plant if it ever does rain.

We have a nice little bunch of cattle now or at least the beginning of one—24 head, all cows and heifers but four. They were getting pretty tired of dry feed but are gaining in milk since I have been watching them on the rye. Last fall we started to name the calves according to the alphabet and had Sweet-Alice and Annabel Lee. This spring we have Ben Bolt, Booker, Beauty, Buttercup and a new comer yesterday who is not yet named. Cream has kept up in price better than usual. Until just recently we have been receiving 30 [cents per gallon], and eggs, astonishing to tell, are still 15 [cents per dozen]! Usually by this time they have been down to 10 or sometimes 8-⅓. The cream and eggs keep a little ahead of the grocery bill so that is quite a help. I wonder sometimes how really poor people in towns manage to get enough to eat these days when nearly everything is so high in price.

We have made one improvement this spring which is a great help to me—that is getting the water pumped into the house. I suppose we shouldn't have dared to do it if we had known how the season was going to be but after all, I am glad we did for it saves so much time and strength. We are fortunate in having kept over enough grain and I think enough roughage to winter the stock if we can only have a little pasture for them this summer.

The great excitement in this community recently has been the sale of the state school lands, sections 16 and 36 in each township in 160 A[cre] tracts. 5% down and forty years time on the rest (if desired) with interest at 5%. The lands have sold well for this new country considering the very unfavorable nature of the spring. The section across the road from us—just bare raw land—brought [$]5,300 . . . some brought more still. It would seem cheap to Easterners, but is considered a good price here.[11]

Eleanor is growing up into a very helpful little girl with a great love for all the beautiful world and all sorts of funny notions in her little head. . . . This morning I didn't feel a bit well and with a child's quick perception she noticed it and wanted to help. She said, "Mother, I won't ask you this morning to show me how the chicken makes its legs go." That was really a great act of self-denial for her and duly appreciated for I was dressing a chicken for dinner and it is always a matter of absorbing interest to her, especially the smooth working of the little joints. Well I see my cows are starting in and I must follow or they will go to the stacks. I hope your farming prospects are more favorable than ours and that you may have a pleasant prospering year. I wonder, if the girls will be home for the summer. I think of you all often.

⤙

JUNE 1916

"THE HOMESTEAD LADY'S SCRIBBLING PAD," *LADIES' WORLD*

. . . A mother said recently: "We hope to give our children an education. It is all we shall be able to do for them." I knew what she meant, and sympathized with the motive. Yet sometimes we speak and feel too much as if "an education" were a finished product, to be bought and paid for, often with great sacrifice, and bestowed. In reality, education can only be attained by personal effort, and should be for each a continuing process, ending only with life itself, or possibly then just well begun. There are fortunately many roads to personal culture and usefulness, and not all lead through the college campus. Some go by solitary ways and some by the crowded ways, where the struggle of life is keen and exciting. Whatever the road, the most important thing is our heart's desire that life may teach us some portion of its truth, that we in turn may give back of what we have for the enrichment of life again. . . .

For several years we have found pleasure in keeping each family birthday by the gift of a book. Fortunately, good books are about the least expensive of gifts, and are of permanent value in the home. I have just been reading one of the books for this year—John Muir's "Stickeen."[12] No friend of dogs should fail to read this true story of the beautiful little dog (named for a tribe of northern Indians), who, we might almost say, found his rejoicing soul in a matchless adventure for life or death on a storm-swept Alaskan glacier. . . .

Each year as I struggle to have a flower-garden, dig the earth and carry water, shade the tiny plants and screen them from "hoppers" and blister beetles, I reflect with growing tolerance upon the maxim of a distant relative. Her rule of conduct was: "Never do anything that doesn't pay." I resolve that next year I will be sensible and save that hard work. But the next year I do it all again. For later on, when a stranger at the well speaks of the pretty flowers, and the fragrance of the petunias meets us away down the road as we bring home the cows, I realize that nothing I have done has "paid" any better. . . .

JULY 1916
"THE HOMESTEAD LADY'S SCRIBBLING PAD," *LADIES' WORLD*

One hundred and forty years are all but gone since the July day when fifty-five representatives of the colonies stood together and signed the document creating the United States of America. We may well pause at times and ask ourselves whether the ideals of democracy then set forth have meaning for us still; whether as individuals our ways of living justly express our faith; whether for the maintenance of those ideals we should be willing to-day as they were willing then to pledge to each other "our lives, our fortunes, and our sacred honor."

. . . The widespread discussion regarding preparedness has had, I believe, one very definite patriotic value. Upon such a concrete question everyone must form some opinion. Even here in our own remote corner people discuss it as I cannot remember their discussing any other public question; a feeling of personal interest in the national government develops, and a feeling of responsibility in helping to form that real but intangible thing known as public opinion. . . .

⤙⤚

"THE HOMESTEAD LADY'S SCRIBBLING PAD," *LADIES' WORLD*

. . . In these troubled days I think often of a little maiden lady whom I know. She is very frail and bent with a life of hard work and the weight of her more than eighty years. But since the war began, she has faithfully done the one thing she could do, and has now knit over eighty pairs of socks for the soldiers over the sea. I wonder sometimes what she thinks of as her needles weave the stitches, and whether in her heart she does not "mother" the boys who will wear the stout wool socks, and so through this patient toil enter into one of the deep experiences of her life.

Would that each of us might learn from the terrible struggle, by doing what we can to lessen its misery, some new and lasting lesson of love of sympathy, of the needs and the heroism of our common humanity! . . .

⤙⤚

"THE HOMESTEAD LADY'S SCRIBBLING PAD," *LADIES' WORLD*

The question is no longer, "What would you do if America were at war?" but "What are you doing?" For in this struggle, which concerns so profoundly the destiny of our country and the world, there is need of the most unselfish effort of each and all. We cannot know now whether few or many of our people may be called upon for the supreme sacrifice—life itself, or the giving up of those far dearer than life. But to some certainly will come this call. Inspired by the gallantry and devotion of their response, surely the rest of us should humbly welcome any chance to serve and show our loyalty to those high ideals in which America has its being.

Work, if possible, with others and under the direction of those who know exactly what is needed. The Red Cross earnestly desires new members, and suggests many and varied lines of helpful activity. If you must work alone at home, at least keep the spirit of cooperation, for the task before us requires an "all-together" effort.

If you can give no other direct service, at least you can help by your own personal attitude to keep America steady in purpose and action. If ever a nation went to war unencumbered by feelings of personal rancor and bitterness, I believe our country is doing it to-day.

Let us keep it so, remembering that, confusing as it may seem we are fighting for peace, for a world "made safe for democracy." So may our minds and hearts be equal to the greatness of our task. So may we also be prepared for the patient work and sacrifices that must follow the war if the world is truly to be set free; if all peoples are to be united by bonds of sympathy and mutual service; if the nations are to be prepared to become at last "the kingdoms of our Lord and His Christ."

. . . Doubtless many of us will find our most direct service in preventing waste in our own homes. As a nation, we have had spendthrift ways. . . . I believe we shall prove our patriotism and our adaptability by learning the value of things and by adopting in practice the new slogan of the Department of Agriculture: Let saving, not spending, be your social standard. . . .

SEPTEMBER 1917
"THE HOMESTEAD LADY'S SCRIBBLING PAD," *LADIES' WORLD*

There is a friendly picture in these words from an old prophecy: "They helped everyone his neighbor; and everyone said to his brother, 'Be of good courage.'" So the carpenter encouraged the goldsmith, and he that smootheth with the hammer him that smote the anvil."[13]

What an ideal of unity in national life! It suggests occupations as varied as human talents, yet all contributing to a common purpose; each worker valuing his own task, yet regarding also the worth of his neighbors' toil.

. . . I cannot help hoping that when the dark shadows of this terrible storm of war have passed by, we shall have come here in this world, even through sorrow and sacrifice, to a fuller knowledge of human worth and aspirations, human capacity for heroism and "patient endurance," to a more abundant sympathy, a more forgiving love. . . .

I rejoice to think that already our American Red Cross has organized work for reconstruction in the desolated regions of France. They welcome every gift, however small, and use it with the utmost economy for this or any indicated purpose.

In these days of high-cost sugar there is real economy in the use of those fruits which contain their own sweetening. . . .

In the far-away spring after the great war began, we had a violent wind storm. Soon after we walked to the little group of trees about the pool where the water flowers grow. The ground was strewn with the fragments of broken nests and poor, little dead birds. Well, I cried over the pity of it. Then, as I thought of the infinitely greater sorrow of the broken homes and battle-fields of Europe, I questioned how human hearts could ever endure such pain.

Now, as the birds are rearing their young again, it seems incredible that I, who cried over the ruined nests, should have given even silent assent to the thought of war for our own country. Yet I realize that I am not alone; that many who hate the thought of war as bitterly as I do, must also have looked upon it now as the one possible means of redeeming and establishing more firmly the liberties of mankind, painfully attained through centuries of struggle. Therefore, with pride I salute the boys who are honored by the nation's choice to guard the precious treasures of civilization. With honor and heart-aching sympathy, I salute the fathers and mothers who give their sons for this service.

⌒⇒⌒

NOVEMBER 1917

"THE HOMESTEAD LADY'S SCRIBBLING PAD," *LADIES' WORLD*

Few things in every-day experience are harder than just to keep pegging away at a task which seems doomed to failure, yet which we cannot in conscience abandon. Practically, I have to admit the possibility of outward failure. I have never attained to the kind of optimism which assures one that he can do anything he sets out for. He might set out for the wrong thing. But in the long, long run, a lifetime or two, if one's task is something that ought to be done, and he has in one way or another become clearly responsible for it, then if he will give that work, irksome though it may be, his most persistent and thoughtful effort, he may not attain exactly his desired goal, but he will gain something well worth while.

Many a man has died—many another will die—not knowing whether the battle in which he fell proved a step toward final victory for the cause he fought for. In a sense, we are all "under orders." The fact that we cannot see the end does not relieve us of our obligation to press forward, to gain every inch we can in humanity's forward march. . . .

If one grows hopeless and impatient over the slow progress of our struggling world, let him read some book on geology and take courage. . . . The mind stops at the thought of the vast reaches of time required for these processes. Surely we need not feel too greatly downcast that human hearts, in some respects more unmanageable than rocks and stones, have not yet risen to their perfect statures. . . .

⟜∾⟞

"THE HOMESTEAD LADY'S SCRIBBLING PAD," *LADIES' WORLD*

We have seen no soldier and few flags but our own. We have heard no bugle calls, no band playing "The Star Spangled Banner," nor even a congregation singing "America" or the noble "Battle Hymn of the Republic." We have heard no patriotic speeches, nor have we felt the thrill of some great assemblage, where each man's strength seems as the "strength of ten," because for the moment at least, each heart is purified from thoughts of self, and all together rise above their common level. Our gardening, canning and Red Cross work have, of necessity, been done alone. Yet wonderfully we have been made to feel that even we, in our remoteness, and millions, like ourselves, have a part in the great work for liberty. The earnest words of our Commander-in-Chief, the unexpected note of encouragement from Red Cross people, the loyal, helpful services of newspapers and magazines—these have assured us that all, even the humblest, must now share together in privilege and responsibility.

Some day this war will be over. Remembering the uplift of heart that has come through common effort and sacrifice, may we not then retain this "unity of the spirit which is the bond of peace,"[14] and still work together for a greater, freer, more beloved America?

Our Allies are giving us generous credit for all we are doing. "There is glory enough for all." Only once, and then in a private letter, have I seen the suggestion that we might have entered the struggle sooner. But we must never forget that while our hearts were aching over the war, theirs were bleeding or broken. While we, in all sincerity, were not yet convinced that it was our war, too, they were bearing "the burden and heat of the day."[15]

Our long-proposed telephone line is at last a reality. Those to whom such service has long been a commonplace can hardly realize all that is suggested to scattered, lonely people by the singing wires and the possibility of this daily miracle.

For several years we have found very practical economy in the use of a small hand-mill exactly like the one pictured in *Ladies' World* for October. There is no cereal we all like as well as the home-ground wheat. It should be left a little gritty—not ground too fine—and is most easily cooked in a double boiler. For variety, equal quantities of wheat, corn and rice (mixed after grinding), make a very fine-flavored breakfast food. For patriotic reasons, we now frequently substitute rye or maize for part or all of the wheat. Corn, freshly-ground at home, hearts and all, is far superior to commercial cornmeal from which the hearts have been removed to make the meal keep better in storage. . . .

One of our preachers said, not long ago, that were it not for his hope of heaven, he should not be trying to live a Christian life. That kind of religion makes me think of a drawerful of beautiful garments once shown to me by an aged friend. They were white and fine, wrought with all care, and folded away until her own work—and that of all her daughters—should be done, and they should rest from their labors. If a man is regarding his Christianity *only* as a covering to make him presentable at heaven's gate, he can hardly expect it to be more serviceable for the great world's storm and stress than those garments so carefully laid away in the bureau drawer. He is missing the appeal of the most valiant, courageous life the world has ever known.

FEB. 17, 1918

RECEIVED AND EXCERPTED BY ROSE ALDEN

Little Eleanor was much pleased with the fine pencils, especially the red, white, and blue, which exactly fitted into the Japanese paint pencil box her Grandma sent by Santa Claus. And I can hardly tell you of the uplift I felt in reading Lieut. Dawson's letters, so appealing in their high purpose, and all the more effective for being written with no thought of publication. We both read them while out "herding," before the new fence around the farm could be completed. . . .

Among the cousins and second cousins are seven that I know of in the service. The young Canadian cousin has seen nearly three years of it now and recently received some service medal, and writes that he is now a "Blooming staff officer."—-

The year 1917 was contrary from beginning to end. Either we or the weather always did exactly the wrong thing. The winter had brought no snow or other moisture. The spring gave us only the lightest of showers, so that crops came poorly or not at all. In July we had a fairly decent rain, and planted more and replanted. Then followed a long drought with intense heat, so that what had started came to a dead standstill. When rains and hail came in August the stuff had to begin growing all over again.—The frost came right on time, and one thousand bushels of maize turned into chaff over night. Our usually lovely month of October was a succession of tempests which blew flat even the fodder we had hoped to cut. We had managed to cut and bind the late planted broom corn and are still not quite through the laborious task of pulling the brush from the bundle, but hope to complete that work this week. The blowing down of the fodder made imperative the fencing of the farm, so as to pasture out the feed in the field. That extra and unplanned for labor and expense with the broom-corn pulling and the rigors of the winter have again upset all my plans for a rather restful winter. . . .

My garden suffered with other things from the bad season, but I raised beans, carrots, parsnips, beets, and pumpkins enough for the winter, and we have made use of everything. I think there will be sufficient fodder from Kafir and broom corn and millet hay to carry the cattle through, and that is the most important thing. We have five new babies since the new year, which brings our little herd up to 47, which means a whole lot of work for two people caring for them.

One improvement during the year was the putting in of a telephone line which connects us with a great many of our neighbors and our market town of Elkhart . . . .

It is very quiet here—only the wind, which rarely rests, and the fire make any sound. . . .

⟨❧⟩

APRIL 13, 1919

RECEIVED AND EXCERPTED BY ROSE ALDEN

Some train of thought which I could not retrace brought me to you as I walked home from the pasture across the road with my pail of milk. So when I reached the house it was a pleasant surprise to find your letter on the table as if I had unexpectedly met someone whom I supposed to be far away.

. . . You have heard something of the earlier part of the winter. The latter part has been so much worse, with its almost continuous storms of snow, rain, sleet, and violent wind, losses among the stock, and general weariness and disheartenment that I will spare you the details. Though perhaps it would surprise you to know that in Oklahoma, supposed to be a southern state, after a winter begun in November we have just this week had another dreadful blizzard, directly responsible for the loss of over a hundred cattle in its smothering drifts, just right around within a few miles of here. We lost none in the storm, but a few which were already weakened by this unprecedented season were naturally not helped, and I fear may yet have to go. . . . Try as we would, and we have almost worn ourselves out with hard work and exposure, yet we, their only providence, must so fail them in their time of need. . . . Please tell your people when you write that we have received and enjoyed both Outlooks and picture papers, which we always pass on so that some one else may enjoy them too. They sent the pictures of the great welcome to New York soldiers, and it was all very interesting and appealing, especially the thin line of soldiers of the Civil War saluting the flag of the marching boys of the twenty-seventh. . . .

⮐⁓

NOVEMBER 15, 1927

"THE WOMAN WHO RAISED HER HAND," *CHRISTIAN REGISTER*

TO THE EDITOR:

Through the kindness of Unitarian friends we frequently receive copies of *The Christian Register*. I am so impressed by the fair-minded intelligence and spiritual sympathy of your editorial writing that I am appealing to you for help in solving a problem in Christian ethics. It has seemed that in your wide experience you may have known of some one in a similar situation who found peace of mind and inspiration for service through a right decision. I will condense the story as much as seems consistent with clearness.

For almost twenty years we have lived here on our "homestead" in the heart of old "No Man's Land." . . . There is only one religious organization within reach (as we are fifteen miles from town and any other church). . . . About twelve or thirteen years ago we joined this [United Brethren] church, more because we wished to be associated with Christian people in worship and work for community welfare than because we had given close attention to the theology of the church.

With more of the discipline of living, more reading and thinking, and more listening to the preachers sent to this community, we have realized the impossibility of believing much that is presented as God's truth. I kept trying to persuade myself that the unity of a common purpose is more important than the unity of a common belief, or method of interpretation. Still, we felt dissatisfied. One night in the early spring, at prayer-meeting, I told the people of our difficulty and left it with them as to whether they still wished to retain in membership people with ideas so different from their own.

I spoke especially of four points.

I told them that we could believe in the Bible as *one* revelation of God's truth, but not a final or even a perfect revelation. I believe we should look for truth everywhere, in nature, in history, in human life and character.

I told them that we could not believe in everlasting purposeless torture for all who failed in this so brief human experience to accept a certain formula of salvation. To me the life of the spirit is continuous, and everywhere and always within the care and influence of Infinite Love.

I told them that salvation seemed to us a matter of *life*, showing forth day by day the spirit of Jesus, rather than claiming purification by "blood atonement."

Lastly, and I think most shockingly, I spoke of our acceptance of Jesus as the great teacher and leader and example for our lives and for *all* who have come to know the great compelling principles of his life and teachings. But it had become impossible for us to think of Jesus as Almighty God.

Though this all seemed entirely contrary to their own beliefs, at a later meeting the official board of the church unanimously voted that our membership in the church should be continued. Doubtless we should have gone on in that way, expecting no more than bare tolerance, yet striving by our lives to show forth the faith that is in us, had not a later occurrence seemed to make that all but an impossible course.

In April the church held a revival meeting conducted by the state evangelist. . . . If you have ever chanced to read Carl Sandburg's address, "To a Contemporary Bunkshooter," you can visualize the type of man perfectly. It is all there, even to the kicking over of chairs and the throwing around of furniture. . . . One night he pictured dramatically the scene on the *Lusitania* (the mistake is his!), when the vessel rammed the iceberg and everybody in the wild confusion was dashing about shouting, "What shall I do to be saved?"[16] . . . I do not mean to be irreverent by saying that Christianity was altogether presented not as a way of life, but as a cheap form of fire insurance for the world to come.

. . . The last night came. The subject was announced: "Hell, What It Is. Where It Is. Who Goes There."

Even if I could write every word, I could scarcely suggest the unloving tone and manner of presentation, the vulgarity and crude materialism of the whole thing. The geological location, the names of people now there (in his opinion, stated without reservation), the vile denunciation of others, the stickiness of melted brimstone, the *red* (?) flames of burning sulphur—it was all but intolerable. Presently he thought of something else, and asked a man on the platform for matches. My mind flew to "The Bonnie Brier Bush," and the story of the evangelist who terrified the little children by burning the paper. I thought he would try something of the sort to impress the boys and girls, of whom many were present. But instead he asked in a loud challenging voice whether there was anyone before him who did not believe in hell. I raised my hand, just as a matter of common honesty and of standing by my belief in God as the Spirit of Love pervading the universe.

This apparently infuriated the speaker. He came charging down from the platform and asked me to hold out my hand. He struck his match, held it below my hand, and asked if it would burn. Of course I said it would. He then applied the flame to my finger and kept asking, "Does it burn?" "Is it hurting?" And finally, "Do you believe now that you can burn?" I told him that one's body can be burned, and he returned to the platform apparently satisfied that he had proved something. "Yes," he said, "one can burn all right. That finger may be blistered now for all I know" (as of course it was).

He went on with increased violence and said that some people thought they were too smart to believe the Bible, but that the *only* people who did not believe in hell were living sinful lives, and were already far on their way to that destination. He warned the people that such persons were a menace to the community, and especially that they should teach their children to scorn and avoid them as those doing the works of the Devil. With passionate vehemence and violent gesticulations, he declared that if he became convinced that there is no hell, he would "*damn God*" and abandon all restraints. He said he didn't *want* to go to Heaven, if the scum of the earth were to be admitted. And so on and on.

Finally, the invitation hymn was given out—"There's Power in the Blood." But sermon, hymn, and the almost frenzied pleadings of both evangelist and pastor were without effect. At last, when all hope of response seemed gone, he asked that all who believed he had preached the truth would march around and shake hands with him as a sign of their approval. Not all, but nearly all of the congregation responded to this request with apparent enthusiasm. . . .

That was May 1, 1927. Since then I have never been to church nor anywhere in the neighborhood except a few minutes once at the parsonage, and to one other home by special invitation. Yet our names are still on the book of the church, and there comes the question of our future course.

Ought we as a matter of Christian duty to relieve this church of the fear of our possible influence and seek even a distant fellowship with some Unitarian church? Or ought we to go on and disregard the action of the church in approving the evangelist's denunciation, and hope to live long enough to show by good will and upright living that "where the spirit of the Lord is, there is liberty?" At fifty years of age, that looks like a faint hope.

The problem is complicated by several things. . . . In four months, neither the pastor nor any member of the church has expressed to us any doubt as to our dangerous character, and the pastor had the same evangelist out here for a meeting at a different preaching appointment. Yet we carried through by correspondence a project planned last winter for the boys and girls—giving Bibles to all who completed a certain study course. On August 29, we invited these boys and girls and all the people of the community to come to our home for the presentation. Nearly all the church people of the immediate neighborhood came, and all was friendliness and appreciation. . . .

One other consideration is perhaps the result of my Scotch and Connecticut Yankee ancestry. I can't help wondering about the financial part of it. We have so little to give, rarely over a hundred dollars in a year, that we can spare from the plainest living and the ever-present necessities of building up and improving the farm and its operation. Are we wrong in giving the greater part of this to a church which sends out the type of man I have described to represent the Christian religion? Or ought we to go on supporting it on the ground that it is the only organized religious effort within reach, that the people in it are good people and working with good intentions, even if from our point of view they are misled?

There must be some clear way through, but we are perhaps too close to discover the principle that would make it all plain. . . . And if you could help us to a soul-satisfying decision, I could not express my gratitude. . . .

DEC. 19, 1928

DEAR ROSE:

It has been a long time since I have written to you. I do not feel sure whether I ever thanked you for the beautiful copy of "The Haunted Bookshop,"[17] so delightful both inside and out. If not let me do so now most sincerely, for we are more and more alone and books—even when we cannot consult them are our friends. Here, too, I will mention the parcel received recently and put away for the great day. Later I shall try to thank you for it more especially.

1928 has been another year of trying our wits against the weather and on the whole being quite definitely but not disgracefully outplayed. No two seasons here are alike. There seems no limit to the number of combinations. This year for variety an unprecedented amount of rain and snow with severely cold weather through the fall and early winter has prevented us thus far from gathering in and saving such crops as did survive earlier misfortunes. But the unusual moisture lures us on to hope for a wheat crop in 1929. I have not seen "Giants of the Earth" and on the whole should judge our own ventures to be more like those of pygmies. But perhaps I can guess at the thought through some quotations Eleanor sent me from Hamsun's "Growth of the Soil" which she read recently.[18]

Yes, "The Prairie Years"[19]—received from the Oklahoma Traveling Library—had seemed wonderful to us too. I wondered how a man could know and write the chapter about Nancy Hanks and the wild apple blossoms. I hope it will not be shocking to you to know that quite independently, without outside pressure, we have become more and more Unitarian in our way of thinking. . . .

It has been a year of many changes and much effort. In the spring we consented to Eleanor's trying for a Watkins' Hall scholarship which would give her all the privileges of a very fine cooperative residence hall under the control of the University of Kansas. She was successful in gaining the scholarship, so the summer was full of unaccustomed plans and preparations. . . .

. . . We made a tremendous effort and took our first vacation in September taking Eleanor to Lawrence by way of the old Ford truck. It is a very pretty place built in the hills and among forests of trees so that from the high window of [university] buildings one can scarcely see the town. We stayed through the opening days and found little to remind one of the opening of Mount Holyoke in 1897. Yet I was pleased to find that the individual student receives more of personal help and direction in the choosing and planning of courses etc. than we did. And the emphasis of all responsible people was upon the enduring realities. I was much impressed by the Chancellor's addresses and by the efforts made to start the young people in wisdom's paths. Just from the composite impression I received, however, of the 4000, a good many will prefer the side paths for a time at least.

From Wichita we brought home with us my mother who is now past 85 and a very great responsibility. She feels that she must assume the direction of everything here and every day brings up new problems. So we all get our training. My plants are blooming for Christmas. We shall try to make all we can of the day. Your letters are delightful and I always feel a little taller when I receive one. We sent a note to your mother and shall try to do better a little later. "For auld lang syne, my dear."

Chapter 3

Clouded Horizons, 1929–1934

Caroline's studies at the University of Kansas from 1930 to 1931 led directly to her second series of publications. Although this phase of her career would not last as long as her tenure with *Ladies' World*, it led to far greater recognition, in part because this time she wrote under her own name. More importantly, her writing documented the impact of two devastating blows to the Great Plains: the Great Depression and dust bowl.

Although Caroline had initially moved to the university to accompany her daughter, once there, she seized upon the opportunity to increase her own education as well. Assignments in her graduate English classes produced her first formal writing in decades, and she quickly demonstrated that she retained the qualities that had led to her career with *Ladies' World*.

The English faculty encouraged her to write about both personal and regional experiences, as seen in "The Day When the Well Runs Dry"—the one known example from her college writing, included herein. Professor R. D. O'Leary probably wrote the comments on that paper: "This very fine, this rarely fine and fresh paper should be printed."[1] Comparable comments on other papers probably led Caroline to submit her work to the *Atlantic Monthly*, thus beginning several years of publication with that periodical.

In turn, Caroline's first article with the *Atlantic Monthly* led to her correspondence with Evelyn Harris, a Maryland widow and farmer. Widowed in 1924, Harris had been left with the task of managing three farms. Despite the obvious challenge, she had in large part succeeded until the Great Depression led to sharp declines in farm prices. Harris responded by trying to earn money from writing and by extensive bartering to supplement her income. She initiated correspondence with Caroline in 1932 with the goal of publishing their exchange of letters. Caroline finally consented to the arrangement, in part because she had begun her own conscious search for new income sources as sharp declines in crop prices disrupted the family's finances.

When the women's first submission was rejected by the *Country Gentleman,* Caroline assumed that her expression of interest in the "Russian experiment" in her letter of May 2, 1932, may have been the cause. In contrast, Caroline's prior recognition among *Atlantic Monthly* editors may have contributed to their acceptance of the letters, published serially in August and September, 1933, as "Letters from Two Women Farmers".[2]

Caroline's letters to the Aldens during this period supplement her formal accounts of family and regional responses to the Great Depression. They also provide interesting comparisons between her formal writing and the letters she wrote to friends while offering some of the earliest accounts of what can now be recognized as the beginning of dust bowl conditions on the southern plains. Together, these writings reveal a woman who was still helping to combine crops, enjoying the stark beauty of the plains, and taking pride in her daughter's accomplishments. Those activities and pleasures sustained her, even as she acknowledged that she had lost her self-respect because of the privations forced by the Depression. Unfortunately, at least six years of struggle remained when she wrote the concluding letter to Mrs. Alden in December 1933.

~~~

DEC. 22, 1930

DEAR ROSE:

Our thanks for the very lovely greeting card which awaited our home-coming Saturday evening. I think it is one of the prettiest cards I have seen and suggests a beautiful thought. You will wonder why and how people who are so tied up at home could have a home-coming. It of course looks strange that a white haired, tired-looking person like myself should start out and go to school again with no expectation of turning the work to any economic account. And I have almost stopped trying to explain. But on the whole it has seemed to be "good medicine." The youngsters can out distance me on the climb up Mount Oread where the Kansas University buildings are situated. The street I climb each morning goes about like this - / a little "more so" if anything. But after I get to the top—in my own kind of work I seem to do about as well as the boys and girls.

Eleanor and I have had a small apartment and have managed as economically as possible. It surely seems pleasant, however, to be at home with a real fire and the windows full of green plants. Mr. Henderson seems to want me to go back and finish out the year, but I am not decided yet. The courses that I have taken would count toward a Master's Degree in English if I should want to go on, but that does not now seem probable.

I think Mother will be likely to come out here again in the spring. She recently had her eighty-seventh birthday and keeps surprisingly well, but fails in mind.

I was interested in what you wrote of the books you had read about the life of Jesus. I had seen just one of them—the book by a Jewish scholar, Klausner, I think.[3] A young man from St. Lawrence University who held meetings here during the summer was reading that while he was here and I looked into it a little. I had hoped to do much general reading at Lawrence. They have a fine library, but the assigned work takes so much of my time that there isn't much left for the additional reading that one would enjoy.

I brought home "John Brown's Body" to read in connection with a course in Twentieth Century American Poetry.[4] I wonder whether you have read it. The letter that he quotes word for word about how J.B. had hoped the evil of slavery might be destroyed with only *a little* bloodshed, is in the Memorial History collection at Topeka. We had seen it when we stopped there on the way to Lawrence.

The recognition is what Professor Hopkins of my course in Literary Criticism would call a "book experience." That is the only course I do not like. I have no aptitude for the hair-splitting distinctions. And when I read a book review I want it to tell me something of what the book is about and Professor Hopkins counts that a literary crime.

Old English is bad, though I get it fairly well with more interest, however, in the human side of it, than in the grammatical and philological. Some of the modern poetry I have enjoyed—particularly Robert Frost's. But when it comes to appreciating "essential poetry"— what is left after all thought and human feeling have been studiously eliminated, I am a great failure. Professor Johnson who gives the course is rather conservative and doesn't pretend an enthusiasm for T.S. Eliot and Ezra Pound.

We are to have a white Christmas unless it suddenly turns warm and melts the recent snow. It will be the first time the three of us have been alone together for quite a while. I am so uncertain about going back that I won't give the Lawrence address. But if you write here, it will be forwarded. I always love to hear from you.

⊸⊰⊱⊶

Nov. 1931

"Bringing in the Sheaves," *Atlantic Monthly*

In all this great southwestern plains country the pale gold of the ripened wheat fields has day by day been changing to the duller brown of the cut over stubble. Early and late, from all directions, has resounded the hum of tractors and combines. Trucks have been hastening over the roads, carrying piled-up loads of bright, hard, full-kerneled wheat to granaries or elevators. Toward nightfall in the sunset glow the air has been luminous with the incandescent dust rising in a cloud about each moving combine. I have never seen a more beautiful harvest.

Our own crew would seem at first thought hopelessly inadequate for our heavy task—a man and woman just past middle age and a young girl just graduated from a Middle-Western university. Yet, with the help of a small tractor and a twelve-foot combine, in a little less than four weeks we have harvested for ourselves or for other people six hundred and twenty-five acres of wheat and twenty acres of barley.

As I think back to childhood days in a Northern state, when we spent as much time laboriously harvesting our small fields of wheat, oats, and barley, I realize anew that we are indeed living in a different age. . . . It was the tradition that wheat must "go through the sweat" in the stack if it was to keep in storage.

What would my father think of our temerity in driving around our fields cutting and threshing all at one operation? Certainly he would expect retribution, and perhaps—in a sense—he would be right.

In our harvest crew the man was the only one able to shovel wheat into the granaries. The girl was already somewhat accustomed to handling the tractor, so it fell to me to manage the combine.

I might say, in the words of the old hymn, "Forbid it, Lord, that I should boast"[5] of any mechanical ability. No mature person could well have less. But I could tell if the combine motor for any reason began to play a different tune. I could see when a chain dropped, or a shaft stopped rolling, or the straw spreader ceased to whirl out its cloud of straw and chaff. I could hear the tremendous clatter, if by any chance we picked up a wire yoke dropped by some nonchalant cow that had pastured earlier on the green wheat. I could shout "Whoa!" to the tractor girl, throw out the gear lever, and wait for expert aid if the trouble proved beyond feminine adjustment. . . .

Before the harvest was over, I realized that more of each day's weariness came from the constant need of alertness and from the heat and jar and deafening noise than from the physical work required. I felt a new sympathy for those whose daily toil involves the mere watching and tending of the swiftly moving mechanical servants of our modern industrial life.

The morning work was not unpleasant. We were up early, often eating breakfast by lamplight, and were in the field by six o'clock, fueling and oiling the machinery for the forenoon work. . . .

When all was running well, it proved difficult for me in my inexperience to fix my attention upon the various chains and rollers which it was needful to watch. In spite of myself my mind would wander away into harvest fields of distant ages and places. I seemed to feel the kinship of a common task with the people of ancient Egypt gathering wheat to feed the Roman multitudes. I remembered the bent figures of Millet's *Gleaners* and seemed to share the pride of Ruth, the Moabite maiden, as she beat out her measure of grain gleaned from the barley fields of Boaz. I could in some degree feel the elation of Russian peasants now beginning to straighten their bent backs, "bowed with the weight of centuries," and enter consciously into the world's affairs. . . .

From such reveries a sudden jolt or unwonted sound would rouse me into more active consciousness of my task, and I would find myself grateful for the strength in chains and bolts and keys that had kept everything moving while my mind had been wool-gathering.

When the grain bin was full, the man's hard work began. Hurrying with the old truck to the granary, he scooped the hot wheat in the hot sun through the high windows into the bins.

Often I wondered about the man and girl. What were they thinking about as the little tractor panted along over the sun-bright stubble, or the truck bumped over the rough road with the beautiful wheat? Of only two things could I feel very sure: first, that near as we have been together through more than a score of years, their "streams of consciousness" would not be like my own; and second, that as the shadows pointed more nearly straight north everybody would be growing more and more fiercely hungry, and more eager for the rest and relaxation that come with even plain food thankfully shared.

The afternoon work was much more trying than that of the morning. With temperatures ranging above 100 day after day, the platforms of tractor and combine burned our feet. Every bit of metal was too hot to handle comfortably, and the heat and odor from the exhaust pipes grew almost intolerable.

There were some blessed days when the wind blew at such an angle as to carry the dust past us and away. On other days there seemed no chance to escape the irritation of the prickly chaff and dust which surrounded us in a moving cloud and adhered to our clothing and sweat-damp skin. On such days all one could do was just to endure, to long for nightfall and the evening coolness, to reflect with sympathy upon Rupert Brooke's expression, "the benison of hot water."[6] . . .

So the days passed, full of effort, each adding to our accumulating weariness, even though we made the most of each diversion; enjoyed to the full the beauty of the pink bush morning-glories growing here and there among the wheat; appreciated the pungent odor as we cut through an occasional patch of mountain sage; loved the small rabbits hopping away to safety, and the pair of little mourning doves which I saved from destruction when, warned by their mother's quick flight, I climbed down from the combine and held them for an instant, pin-feathered and hot in my hand, while the combine roared over the tiny hollow which was their home.

When the last day came, the nervous tension increased and the anxiety grew deeper lest some oversight or accident should cause delay and prevent the completion of our task. But all went well. The loads moved regularly to the barn loft where we were storing the last of our crop. The patch of uncut wheat in the center of the field grew steadily smaller and narrowed to a thin wedge, and, as we made the last turn and cut back toward home, disappeared entirely. Our harvest was over.

I was relieved to see that the tractor girl in her blue overalls had enough excess energy left to turn a few handsprings in celebration of the event. The man shoveled the last load into the loft while I brought a broom and swept up the scatterings for chicken feed.

It certainly seemed that "something attempted, something done" ought to have earned at least "a night's repose." Yet repose is just about the last thing any of us has gained from one of the best wheat crops this country has ever produced in our twenty-four years of farming, beginning with the early days of homesteading.

Bewilderment, distraction, despair, would come nearer to suggesting the common state of mind as people are forced into selling their most important means of livelihood for less than the cost of production. Wheat has been going out of our community by the trainload, 162 carloads in two days from a little siding on our new railroad, at around 25 cents a bushel. It has been as low as 21 cents, is to-day 24. . . .

It is safest to talk of what one actually knows, and our own crop will do for an example, though in some respects our report is too favorable to be thoroughly typical. We were farming our own land, were free from indebtedness on land or machinery, used home-grown seed, hired no outside help, and were fortunate enough to produce a crop somewhat above the average—4,500 bushels from 294 acres. I believe the ten-year average for wheat in our state is a little over twelve bushels to the acre.

Yet, with these advantages, the report of our year's work reminds one of the boy's stone bruise. We are too big to cry about it and it hurts us too much to laugh.

Allowing 6 per cent on the value of the actual wheat acreage, figuring in the value of the seed wheat at 50 cents a bushel, and adding the actual cash outlay for fuel and oil for preparing the ground, drilling the wheat, and harvesting and marketing the crop, if, like many others, we had been forced to sell our wheat at 21 cents, we should have had, out of our 4,500 bushels, a margin of $130 to pay for everybody's time and work, to say nothing of the depreciation of machinery or the wear and tear of bones and nerves and muscles.

Of course we hope to pull through somehow, though we hate to think about taxes, which will be around $200 this year. We are grinding our own wheat for breakfast cereal; sifting out the finest meal for muffins and brown bread; trying to keep our grocery bills within the limits of our weekly case of eggs at 7 or 8 cents a dozen; buying nothing that we can do without and still maintain any sort of standard of health and decency.

Yet some things we must buy or go out of business, and here is where we suffer. For example, we had to have repairs on our plough. Three little oil cups and an axle as long as my arm and thick as my wrist cost us yesterday $12.60—fifty-two bushels of wheat. Apparently the infant industries are receiving the usual tender care and solicitous protection.

We shall, I think, keep on some way. But what of the people who are paying rent, who are in debt for legitimate expenditures, who have the expense of illness or larger families to provide for and educate? . . .

It might perhaps be easier for us all to take our bitter medicine if we felt that we had been guilty of fault or folly, if we knew that there was really too much wheat to satisfy the world's hunger and sow the fields again. We shouldn't mourn over the losses of a man who persisted in establishing hairpin factories in a bobbed-haired world. But we can't see the wheat situation that way, no matter what we hear or read about it. . . .

Surely there must be some better way than this to realize the ideal of contented, productive effort—the ideal which was so well put by one in olden times: "And to rejoice in his labour; this is the gift of God."[7]

⤛⤜

March 19, 1931

"The Day When The Well Runs Dry," the University of Kansas

Long ago when home-made bread was more common than it is now, I once read a poem whose aim was to suggest the gloom pervading a household "On the Day When the Bread Doesn't Rise."[8] A similar atmosphere of despair settles down on our home, when the man of the family announces before breakfast that the windmill has stopped pumping water.

With somewhat the same foolish impulse which sends the despairing searcher of some lost article back to look again in the place where he first missed his treasure, I rush out to the well. I must verify the dis-aster with my own eyes. The windmill wheel is turning smoothly; the jet-rod is rising and falling, but no drop of water flows. The pipe lead-ing to the water-barrel is not even damp.

Rather half-heartedly, we try striking the well pipe with the axe, hoping to set free the check-valve if by some chance it has become wedged in its little cage far down in the bottom of our deep well. This does no good, and we decide to eat breakfast before we attack the problem more actively. But it is a hurried and somber meal.

I then hurry through my morning work, while the man gathers chains, wrenches, pump-leathers, block and tackle—whatever we may need for the work before us. Judging by all past experience, there is a high degree of probability that these crises will occur on days notable for extreme heat or cold or violent wind, when there is already a scarcity of water for the household and for the stock, because of sev-eral preceding days of calm weather.

But whatever the circumstances, we must try to face them. At best, it will take time and all our strength and some measure of knowledge and experience to make the right adjustments. My own part is small— to maintain an unwonted silence; to try earnestly to see and supply whatever tool or effort is needed at a particular moment, and to do quickly just what I am told. It is my part neither "to make reply" nor "to reason why."

When all is ready, we begin our united attempt to raise the long wooden plunge-rod. It is heavy to begin with and requires all the lift-ing power of both of us to raise it. When a joint comes in sight, I quickly slip a wrench around the neck of the iron coupling to hold the rod while we rest and take breath. Loosening the upper rod, we lay it aside and lift again.

Slowly the rods come up. I must not distract my companion's attention by talking, but I can't help thinking, and often, as we work, I wonder where the ash trees grew, from whose trunks these long straight-grained rods were fashioned; or where the iron was mined which furnished the fittings. The realization of our absolute depend-ence upon a supply of water seems to make me more sensitive than usual to the thought of the interdependence of all our lives.

But I mustn't dream too long. The lower rods which have been underneath the water are slippery, and we have to hold fast. Each one lightens the load, and at last we bring out the lowest rod and examine carefully the section of the pump attached to it.

If the cup leathers are too badly worn to hold the water, or if the leather on the little brass plunger needs replacing, or if we find some bit of wood or metal wedged under the valve, we are happy, for we think we have found the cause of our trouble. But if we can find no defects here we must put the rods all back together and try to bring up the lower valve from the cylinder.

We must not delay, for by this time the cattle have come for water. They quickly drink the small supply in their tank and crowd up to the fence begging loudly for more. We can't comfort them with assurances that "prosperity is just around the corner."[9] So we hurry on with the work, while they express their displeasure in their own distressing way.

If the lower valve also seems in perfect condition, nothing remains but to pull up the pipe for examination, a difficult and even dangerous proceeding. This, of course, we cannot do without help. We must call to our aid the good old truck, "Henry I." There is no time to stop for dinner. We must hasten if we are to get through before night.

When all the necessary connections of blocks and chains and pulleys are completed, and the lifting rope is tied securely to the truck frame, the man starts the truck and drives slowly ahead until the rope can stretch no more. There is an instant's pause and then as the truck moves on, the pipe begins to rise slowly. I stand ready to give the "stop" signal as soon as the coupling is above the ground. We quickly tighten the clamp below the coupling, to hold the pipe while we unscrew the joints.

Over and over we repeat this nerve-trying procedure. The last length of pipe comes up with the brass cylinder attached. We are breathless with effort and with anxiety as to the cause of all our trouble. The pipe may have rusted through somewhere; there may be a crack in the cylinder; some change of condition may have caused sand or mud to accumulate so as to hinder the action of the valves.

If on examination we find that a portion of the pipe or the cylinder must be replaced, the completion of our task will have to wait— and the cows will have to bawl—until the next day. But if a thorough cleaning and perhaps raising of the pipe seems to be all that is needed, we go to work hopefully to reverse the process just completed. One by one the heavy pipes and then the wooden rods go back into the well. We connect the rods and the windmill. If the wind keeps on blowing, we shall soon learn the result of our labor. We are hungry and tired and uneasy, for fear that we may have overlooked some factor in the problem.

Dusk is gathering about us now. All the usual tasks of evening are waiting for us, regardless of our weariness. Yet when the longed-for water really gushes forth from the pipe, we are rather foolish in our sense of lightness and relief. The man tells me I am worth a nickel, and we gather up our tools and go about our work preparing for the night.

DEC. 15, 1931

DEAR ROSE:

I am hoping that this may reach you before you leave Newark for your holiday vacation. Your friendly note was the first intimation I had received that the Atlantic had really made use of our little harvest story. Though they had accepted it promptly and paid me too much for it, I had heard no more about it and had begun to think they had come to themselves and that I should have to recover and return the amount of their pretty blue check. It was most kind of you to write, and a few messages from friends old and new who felt interested in the wheat situation have helped wonderfully to brighten what has otherwise seemed a pretty trying experience. Very many thanks.

As to your implied question about other work, there isn't much to tell. I think I sent your mother a little account of one of our short vacation trips published in *The Christian Leader*. The same paper published a short account of the seventy-fifth anniversary of the founding of the Unitarian Church in Lawrence, one of the very first churches established in the new territory of Kansas.[10] But I didn't write it with any idea of publication. In fact it was really prepared for an English class, and I just thought the editor might be interested as he is a former Kansan—used to teach English at Emporia.

I rarely feel any impulse and never any consciousness of ability to write for publication. It really seemed as if some one ought to try to suggest the human side of the wheat situation and it was, I think, only a fortunate accident that caused the acceptance of so matter-of-fact a narrative.

Conditions are still difficult, in some ways increasingly so, because as the months pass without any important signs of improvement, we begin to fear that after all we shall have to sacrifice our wheat for whatever it will bring. The price is now hovering around thirty cents, which represents a definite loss if ones' time and work are worth anything whatever. And the real hardship here arises from the fact that while wheat is not a <u>sure</u> crop, with reasonable management it comes nearer to certainty than the crops which depend on summer rainfall. For several years now rain in the growing season has been scarce indeed and spring planted crops invariably fall short. Cattle, hogs, and poultry products have gone on down with wheat, so it is a real problem how to pay taxes and keep up expenses.

We are so glad that Eleanor finished her course at Lawrence before things became as bad as they are now. . . .

Eleanor had been invited to join the Phi Beta Kappa and had already received the promise of technician work in one of the laboratories if she wished to return for graduate work so we felt very proud of our little girl, and I think it was really a very happy time for her. . . .

In August we took a week off for a very pleasant vacation. The little old second-hand Ford took us over about 900 miles of wonderfully varied and beautiful country in Colorado and north-eastern New Mexico. We revisited Mount Capulin with its deep crater in such contrast to the luxuriant greenness of the vegetation where the cindery mass of the mountain has weathered on the surface to life-giving soil. We picked up marine fossils on Raton Pass about nine thousand feet above sea level. Around Trinidad we passed through several coal-mining settlements and I recalled Miss Soule's[11] saying that the substitution of some other source of energy than coal was one of the great problems of a better civilization. We camped over night in sight of the beautiful Spanish Peaks. About noon the next day we crossed the mountain range at La Veta pass, one of the loveliest and most impressive parts of our journey. . . .

Now we are looking eagerly forward to Eleanor's home coming on Saturday. I have washed the curtains in her room and made up her bed with a fresh blanket. The geraniums and one carnation are blooming nicely, the Christmas cactus is budded—also some narcissus bulbs, and we anticipate a happy time together even if there is much to be anxious about, not only for ourselves but even more for many people we know who are under even heavier pressures.

I wonder how your brothers find conditions in Iowa and New Jersey, and what do you people think is the way out. Hoover seems to me too complacent. He insisted too long that everything was all right when we all knew that much was altogether wrong. The mere fact of a nation like our own with every natural resource in abundance going billions of dollars behind on current expense in time of peace doesn't look right to one of Scotch and New England ancestry.

Does the disturbed condition of the times affect your work in any way? I hope you are gradually recovering from the effects of your operation and gaining strength for all the heavy work. There is surely nothing that requires more constant effort than teaching and I doubt whether I could do it again at all.

The fire is out and the room is growing cold so I really must stop. I shall try to write to your mother by Christmas time. We hope you may have a good vacation with whatever you most need of rest or other recreation, of Society or Solitude. With every good wish for Christmas and a better year for everybody in 1932. I am still Your old friend

DEC. 21, 1931

DEAR MRS. ALDEN:

We were very glad to receive your letters and to hear something of all the family. I hope that at least the nearer ones can be home for Christmas and that you may have a good day together.

Conditions are so extremely difficult for many people that for many of us it can't be exactly a merry occasion. But there are always the children to help us to look forward; and perhaps they will be able, little by little, to right some of the wrongs which darken this holiday time.

Eleanor came home Saturday for two weeks, a little thinner and more tired than I like to see her. We hope the rest and change may help her to gain some weight and that she may lighten up a little on her work for the rest of the year. Perhaps I haven't ever told you that after a busy summer here she returned to Lawrence for graduate work. She has been making her own way by doing technician work—mostly microscope slides—for the anatomy department in the medical school. It is work which should help her in what she thinks she would like to do later. . . .

Things go on about as usual in Wichita. Susie still has to be very careful about any extra exertion. I fear she will always have a bad heart, but her husband fortunately has the steady and well-paid work of a city mail carrier. . . . Robert is a big boy, doing well with his school and music lessons. Mother is very little changed from a year ago. . . . Is really surprisingly well for her eighty-eight years and takes the greatest pride in her two grandchildren.

Since I wrote to Rose, we have had a very welcome snow which has brought at least some moisture to our dry fields. The late summer and autumn had been so extremely dry that our fall-sown wheat had not even sprouted.

Well, if we are to have breakfast in time for Mr. Henderson to get this to the morning mail, I must stop. Take things as lightly as you can. I think of you a great deal even though I do not write and am so glad to have known you and Mr. Alden and all the family. Our best wishes to each and all.

⌐⥰⌐

AUGUST 1933

"LETTERS OF TWO WOMEN FARMERS I," *ATLANTIC MONTHLY*

MAY 2, 1932

MY DEAR EVELYN,

Last week I caught a glimpse of what must have been the real blue-bird of happiness—a flash of deepest azure brightening the misty morning on which he appeared among the branches of our locust trees. We were more than glad to welcome this messenger of spring, for the "winter of our discontent"[12] has been long and stormy and persistent. Even this past week, when we should have been making May baskets, the lilac blossoms, which had survived the March blizzards and the April gales, and the rosebuds, just beginning to show their color, were coated with ice and tinkled like glass in the shifting winds. One day of the week before, four freight cars on our new railway went hurtling along the track for about forty miles, set in motion and carried forward solely by the violence of the wind and their own momentum.

These days of furious wind, which we must expect in the early spring, have a nervously exciting effect on both man and beast. On one of the worst days recently, our little Leghorns fought like fiends from dawn till roosting time, and when I went out in the night, as usual, to see about the brooder fire, they got up and promptly went at it again.

You ask about farming prospects out here. Well, we are going ahead with our spring work, but in a rather hesitating way. Unfavorable weather, lack of moisture, and wretched business conditions have slowed up everything. We cannot afford expensive mistakes, and are trying to proceed cautiously, with the least possible outlay. Our stored wheat from last year's crop is all we have to depend on to keep things going, except the small returns from dairy and poultry products. It would require a lot of close accounting to prove which involves the greatest loss—wheat at 31 cents a bushel, eggs at 7 cents a dozen (in trade), hens at 8 cents a pound, calves at 3 cents, steers at 2 cents, or milo, maize and Kafir corn at around 30 cents a hundredweight.

In nothing that we can produce here is there at present the slightest chance of any return on our labor. Yet we keep on working—really harder than ever. I wonder sometimes whether we are any wiser than the ants that William Beebe writes about in one of his books.[13] He joined the ends of a marching column, and the ants went milling around in that circle without sense to stop or break from the line until they died of complete exhaustion. I'll have to confess that at times the endless round of our daily duties seems quite as meaningless and unprofitable. Just now, all by our two selves, besides trying to plant the garden and truck patch and prepare for feed crops and summer fallowing on 240 acres, Will and I are milking 9 cows, caring for 41 head of cattle, about 100 hens and 240 young chicks, grinding and mixing our own feeds, and struggling to make a few improvements about the place.

This spring we have set out about 300 small trees—Chinese elms, mulberries, and arbor vitae. Our State Forestry Department is generous with seedlings for hedge and windbreak planting, and my own feeling is like the parting advice of Sir Walter Scott's wicked old laird of Dumbiedikes in *The Heart of Midlothian*: "Jock, when ye hae naething else to do, ye may be aye sticking in a tree; it will be growing, Jock, when ye're sleeping."[14]

Through this most lonely and disheartening of all winters, I have found my greatest inspiration and encouragement in the blossoming plants in our windows. . . . Insignificant little things these are, I realize; yet they have seemed to reassure me that sunshine and rain, the laws of life and growth, seedtime and harvest, are in a general way dependable; that our earthly heritage is still rich in possibilities; and that most of our troubles are caused by human faults and follies, and are therefore capable of correction—if only we care enough, and are brave enough, to demand and to work personally for justice and mercy.

During the winter we have had several letters from a young friend engaged in social work in Chicago.[15] Trying as our situation here often seems, I feel ashamed of my own bitterness when we read of conditions there. She writes of homes "where only oatmeal has been eaten for days, where a loaf of bread must serve six children for a meal until relief comes," and of schools where "children sit in men's clothing and overshoes. . . . They have gone without food until they do not feel hunger pangs any longer."

Granting that much of this misery is brought on by personal inefficiency and mismanagement, are not such conditions a challenge to us all? Some of my friends are uneasy about my interest in the Russian experiment[16]—as if Americans had never tried daring adventures! The Russians may fail, but I see no reason why we should nationally assume a self-righteous attitude and pour contempt upon them for having dreamed of a new order under which men should work for the joy of the working and for the common good. Someone—I think it was Professor Carver of Harvard—has recently said that the Russians have equality without liberty, and we have liberty without equality, but that we might, by the application of intelligence to our own problems, have a fair measure of both.[17] I believe that.

I judge that hardening of the heart is about as common among bankers in the East as in the West. They say that they are making no new loans here except occasionally, in very small sums and for a short time. The State Banking Commission has been taking care of a part of our small resources since October, and we cannot even get a reply to our inquiry as to whether the depositors of the closed bank may expect any return whatever.

Our own programme contains nothing new or original, but is largely an intensification of effort along the lines we have previously followed. We try to spend money only when the loss from doing without the needed supplies would be greater than the loss on the wheat that must be sold to purchase them. Some things, like coal for the brooder at $20 a ton, seem necessary regardless of the loss. We are trying, so far as possible, to keep things in reasonable repair. We have bought fencing to protect the yard and garden, and have even squandered a load of wheat on paint. So you see we are not among the much-berated hoarders—though I wish we had something to hoard for taxes and emergencies. Our own personal "use-what-you-have" movement had been going on for a long time before anyone thought up the hateful phrase, "anti-hoarding."[18] It is surprising how many things temporarily out of use we have been able to fix up and turn to some account for ourselves or for other people.

And we mean to help where we can—especially to help young people who might grow disheartened under the stress of existing conditions. I hope your boys and girls are all doing well in whatever interests them, and that somehow we shall all find courage for the tasks ahead. I often think of Christina Rossetti's little poem, "Uphill," and begin to realize its truth: —Does the road wind up-hill all the way? Yes, to the very end. Will the day's journey take the whole long day? From morn to night, my friend.—[19]

Our best wishes to you for all of the journey.

JUNE 10, 1932

MY DEAR EVELYN,

You must have been writing to me on the very evening when I was thinking especially of you, and wondering whether farming in Maryland is as different as it is here on the great plains. We had had no rain for weeks. The wind, which had raged all through April, seemed to have blown itself out, and for several days the breeze had been too light to stir the windmill upon which we depend for water. The tanks were all empty, and my lettuce bed was drying up. So after dark one night we put a cream can in the back of the old Model T and drove to a shallow pool in the south pasture to dip up water for the thirsty plants.

The pool is supplied by a deep well, one of the earliest in all the neighborhood. The people who drilled it "on the lone prairie" have moved on long ago, but that much of their work remains. The cottonwoods which they planted about the little pool rustled silkily. A pair of killdeers, disturbed by our adventuring, filled the air with their answering cries. A young moon, with Venus and Jupiter blazing in the west, gave light for our undertaking. The lettuce revived, and with later watering have provided a welcome addition to our "iron ration." . . .

Out here we thought the depths of the depression had been fathomed some time ago when the sheriff subtracted from the very personal possessions of one of our neighbors a set of false teeth that he had been unable to pay for. But we were too sanguine. While we were again distracted by lack of wind to pump our water and by apparently futile but finally successful efforts to recondition a small gasoline engine for that work, we received in the mail a lengthy document explaining why our only intangible possession—a real estate bond for $1000—had become valuable principally as a souvenir and a warning. It appeared that the only hope of any ultimate recovery lay in turning over the bond to a committee whose autocratic powers would make Mussolini ashamed of himself. The committee seemed to have in mind some plan of reorganization incapable of completion until long after we shall have ceased to care about bonds or anything else.

The same week another disaster overtook us. One day when the men were busy in the fields, a terrifying cloud came rolling up from the south. Though I tried hard to get the small chicks into their shelter, they turned away, not realizing their danger, and were almost instantly beaten to earth by the vicious pelting of hail which burst from the angry-looking cloud. I stayed out through all of it—and how those hailstones did sting!—picking up the helpless chicks. Most of them I was able to revive by wrapping them up in warm cloths, but several were beyond help.

I was so occupied with trying to save the chickens that the storm was nearly over before I realized that garden, truck patch, and wheat fields were all involved in one common ruin. Although stubs and stems remained almost everything above the ground except the screened-over lettuce and tomato plants was either destroyed or so seriously damaged as to give little hope of recovery. What to do? We hardly know, but, as the saying goes, we have the bear by the tail and it looks like a poor time to let go. I have replanted some of the quicker-growing seeds and hoed the entire garden to give all possible encouragement to the scattered, broken plants that remain. Fortunately, our cantaloupes and Mississippi peanuts were just coming up, and most of them escaped injury. Will is going on with his field work, and expects to finish his milo and maize planting and to replant the Mexican and Tepary beans to-day.

As for our wheat, it was poor at best, but we hoped for a little feed for the cattle and poultry from what the cutworms had left. No farmer can feel any enthusiasm over ploughing out a third of his cotton or seeing a hailstorm harvest a large share of his wheat, particularly when he knows that people are ragged and hungry through no fault of their own.

But of all our losses in recent years the most distressing is the loss of our self-respect. How can we feel that our work here has any dignity or importance when the world places so low a value on the products of our toil? We are humiliated every time we have to dole out another load of wheat at a price below production costs, but we must do it to meet our current expenses. We did stop selling cream and dairy products when prices fell, but we may yet look back to the good old days when butter fat was worth 9 cents a pound.

By sacrificing the small reserves we had held against the days of drought or disaster, we have succeeded so far in keeping on a cash basis. We have disconnected the telephone, our only insurance in case of accident or emergency;[20] stopped the daily paper; postponed our annual gift to the Grenfell Mission until wheat reaches 50 cents, if it ever does again; made hand towels out of the cement sacks which are no longer returnable; substituted cheap lye for washing powder, so that my hands are rough and uncomfortable from week to week; abandoned regretfully our emergency shelf in the cupboard. If the President were to drop in for dinner some day, he would have to eat wheat porridge or beans or potatoes or cheese or eggs along with the rest of us, unless there were time to prepare a worthless chicken.

I am sure you are quite right about the seriousness of the transportation problem. It affects to our disadvantage the price of everything we buy or sell. In the April number of the *Nation's Business* a staff writer refers to the price of wheat as "around 70 cents." At that time the price here was hovering around 30 cents. The difference of 40 cents a bushel must have gone into transportation and handling costs, with possibly a margin for gamblers' gains.

You ask about government appropriations for fighting grasshoppers.[21] We have heard nothing about it here. As yet, insects have been less troublesome than usual, perhaps because of the severe winter. But if our crops *were* threatened by grasshoppers, I feel reasonably sure that we should have to provide our own poison, together with bran, lemons, and molasses, mix the loathsome mess, and scatter it broadcast over the fields at nightfall just as we did during the early summer of 1918. Government action in such emergencies ought to be the most economical and effective way to meet the situation. . . . I don't know of anything more destructive of confidence, the lack of which is so frequently deplored by our leaders, than the knowledge that government, whose chief aim should be to "promote the general welfare," is being used for selfish, personal ends.

But confidence may be sacrificed in other ways, too. Last November we received an appeal signed by our county agent and the chairman of our county advisory committee. It was headed, "Wheat Donation for Red Cross," and went on to explain that the American Red Cross had asked our state "to donate 25 carloads of wheat for relief work in the Northern states where crop failures had been all but complete." The letter stated that railroads and mills had agreed to transport and make this wheat into flour free of any charge. The farmers of our county were urged to give whatever wheat they felt they could spare for this purpose—"to aid farmers who, because of drought and grasshoppers, must have help."

The day before Thanksgiving was appointed for collection. It was a bitter day, and we had a desperate time getting the old truck started. At last, however, we got the wheat loaded, hauled it to the elevator, and were given a pink receipt marked "Wheat for Red Cross." We warmed ourselves with the thought that a little of our concentrated Southwestern sunshine would be going North where it was needed for the cold winter.

We heard nothing more of the project until late in February. The county agent was here one day, and we asked him about the success of the appeal. He seemed chagrined to have to tell us that we had all been let down together. After the wheat was collected—there were something like 1,200 bushels—the railroads refused to move it, and the nearest general division of the Red Cross could furnish no funds for transportation. There was nothing to do but sell the wheat, and either to turn the proceeds into the general treasury of the Red Cross without assurance that it would ever reach the people for whom it was intended, or to hold the money—about $400—until somebody could decide which community stood in the greatest need of it. The second course was chosen, and in February, with the winter nearly over, the money was still on deposit in a bank at the county seat. Though it was later turned over to Red Cross officials in South Dakota, the plan proposed in the original appeal was not carried out, and the intrinsic value of the donated wheat would have been far greater in flour and feed than the small sum received for it at the low market price. . . .

The sun is getting low. It's chicken time and cow time and supper time and time for the tractor man to come home from his hot, dusty work. Would you like to know what has been running in my mind today? Two lines from Shelley, the lover of all beauty: "Ay, many flowering islands lie In the waters of wide Agony."[22] Perhaps you wonder whether, amid all our futile efforts and disappointments, we do find any flowering islands, any place of rest and refreshment for continuing the struggle. Yes, we do.

I wish you could have been with us one day when we had to make a trip to town to see about repairing the tractor. You would have noticed the blue lakes of the mirage as they appeared and faded in the road ahead, and you might have thought that our hopes for the future were quite as insubstantial. But you would have taken pleasure, as we did, in the fields of golden coreopsis, in the banks of salmon-colored mallow, in the mats of vivid purple verbena, in scattered plants here and there of white and lilac beard tongue, and in several varieties of evening primrose—lemon yellow, pink, and white. . . .

Yes, we find respite in many simple things like these. Of those green and flowering islands, each of us must, I think, be his own discoverer.

Sept. 1933
"Letters of Two Women Farmers II," *Atlantic Monthly*

June 21, 1932

My Dear Evelyn,

Will and I were both interested in what you wrote about farm relief. We, fortunately, have managed to keep out of debt, but otherwise the shoe pinches us in the same place it pinches you. We do not need credit so much as we need some reasonable ratio of exchange between our farm products and the things we must buy. At present, the proportions are all against us: sixteen dozen eggs for a pair of overalls, more than a bushel of wheat for a wick for the oil stove, two pounds of butter for a small felt washer for the tractor, and so on indefinitely.

I do not know how or when a fairer system of exchange can be brought about. A professor of sociology at one of our Western state universities says that it will take ten thousand years to secure any general acceptance of the idea that the good of each is dependent on the good of all. It's a long time to wait. . . .

Out here on the plains we are hedged about with such difficulties as we have never before known. We cannot see our way ahead, but still we hope. Doubtless you remember the artist's conception of Hope—blindfolded, with a broken lyre. That is a symbol of our state of mind. Our hopes may prove to be what your neighbor, Mr. Cabell, would call "dynamic illusions," yet they serve to spur us on to continued endeavor.

A few specific things have tended, of late, to make us more cheerful. We have once more paid our taxes, and were grateful to find, instead of the expected increase, a decrease of about 40 per cent. There has been wide-spread indignation throughout the West over governmental waste and official laziness, and apparently it has had some effect. In our county a citizens' petition recently brought about a saving of $12,000 in the allowance for deputies, and some of the candidates for office are promising, if elected, to do their work themselves. Taxpayers' leagues have sprung up all over the state, and they seem to be getting results.

Even more cheering than our tax receipt was the life-restoring rain. The growing season here has been unusually late because of the dry spring. On this, the longest day of the year, many of the planted fields are still bare and brown. For days two lines of Masefield had been in my mind: "Let me have wisdom, Beauty, wisdom and passion, Bread to the soul, rain when the summers parch."[23] And then the rain came at last, gently and graciously, and it seemed as if the earth breathed a great sigh of relief. The buffalo grass has now started in the pastures; the yard is gay with wild flowers, starred all over with brilliant, rose-colored cactus blossoms; the trumpet vine is trumpeting, and even the garden, so badly damaged by hail, has recovered more than at first seemed possible.

Our daughter Eleanor has just come home from the University where she has been combining the work of a student with that of a laboratory assistant. She tells of a plan that was carried out at Commencement time. On the south slope of the campus, overlooking a broad valley, lies a plot of ground never yet disturbed by plough or spade, green and flowering with the coming of each new spring. It was beautiful again this year with spiderwort and poppy, wild roses and geraniums, dotted about among the tall grasses. A group of the older alumnae arranged for the dedication of this spot as "The Prairie Acre," and marked it with a tablet set in a block of native limestone. Through the years to come that acre will retain its untouched natural beauty— a reminder of pioneer days, whose difficult problems called for resolute action like those of our own time. . . .

JULY 19, 1932

MY DEAR EVELYN,

I am sure you know enough about the uncertainties of farming not to have been unduly elated over my last more hopeful letter. It had hardly been mailed before trouble began.

One of our neighbors was trying to cut down tractor expenses by using horses to cultivate his crop. He lacked one team, so we let him have Ned and Star. Since we bought our tractor they have not had much to do, but Will has always said that the horses made for us the little we have, and that they were welcome to live out their old age in peace, helping us now and then in the lighter tasks. They worked well enough for a week, and our friend said they seemed all right when he turned them into the pasture Sunday evening. Monday morning Star lay there dead.

Some people say that animals do not suffer keenly and have no dread of death. I hope it is so, and certainly I am glad for gentle, faithful Star that there can be for her no more sweat and dust and tugging at loads the importance of which she could not understand. But horses hate to leave their homes; they know their friends; and I suppose it will always hurt me to think that perhaps Star wondered why we didn't come in her hour of need. I am afraid she will always seem a sacrifice to the demands of this cruel time.

How we should welcome a small part of your surplus rain! We have had none in a month. The extreme heat and almost constant high winds have destroyed all hope of a satisfying return from the garden. The potatoes were set back seriously by the early hail, and, though the vines grew out, they are now dying down, with little potatoes like marbles half cooked in the parched ground. Canada field peas, which we hoped would provide a late crop after the earlier peas were gone, blossomed fully, but, like the tomatoes, were blighted by the withering winds. Cowpeas and peanuts are standing the heat the best of anything, and, along with the field crops, *may* hold out until rain comes. No one knows. The cattle still have sufficient pasturage on the weeds and grasses among the ruined wheat, but the prairie grass is brown again and crackles under one's feet.

This has been another long day of wild wind and blistering heat. Tonight I am quite alone—a mile and a half from anybody. The wind has gone down and the quietness makes me think of Will's memories of his old cowboy days, of silences out on the open plains so intense that one's ears would ache with listening.

Will and Eleanor, with a neighbor's boy to help them, have gone with truck, car, tractor, combine, and oil wagon to harvest a half section of wheat for some people out in the adjoining county, seventeen miles from home. Money is scarcer than ever with us, and they are taking their pay in wheat at three bushels for the acre. Whether they will make anything to compensate for their exhausting effort and for the expense and depreciation of the machinery depends on the future wheat market.

The wheat yield is disheartening all through this part of the country; there is hardly one stalk where three or four grew last year. The man for whom our folks are harvesting counted on about twelve bushels to the acre and is getting less than five. It puzzles everyone to know how to manage these poor crops. They will not pay handling expenses. . . . Many fields will not be cut at all. On three sides of our own home farm are 330 acres left for the birds—potentially something like a thousand sacks of flour poured out on the ground in a hungry world!

People still toil amazingly and make a conscious effort to keep cheerful. But it seems to me that the effort grows more apparent. Behind the characteristic American nonchalance one detects a growing anxiety, especially about the coming winter. People speak openly of their dread of cold weather. I am told by a man who is familiar with neighborhood conditions that many farmers once regarded as well-to-do will not be able to put in another crop on their own resources. City folk talk lightly of the obvious remedy. "Let the farmers stop producing if they can market their stuff only at a loss," they say. But the thing is not as simple as that. When all of one's investment is in land and equipment for working it, there is nothing else to depend on for taxes, repairs, the upkeep of buildings and fences, and the maintenance and education of a family.

But it is useless to tackle that problem tonight. It is already late, and day comes soon. Tomorrow I must care for the new shorthorn I found this evening when I went for the cows; look over the winter-squash vines for bugs; go around a mile and a half of fence and put in missing staples; finish hoeing and working the ground around the small trees which we are trying to save through the drought. Why do people speak of "the monotony of farm life?"

SEPTEMBER 17, 1932

MY DEAR EVELYN,

You and your responsibilities have been much in my thoughts as the season's work draws to a close. All about us, in maturing seeds, in asters and goldenrod and yellowing leaves, in some indefinable, lingering, caressing quality in the sunlight, we see reminders that "the harvest is past, the summer is ended."[24] And we, like you, have little enough to show for it. Judging by any standards that the world would recognize, we should have been further ahead if we could have spent the year in sleep.

The harvesting away from home was at last completed. Of the wheat received in payment we sold several loads to cover repairs and other expenses, and we have left 400 bushels, worth to-day 33 cents. Will and I gleaned by ourselves the small amount of wheat that was spared for our own harvest by the hailstorm and the cutworms. From the hundred-acre field which yielded 1800 bushels last year we salvaged about 215 bushels, most of it of poor quality.

Lest you think that we are the sole darlings of misfortune, I might mention the neighboring farmer who sold his crop from 75 acres at 30 cents and had $12 left above combining expenses to pay for his seed, for the use of his land, for the labor of preparing the ground, drilling the wheat, marketing the crop, and for board for the combine hands; or another neighbor who sold $49 worth of wheat from 250 acres and owed one fourth of it for rent. Sadder still, I might tell of the man who kept on persistently trying to raise wheat before anyone else here thought it practicable. He did at last succeed in showing that over a series of years wheat is probably our most dependable crop. But troubles in his family, some years of short crops, and the low prices of the past three seasons have broken him. He has lost his 960 acres of land and most of his stock. He is now trying desperately, and I think without much chance of success, to get a government loan to buy back a few of his cattle and start all over again—old, half-blind, almost barehanded—in a Texas valley, where, as he told us, he hopes to avoid the mistakes he has made here.

The rain for which we were hoping so eagerly when I wrote last has never come. Indeed, we have had no effective moisture since early in June. One good rain during the summer would have given us at least roughage for our stock. As it is, the sowed cane and Sudan grass died down when it was six inches high, and our crops of maize and Kafir corn are little better—hardly a start on what we shall require for winter feed. I really do not know what we shall do. Our choice seems to lie between sacrificing the cattle at the ruinous prices now prevailing—we recently sold five well-grown young steers for $122.50—or trying in some as yet unthought-of way to get roughage for them through the winter.

The situation throughout the country is much more serious, I believe, than many people suppose. Think of the loss of homes, the decrease in land values, the idle shops and idle men, the closed banks, delinquent taxes, rents hopelessly overdue, children deprived of school privileges, thousands of young men and women roaming over the country freed from the normal restraints of orderly social conditions. A neighbor recently told us that he had counted eighty-five such wanderers on one freight train in northern Texas. Just a few days ago I talked with a merchant who was elated because, as he said, even the most destitute folk in St. Louis are making no complaints about their condition. He regarded this as a hopeful sign, but it seems to me a sign of lethargy unworthy of a people with the history and traditions of America behind them.

I, too, have been interested in the farmers' movement in Iowa, both for its own sake and because it centers around the vicinity of my girlhood home.[25] In these days, when canned fruits and vegetables and condensed milk and supplies of all sorts can so easily be transported, if not in one way, then in several others, the farmers' holiday plan, if I understand it, seems doomed to failure as a practical measure for securing any widespread or permanent increase in prices. It may have some value in directing attention to the crisis in the farming situation in general.

If there are any definite reasons for farmers to be hopeful, they would seem to lie in their habitual capacity for keeping at work in spite of failure and loss, their lifelong training in facing hard facts, their comparative adaptability, and their opportunities under normal conditions to produce at least a great part of their own necessities of life. These are all characteristics favorable to survival. At best, however, agricultural recovery must, I think, be slow, variable in rate and method, "here a little, there a little," depending largely on individual planning and initiative to meet local conditions. Permanent gains will require an awakened spirit of fair play, passion for the common welfare, sympathy and cooperation, both among farmers themselves and among the American people as a whole. In creating and expressing this spirit, everyone, whether of town or country, may have a share.

As for us, you must not feel unduly anxious. We have traveled rough roads before. Many cherished plans have failed. Not only radio and telephone, but running water in the house, furnace heat, modern lighting and refrigeration, have all passed beyond our dreaming. Even the three-cent postage is a burden. Obviously the national budget had to be balanced, but I could use the new stamps more cheerfully if they would print on each the old Scotch proverb, "Willful waste makes woeful want." Estimates at our state school of agriculture show that it took *ten times as much wheat* to pay the 1931 taxes as it did to pay the average tax in the years between 1916 and 1921! The road ahead seems blocked. All sense of security for our old age has vanished. But we have not given up.

In some way—I hardly see how myself—we have managed to keep out of debt. We can still eat home-ground wheat cereal. The spring pullets are beginning to lay and the fall calves to arrive. We plan to gather driftwood from the distant river and "cow chips" from our pastures to help out on the winter's fuel supply. We take courage from thinking that, while we rarely have two good seasons together here, we have never had two as disheartening as this in direct succession. I believe that the experiences of the past two years have made us somewhat more sensitive to "the still, sad music of humanity."[26] Above all, we have shining memories to brighten gloomy days, and friendships beyond our deserving.

Perhaps, in what many people would count ignoble poverty, we are rich after all.

⇌

DEC. 12, 1932

DEAR ROSE:

I have just been re-reading your letter and enjoying again the glimpses of your home, of old friends, and of what must have been a delightful fortnight last summer in Vermont. . . .

A few days after your letter came The Good Earth.[27] Will got started on it first and became so absorbed in it that I could hardly get him away from it at all until he was through. And when I began it myself, I could understand his feeling. It is rarely that one finds a person able to understand and sympathize with the primitive feeling of kinship with the earth—our common mother. Still more rarely can such a person express that feeling so that other people may realize and possibly share it. We are both near enough to pagans to have a good deal of that instinctive love for the earth. I think that has had much to do with our continuing the long struggle here. So the book had for both of us a strong appeal and we appreciate deeply the generous gift. Indeed, it seems almost too generous in these difficult days. . . .

I had to laugh when I came to your question about the candidates for President. I told Will then what I hadn't admitted before,—that I had been sure my sin would find me out. In other words, I didn't vote for either Hoover or Roosevelt. Of what seemed to me two evils, I chose neither. I have never questioned Hoover's personal integrity or idealism, but I felt as I imagine you did that he was tied in with a bad bunch, and practically committed to policies which in my judgment are largely responsible for the status quo. . . . So when the Democrats nominated Roosevelt who seems to me quite inadequate for the position, I decided to vote for Norman Thomas, who seemed to me more free than either of the others to work for "a new deal" all around. We have been through too much to be alarmed or charmed by mere words. I am not crazy about normalcy which we are beginning to understand now has always meant misery for millions. Nor am I afraid of the name socialism. Most of the more progressive legislation of recent years, looking toward fairer conditions for all has at some time been called socialistic. I was so certain that I should vote in protest against both the old parties that when we reached the polling place and learned . . . an "outrageous decision of the Oklahoma Supreme Court" would make it impossible to vote for Thomas, I decided to let the people who thought they knew what was best decide the election. Evidently there were a lot of them, and I can only hope Roosevelt may do much better than I believe he is capable of doing.

It has been a tough year for us with cut worms, hail, drought and short crops, losses of small savings and investments and always the problem of trying to adjust expenses to the incredibly low prices that have prevailed through the entire year. Yet as we compare even our modest and often very pinching comfort with the boys—and girls, too—roaming over the country in freight cars, with the man and woman Eleanor saw on Thanksgiving Day footing it along the highway, dragging a little wagon and two small children, or with people here in our own community destitute of the simplest things such as sheets, night clothing, clothes pins—or even a can-opener!—we think we ought not to complain. We are trying to put our socialism into practice by helping where we can, and there is of course, no end to the bitter need.

A peculiarly distressing case recently has taken time and effort and much thought. We spent Thanksgiving Day trying to help in a sorely afflicted family. Five of the children were down at once with typhoid fever in a family who had already lost their stock, truck, car, tractor, and some say their farm. One boy had already died and two girls since, with two young men still very low. We haven't heard from them for a day or two now. And such utter lack of every thing to make life decent or endurable, I hope you have never seen. One feels quite helpless in the face of such misery. The neighborhood and county are having to bear the entire expense for they haven't a thing left from comparative prosperity. Just an instance of the sort of thing that has been happening all over, I suppose. It wouldn't be fair to blame the Lord or the government for all of it, because anyone could see that there had been poor management. But the question now is, what is going to become of such people. Personally, I can't see any way out for them. The new comforter I am making them for Christmas is but a feeble gesture. . . .

If you see the Atlantic you may after a time hear a little more of our year's endeavors. I am not at all satisfied with the project which was not of my own seeking. I feel rather apologetic about it. A lady in Maryland, who has had a much wider experience that I both in living and farming, was interested in our little harvest story last year. I wrote a friendly letter. This spring, being in pretty desperate shape financially, she proposed a joint effort—a series of letters telling the "low down of present farming conditions," which the editor of the Country Gentleman had promised to consider. I wasn't very strong for it and felt that it would not be accepted, but hated to refuse to make the attempt. The Country Gentleman politely returned the stuff. I think a mild expression of my own of interest in the outcome of the Russian experiment—helped to settle our hash. Without even consulting me Mrs. Harris submitted the same material to The Atlantic, who professed interest in the scheme. They wished us to write a mass of material from which they might make selection, editing in continuous form, though keeping the letter framework. . . .

I have written wearisomely I fear, waiting for Will to return from a belated trip to the south farm to shut off the wind mill there, for fear of damage from a threatened storm. We have had unusually severe weather lately. Yesterday after I had had the fire burning for some time in the kitchen the thermometer stood at only 10 degrees above zero! Our thanks and best wishes for a restful vacation and a good Christmas.

DEC. 19, 1932

DEAR MRS. ALDEN:

Many circumstances have combined to delay my Christmas writing so now I must hurry if I do it at all. We have just passed through a season of severe storms and extremely cold weather. Our country is still "frosted like a wedding cake." Tanks froze solid and then the wind ceased so that watering the stock has been a problem and for two or three days we had no water—even for drinking—except what we could melt from snow or ice. Two new roan sisters have appeared at the barn in the midst of these bad weather conditions, and you may be shocked but we had to let one of them stay on a pile of sacks in the kitchen through her first night. It was too severely cold to risk her out at the barn.

We have been holding the fort in one room—the dining room and so far have kept the plants from freezing. But it seems as if everything in the house circles around and gets drawn into the dining room like a whirlpool. It keeps me busy carrying things back where they belong.

We are feeling blue and lonely tonight. We had expected Eleanor home last Saturday but instead of the girl came a telegram saying she could not leave before the twenty-fifth. This evening we received a card explaining that she is down with the flu which has been very prevalent at Lawrence. So we are anxious and disappointed—more than I can tell. . . .

If we only had her safely home, I think we should feel rich tonight in spite of all the disappointments of this most depressing and distressing year—the worst from a farming standpoint since 1913. Cutworms in the early spring and a heavy hail storm in May combined to ruin the wheat. The long summer drought brought to nothing all our labor on garden, truck patch and forage crops. We have a dangerously small amount of roughage to see the cattle through the winter and, like everything else, they are worthless to sell. . . .

⌒⇒⌒

DEC. 14, 1933[?]

DEAR MRS. ALDEN,

And so another year has sped away before we had time to get used to the new number! It scarcely seems possible. We have appreciated your letters of good will and encouragement during the year. How could we ever have kept on here at all without the feeling that friends here and there had an interest in our endeavors?

I wonder whether the eastern papers have had any accounts of the really desperate conditions through this section during 1933? To begin with we had no winter moisture to give the fall sown wheat a chance. Subsoil moisture was already exhausted by the hot dry summer. In January we had the beginning of a long continued series of violent wind and dust storms which for the summer turned this plains country into a veritable desert. We had no wheat, no garden, not even grass in the pastures and only the scantiest feed crop which came after August 1 when the 14 months of drought finally broke with a number of most welcome rains. They came too late, however, to save our little grove of locusts which had given a bit of distinction to our corner and represented a deal of labor and loving care through many years.

Today we went to Texhoma—26 miles from home to see about some necessary repairs for the tractor and were dismayed to find ourselves out in another of the raging dust storms which have made life miserable here for so long. We hoped they were over; but they were turning on lights in all the stores by 1:30. We left town about 2:00 and had to creep along burning our lights all the way home. Often we could hardly see the length of the car ahead of us through the clouds of pulverized soil. Really not much wonder that Secretary Ickes advised wholesale deportation![28]

By saving two big stacks of Russian thistles, which seem able to grow without rain, and every bit of feed that grew we hope to be able to get our herd of cattle through the winter as they are worthless on the market at present.

I had good success with chickens but they too scarcely pay expenses. Light hens and "springs" are worth 4 cents now; heavies bring 6 cents; I sold eggs today for 18 cents, but from March to September they were only 6 cents. Like most people here we signed the contracts for wheat acreage reduction, taking out 39 acres for 1934, but so far no checks have been received in this county. I suppose they will get around some time and ought to be a great help, not only to the farmers but to the business men in all the little towns which depend exclusively on farm trade.

Perhaps we told you that Eleanor took her Master's degree in June and for the first time in several years was free from necessary study through the summer. She is back at Lawrence, working harder than ever in the medical school. She feels now that she has gradually been tending toward that work and seems satisfied with her choice. . . .

We are very quiet old people here now. Often for many days at a time I see no one but Mr. Henderson, not even anyone passing on our little used road. We have two very cunning pets, a guinea pig that survived a course in Immunity last winter and has become a very wise little creature; and a mountain plover whose broken wing Eleanor mended successfully last summer. If he lives till spring we will let him go free when his brothers return from their long migration. He is a wonderfully intelligent little thing and we love him dearly.

It is fine that your family are most of them near enough that you can see them often. I am sure you take great satisfaction in the progress of the grandchildren. I had a nice long letter today from Mabel Gilbert Schutt and she spoke so nicely of her special admiration and affection for Rose.

We think of you often. Eleanor said that having to plunge into this new work just before the vacation would make it impossible for her to carry out any Christmas plans. But perhaps she can get around to writing a little later. Mr. Henderson is reading a good book—John Muir's "Boyhood of a Naturalist."[29] But he joins in all friendly wishes for a happy Christmas to you and all your family.

❧

Dec. 14, 1933

Dear Rose:

I meant to answer your summer letter right away. But the days slip by, and this year it has seemed more difficult than ever to carry out plans. But anyway. I did appreciate your comments on the <u>Atlantic</u> articles. And I do hope you have gone on and secured publication for the article you mentioned regarding the poultry and egg business. It seemed to me that the more information that people can gain about all sorts of industries and occupations, the sooner we might all hope to come to a most desirable understanding of the other fellow's problems and difficulties. In one of the earlier English courses at the University of Kansas they use a little book of that sort, <u>America at Work</u> by Joseph Husband.[30] It gives brief but really exciting sketches of all sorts of out-of-the-way employments that most of us know nothing about. "Dynamite," "Semaphore" and the work of the man in charge at one of the big electric power stations are three that I happen just now to recall. I have no doubt that the perplexities belonging to a commercial poultry plant need setting forth. We know so little of the price-controlling influences. We only know that all summer 6 cents per dozen was all we could get for eggs—in trade at that! Just to day they are worth 18 cents and seem to be headed for lower prices as they were 20 cents last week. Of course under our conditions poultry is a side line, but it has ceased to hold any hope of profit.

I've just been writing to your mother and telling her a little about this disastrous year, so won't repeat the record of this most disheartening season. We are trying to hope that for all this drought-stricken area, which included parts of five states centering around our Panhandle country, the worst is over. Yet today after we thought the drought had been effectively broken and the wind storms had ceased we had another terrible day of violent wind, drifting clouds of dust, and Russian thistles racing like mad across the plains and piling up in head-high impassable banks and barricades at every fence or other obstruction. The fall sown wheat has been looking fairly well and we do hope that it won't have to try to survive many such days of persecution.

We feel as if the Administration is really making a sincere effort to improve general conditions but they have a tremendous task, made harder of course by all who cling tenaciously to special privileges or opportunities of the past. Personally I'd rather have seen some sort of balance effected on a basis of abundance for all, rather than on the basis of anything like scarcity. But to have scaled prices of all manufactured goods <u>down</u> to meet the low prices of agricultural products resulting from an actual over supply would probably have caused louder out cries than the effort to bring farm products up in price to some sort of level. . . . "Parity price" as they call it. Not that this has yet been accomplished. It is a scandal how the small town merchants here, anticipating the allotment checks due to most farmers in this section for reduced wheat acreage, have increased prices—out of all reason. Wheat is now 65 cents per bushel. Yet today I looked at a piece of print about 14 cent quality at mail order houses, and they were asking 30 cents for it! I didn't buy.

The very trifling little parcel I am sending is a fair sample of the way we are keeping Christmas, with scraps of this and that around the house. But I suppose you have to wash dishes some times and perhaps the little apron will do for that. . . .

As you sent me the book called <u>The Christ of the Indian Road</u>, you might be interested to know that Eleanor heard Mr. Jones recently at a University Convocation at Lawrence.[31] He spoke especially of the awakened East, particularly India which I suppose he knows best. But he also plead for an application of Christian principles to all the problems that darken our days. Sometimes I think it is willingness we lack; at other times I think it is knowledge of <u>how</u> to translate the fundamental principles into the manifold details of every day living. Probably it is both. . . .

I meant to tell you that I recently read <u>Sons</u>, the continuation of <u>The Good Earth</u>.[32] I found it interesting but not so appealing as the earlier book.

We always enjoy your letters and shall hope for one whenever you are in a writing mood. So here must close with the old wish—A Merry Christmas.

Caroline Boa and her sister, Susan, ca. 1885. (Grandstaff Collection)

Caroline and Will at the time of their wedding in 1908. (Grandstaff
Collection)

Caroline (right) and her sister, Susan, ca. 1936. This photograph may have accompanied an article about Caroline in the *Wichita Eagle*. (Grandstaff Collection)

Will and Caroline at a community gathering honoring "old settlers," 1964. (Author's collection, courtesy of Mr. and Mrs. Lee Johnson)

The Henderson home, ca. 1908. (Grandstaff Collection)

Will and Eleanor outside their home, ca. 1911. Note the addition to the home. (Grandstaff Collection)

Children gathering at Center school, where Caroline first taught, ca. 1914. (Grandstaff Collection)

Caroline and Will, July 1958. (Jaffe Collection, Western History Collection, University of Oklahoma Libraries)

Henderson homestead covered by snow, ca. 1911. (Grandstaff Collection)

Caroline with one of her pets, ca. 1930. (Grandstaff Collection)

The Henderson home, ca. 1930. (Grandstaff Collection)

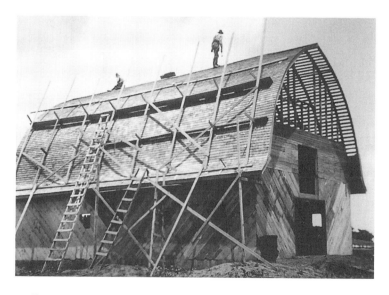

Will Henderson, probably at right, designed and supervised the
construction of the barn, ca. 1925. (Grandstaff Collection)

Buildings and equipment covered by an Oklahoma dust storm,
September 8, 1937. (Minneapolis Public Library Collection,
Archives and Manuscripts Division, Oklahoma Historical Society)

Abandoned farmstead, Texas County, Oklahoma, 1937. (USDA,
Soil Conservation Service, Archives and Manuscripts Division,
Oklahoma Historical Society, Norman, Oklahoma)

A Panhandle orchard covered by drifting dust and sand, ca. 1936.
(FSA Collection, Western History Collection, University of
Oklahoma Libraries, Norman, Oklahoma)

Eleanor sits in a
cart as Will har-
vests broomcorn,
1911. (Grandstaff
Collection)

Drifting dust and sand reached the barn roof on a western Oklahoma farm, April 1935. (World Wide Photos, Inc., Minnesota Public Library Collection, Archives and Manuscripts Division, Oklahoma Historical Society)

Dust storm approaching Hooker, Oklahoma, June 4, 1937. (Photograph by G. L. Risen, Haskell Pruett Collection, Archives and Manuscripts Division, Oklahoma Historical Society)

Residents of Guymon, Oklahoma, watch as "roller" nears, 1937. (Maupin Collection, Western History Collection, University of Oklahoma Libraries)

Dust storm approaching Knowles, Oklahoma, 1935. (Morris Collection, Western History Collection, University of Oklahoma Libraries)

Chapter 4

Dust to Eat, 1935–1937

By 1932, Caroline claimed she had lost her self-respect. The conditions she faced during the next six years compounded her woes and brought her to a new degree of despair, from which she would never fully recover. By 1938, her dream of building a life that fulfilled the Jeffersonian vision had vanished. During these years, when the Hendersons experienced the horrors of raging dust storms and summer temperatures as high as 120 degrees, their farm produced no significant crops. In 1938, they were still saving seed for their next planting, eating boiled wheat cereal, and feeding their remaining livestock from what they saved from the harvest of 1931.

This chapter consists largely of Caroline Henderson's published writing through the dust bowl years. These accounts are complemented by those she wrote to Rose Alden and another letter, entitled "Dust to Eat," dated April 1935. That letter was eventually sent to Secretary of Agriculture Henry A. Wallace, but Caroline may have first submitted it to the *Atlantic Monthly,* which published two more of her articles in 1936 and 1937. The first of these, "Letters from the Dust Bowl," retained the format that she had employed in her joint effort with Evelyn Harris, complete with the salutations to "Dear Evelyn." In this instance, however, the magazine did not print any accompanying letters from Harris, and it is not clear whether any had actually been submitted.

Both "Dust to Eat" and "Letters from the Dust Bowl" contain some of the most vivid descriptions of the dust storms and accompanying devastation ever published. Caroline's talent justified the praise a Wichita writer afforded her in 1936 as a "noted woman writer . . . recognized as one of the nation's best descriptive artists with the English language."[1] Her publications from this period are also important for their recognition of the vital role played by the New Deal, which largely defined both national and regional responses to the Depression and the dust bowl.

From 1933 to 1939, President Franklin D. Roosevelt's New Deal offered an array of programs to address the problems of the Great Depression. Among the most important was the 1933 Agricultural Adjustment Act (AAA), which aided farmers such as the Hendersons with a variety of programs ranging from drought relief to agricultural price stabilization. One controversial policy of the AAA program provided cash incentives to reduce farm acreage, providing a much needed source of cash for farmers while removing marginal lands from production. Although the U.S. Supreme Court ruled the first AAA unconstitutional in 1936, it was reestablished with some modifications in 1938. In the meantime, some of its goals were pursued by the Soil Conservation Service (SCS), which facilitated the creation of Soil Conservation Districts while encouraging new farming methods to conserve the land and reduce the impact of practices that had contributed to the dust bowl.

Farmers also benefited from other relief and recovery measures such as those offered by the Civil Works Administration (CWA), the Federal Emergency Relief Administration (FERA), and the Public Works Administration (PWA), each established in 1933. These agencies offered work to the unemployed in road improvement, public works, and similar projects. The Civilian Conservation Corps (CCC), also created in 1933, expanded on these efforts, as did the Works Project Administration (WPA), created two years later.[2]

These measures would eventually facilitate the recovery of Great Plains agriculture, but two major problems still prevented restoration of the land. First, huge areas of land had been abandoned in preceding years, leaving no one to implement the measures for stabilizing the soil. Caroline supported the new federal measures despite that concern. She also argued, however, that the region's essential problems stemmed from a lack of moisture and that there would be no long-term solution to that dilemma until they received an adequate amount of rain. Her last article for the *Atlantic Monthly*, "Spring in the Dust Bowl," noted that this essential ingredient had yet to arrive by 1937.

In light of the harsh conditions the Hendersons and other

families in the region faced, one might very well wonder why they stayed. Indeed, thousands had already left, although as Caroline notes, they did not have that many choices. Texas County alone shrank from its 1930 population of 14,100 to 9,896 in 1940, and still others had moved from their farms to towns such as Guymon and Goodwell.[3] In contrast, Caroline was reluctant to abandon her home and continued to believe in a better future. This belief no longer included her vision of the Jeffersonian dream that had motivated her originally, but her decision to stay may be best understood in the words she shared with a Wichita reporter: She had come to love her place and "had no intention of leaving."[4]

The first of two bright notes from these dismal years came when Eleanor completed her medical training in 1935. The second was her marriage to August Grandstaff later that year.

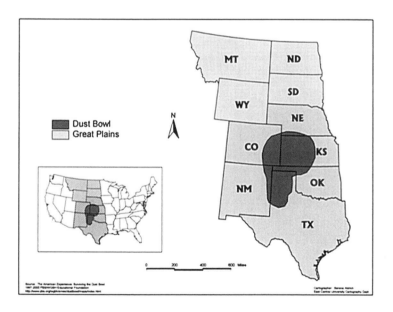

The Dust Bowl, 1933–1939

⌐⇌⌐

JULY 26, 1935

"DUST TO EAT," TO HENRY A. WALLACE, SECRETARY OF AGRICULTURE

> *Who has given to me this sweet*
> *And given my brother dust to eat?*
> *And when will his wage come in?*[5]

. . . For twenty-seven years this little spot on the vast expanses of the great plains has been the center of all our thought and hope and effort. And marvelous are the changes that we have seen and in which we have participated.

The almost unbroken buffalo grass sod has given way to cultivated fields. The small rude huts or dugouts of the early days have been replaced by reasonably comfortable homes. The old trails have become wide graded highways. Railways have been built, reducing our journey to market from thirty miles to fifteen and later to two and a half. Little towns have sprung up with attractive homes, trees, flowers, schools, churches, and hospitals. Automobiles and trucks, tractors and combines have revolutionized methods of farm work and manner of living. The wonderful crop of 1926 when our country alone produced 10,000,000 bushels of wheat—more, it was said, than any other equal area in the world—revealed the possibilities of our productive soil under modern methods of farming. I can shut my eyes and feel yet the rush of an almost painful thankfulness when we looked out over our fields that summer and watched our ripening grain bending, rising, bending again in golden waves swept on interminably by the restless wind. It seemed as if at last our dreams were coming true. . . .

Yet now our daily physical torture, confusion of mind, gradual wearing down of courage, seem to make that long continued hope look like a vanishing dream. For we are in the worst of the dust storm area where William Vaughn Moody's expression, "dust to eat" is not merely a figure of speech as he intended, but the phrasing of a bitter reality, increasing in seriousness with each passing day. Any attempt to suggest the violent discomfort of these storms is likely to be vain except to those who have already experienced them.

There are days when for hours at a time we cannot see the windmill fifty feet from the kitchen door. There are days when for briefer periods one cannot distinguish the windows from the solid wall because of the solid blackness of the raging storm. Only in some

Inferno-like dream could any one visualize the terrifying lurid red light overspreading the sky when portions of Texas are "on the air." This wind-driven dust, fine as the finest flour, penetrates wherever air can go.

After one such storm, I scraped up a dustpanful of this pulverized soil in the first preliminary cleaning of the bathtub! It is a daily task to unload the leaves of the geraniums and other house plants, borne down by the weight of the dust settled upon them, and to excavate the crocuses and violets and other little growing things that we have cherished out of doors. A friend writes of attending a dinner where "the guests were given wet towels to spread over their faces so they could breathe." At the little country store of our neighborhood after one of the worst of these storms, the candies in the show case all looked alike and equally brown. . . . "Dust to eat," and dust to breathe and dust to drink. Dust in the beds and in the flour bin, on dishes and walls and windows, in hair and eyes and ears and teeth and throats, to say nothing of the heaped up accumulation on floors and window sills after one of the bad days.

Yet these personal inconveniences are of slight moment as compared with the larger effects of the persistent drought and wind erosion. The year 1929 brought a good wheat crop and we bought and paid for a small tractor and combine. In 1930 our harvest was cut short by hail. In 1931 we again raised a good crop of wheat and sufficient forage for our stock, but the ruinous prices and heavy expenses left little or nothing in return for our labors. Since 1931 the record has been one of practically unbroken drought resulting in complete exhaustion of subsoil moisture, the stripping of our fields of all protective covering and the progressive pulverization of the surface soil—an effective combination to produce exactly the results from which we are now suffering. In one limited respect we realize that some farmers have themselves contributed to this reaping of the whirlwind. Under the stimulus of war time prices and the humanizing of agriculture through the use of tractors and improved machinery, large areas of buffalo grass and blue-stem pasture lands were broken out for wheat raising. The reduction in the proportionate area of permanent grazing grounds has helped to intensify the serious effect of the long drought and violent winds.

Now we are facing a fourth year of failure. There can be no wheat for us in 1935 in spite of all our careful and expensive work in preparing ground, sowing and resowing our allotted acreage. Native grass pastures are permanently damaged, in many cases hopelessly ruined, smothered under by drifted sand. Fences are buried under banks of thistles and hard packed earth or undermined by the eroding action of the wind and lying flat on the ground. Less traveled roads are impassable, covered deep under sand or the finer silt-like loam. Orchards, groves and hedge-rows cultivated for many years with patient care are dead or dying. The black locusts which once gave something of grace and distinction to our own little corner are now turned into a small pile of fenceposts while the carefully gathered brush has helped to feed our winter fire. . . .

Thousands of acres of carefully and expensively tilled soil show only the drill marks in the hard subsoil to prove that the wheat had been sown. Over much of this area the wind and eroding sand have obliterated even the traces of cultivation. Pastures have changed to barren wastes and dooryards around humble little homes have become scenes of dusty desolation. Small buildings have been almost buried. Stock ponds have in some cases been gradually built up into miniature sand dunes as the dry dust, shaken from the wings of the wind, has settled into water of the pool and later deposits have adhered to the accumulating moist earth.

It might seem that the conditions here suggested were in themselves sufficient cause for discomfort and regret. Yet one must endeavor to resist not only the violence of the physical tempests but also the influence of erratic "winds of doctrine" which seem to blow most vigorously in time of trouble. Some would-be prophets are sure that the days of grace and mercy and rain for this great prairie land are forever past; that the future promises only hopeless and permanent desert conditions. Others, according to their own words, are quite as sure that fervent prayer is the one thing needful to bring relief. Special prayers for rain were offered at our county seat last Sunday morning. The afternoon brought one of the most sudden, dense, and suffocating dust storms of the season. . . . A revival preacher—a true Job's comforter—proclaims that the drought is a direct punishment for our sins. Some regard it as retribution for the ploughing out of cotton hundreds of miles away. . . .

In this time of severe stress, next to the enduring character of our people credit must be given for the continued occupation of the plains country to the various activities of the federal government. Without some such aid as has been furnished, it seems certain that large sections must have been virtually abandoned. As it is, aside from the actual physical effects of the dust clouds, life goes on in a manner surprisingly near to normal, so near in fact that superficial observers have not realized the true situation and have felt that the reports of drought conditions have been exaggerated. One is forced to wonder whether such reporters expected to find people dying of starvation by the roadside! . . .

In our own section, the largest amount of direct cash benefit has come through the rental checks under the wheat acreage control program. I realize perfectly that this whole question is debatable. I do not know of any farmer who can give his whole-hearted approval to policies involving voluntary restriction of production. Such measures are contrary to the whole theory and habitual practice of agriculture. I do not know of any real farmer who would not gladly produce all that his acreage and equipment and the weather would permit him if he were sure of being able to secure by his labor the means of continued production, of clean, reasonably comfortable living, of education for his children, or professional care and some measure of security for the days when "the almond tree shall flourish—and desire shall fail."[6] The important point is not the market price of our products but their actual value in exchange for the things we need. But who would venture to suggest a scaling down of interest, taxes, the cost of manufactured goods, labor, wages, or special services to correspond with the twenty-five cent wheat, ten cent corn, six cent eggs and five cent cotton of recent years? . . .

To ourselves, inured by twenty-seven years of experience to the "plan-as-you-go" system of agriculture, dependent principally upon the vagaries of the shifting seasons, the very flexibility of the [AAA] plans, the apparent willingness of those in charge to adapt the program to new or unforeseen conditions, gives us confidence in the sincerity of the purpose to prepare the way for better days in agriculture. Our personal hope is that eventually the limitation policy may give way to a more ample production program with storage facilities sufficient for all emergencies, planned on the broad basis of human need. A country blessed with America's actual and possible wealth ought to feel humiliated by the thought of a single ragged, undernourished child. . . .

In our own part of the country the voluntary responses to the campaign for controlled production as an experiment for the benefit of farmers was practically unanimous. Undoubtedly the immediate results have been beneficial and we are glad for even one hesitating step toward what has been called "the American dream," the equalizing of opportunity so that even the humblest may be free to develop whatever native gifts he may possess. . . . I did not vote for the New Deal and certainly not for the old one. I can therefore claim no credit for its accomplishments or responsibility for its mistakes. I am not appointed to defend it. But I do like fair play. There are certain accusations made against the present attempts at social reconstruction that are wickedly unjust so far as we can determine from local conditions.

One of these criticisms relates to the alleged wastefulness of relief administration and the useless or damaging work projects attempted. In our county with a population of 14,000, between November 15, 1933, and December 27, 1934, the public work pay rolls under [the CWA and FERA] are reported as totaling $331,760.69. The sum expended seems to us truly enormous, and the extent of aid required is most unusual in a section where pioneer traditions of self-help and neighborly assistance are still strong. Yet certain facts should be considered. In the late summer of 1934 the county relief administration reported that they had been operating on about a 3% margin.[7] . . . This, too, in a county of "magnificent distances" requiring much driving over an area 34 miles wide and 60 long, almost twice as large as the state of Rhode Island and nearly as large as Delaware. Even if this 3% overhead expense were doubled or quadrupled, it would still be far below the cost alleged by some severe critics. . . .

If mere dollars were to be considered, the actually destitute in our section could undoubtedly have been fed and clothed more cheaply than the work projects have been carried out. But in our national economy manhood must be considered as well as money. People employed to do some useful work may retain their self-respect to a degree impossible under cash relief. . . .

A second anxiety, whether real or assumed, relates to the fear of wide-spread and serious degradation of moral character, resulting from the various relief projects. . . . When a man will drive several miles to some FERA project, work with his horses for the required time under any weather conditions, spend most of his earnings for high-priced stock feed so as to conserve the means of his family's livelihood and be ready for farming again whenever rain may come, the danger of his becoming a habitual pauper through government aid seems to me quite negligible. If we must worry so over the ruinous effects of "made work" on people of this type, why haven't we been worrying for generations over the character of the idlers to whom some accident of birth or inheritance has given wealth unmeasured, unearned and unappreciated? If we must continue to protest against the AAA efforts to effect some fair balance between prices of farm and industrial products because of increased cost to the consumer, why haven't we for a century been crying out against the similar effect of protective tariffs, imposed with the conscious purpose of maintaining prices sufficient to build up and increase enormous fortunes for a comparatively few?

A third criticism is based on the overworked idea of "regimentation," concerning which certain syndicate writers and politicians have wasted too much ink and breath . . . over this alleged menace to American liberties. . . . I have attended nearly all of the wheat meetings in our own district and the most distinct impression received was the entire absence of anything like standardization or compulsion. . . . Many of these self-appointed defenders of freedom seem to know nothing of the loss of liberty attendant upon seriously adverse economic conditions. No regimentation is more cruel than that of extreme poverty. The cramped and barren lives of millions of sharecroppers in the southern states, the deplorable conditions in some of the coal-mining areas, the slum districts in almost any large city, are a pitiful contradiction to our boasted "inalienable right to life, liberty, and the pursuit of happiness."

. . . We did not wait ourselves for the government or any one to tell us to go to listing[8] our own fields to control as far as possible the blowing and loss of surface soil. But this work is wearing on both men and machinery and especially hard on our thin pocket book. A prominent political interpreter recently referred to the idea of the possible exhaustion of people's resources as an "alibi." Perhaps he really thinks that small savings renew themselves like the widow's cruse of oil[9] and that people prefer to ask for government aid rather than to depend upon their own efforts. To go back to our listing, we feel that to some extent it has been helpful in holding our own acreage this far. But to be genuinely effective, such a plan must be carried out on a large scale and not left to piecemeal efforts. . . .

Our reduced herds of cattle were carried through the past winter largely on waste materials. Straw had been saved from the meager wheat crop that survived the drought and dust of 1933 and 1934. Crops not worth harvesting were pastured out and utilized to the last stalk. Russian thistles were gathered and stacked; in some cases where wheat was worth harvesting with a combine, the stubble was later cut with a mower and the rough, poor feed laboriously saved. We even hear of bear grass, or "soap weed," the yucca plant of the broken grazing lands, being ground and utilized for stock feed. There is in our section no supine waiting for government assistance. The people we know are meeting a hard situation with vigor, and individual resourcefulness. Yet there is moral support in feeling that agencies more comprehensive and powerful than any one person can control are supplementing our efforts. . . .

To many old-timers like ourselves who have for twenty-five years or more wrought the persistent effort of bodies and minds into the soil of this now barren land, the greatest cause of anxiety is the fear that our county may yet be designated as "submarginal" land and included in the areas now being purchased for public domain. A fourth year of failure such as now seems probable would give added weight to the arguments for such a procedure. Repossession of our land by the federal government and a general migration to more favored localities may be the best way to meet the present disheartening situation. Yet the problem is not one that admits of a simple, off-hand solution. . . . It involves the interests not only of farm people but of the many small towns which have sprung up as trading centers throughout the plains region. . . .

Yet common sense suggests that the regions which are no longer entirely self-supporting cannot rely indefinitely upon government aid. So the problem remains and the one satisfactory solution is beyond all human control. Some of our neighbors with small children, fearing the effects upon their health, have left temporarily "until it rains." Others have left permanently, thinking doubtless that nothing could be worse. Thus far we and most of our friends seem held—for better or for worse—by memory and hope. I can look backward and see our covered wagon drawn up by the door of the cabin in the early light of that May morning long ago, can feel again the sweet fresh breath of the untrodden prairie, and recall for a moment the proud confidence of our youth. But when I try to see the wagon—or the old Model T truck—headed in the opposite direction, away from our home and all our cherished hopes, I can not see it at all. Perhaps it is only because the dust is too dense and blinding.

Meanwhile the longing for rain has become almost an obsession. We remember the gentle all-night rains that used to make a grateful music on the shingles close above our heads, or the showers that came just in time to save a dying crop. We recall the torrents that occasionally burst upon us in sudden storms, making our level farm a temporary lake where only the ducks felt at home. We dream of the faint gurgling sound of dry soil sucking in the grateful moisture of the early or the later rains; of the fresh green of sprouting wheat or barley, the reddish bronze of springing rye. But we waken to another day of wind and dust and hopes deferred, of attempts to use to the utmost every small resource, to care for the stock and poultry as well as we can with our scanty supplies, to keep our balance and to trust that upon some happier day our wage may even yet come in.

⁓

MAY 1936
"LETTERS FROM THE DUST BOWL," *ATLANTIC MONTHLY*

JUNE 30, 1935

MY DEAR EVELYN:

Your continued interest in our effort to "tie a knot in the end of the rope and hang on" is most stimulating. . . . Wearing our shade hats, with handkerchiefs tied over our faces and Vaseline in our nostrils, we have been trying to rescue our home from the accumulations of wind-blown dust which penetrates wherever air can go. It is an almost hopeless task, for there is rarely a day when at some time the dust clouds do not roll over. "Visibility" approaches zero and everything is covered again with a silt-like deposit which may vary in depth from a film to actual ripples on the kitchen floor. I keep oiled cloths on the window sills and between the upper and lower sashes. They help just a little to retard or collect the dust. Some seal the windows with the gummed-paper strips used in wrapping parcels, but no method is fully effective. We buy what appears to be red cedar sawdust with oil added to use in sweeping our floors, and do our best to avoid inhaling the irritating dust.

In telling you of these conditions I realize that I expose myself to charges of disloyalty to this western region. A good Kansas friend suggests that we should imitate the Californian attitude toward earthquakes and keep to ourselves what we know about dust storms. Since the very limited rains of May in this section gave some slight ground for renewed hope, optimism has been the approved policy. Printed articles or statements by journalists, railroad officials, and secretaries of small-town Chambers of Commerce have heralded too enthusiastically the return of prosperity to the drouth region. . . . But you wished to know the truth, so I am telling you the actual situation, though I freely admit that the facts are themselves often contradictory and confusing.

Early in May, with no more grass or even weeds on our 640 acres than on your kitchen floor, and even the scanty remnants of dried grasses from last year cut off and blown away, we decided, like most of our neighbors, to ship our cattle to grass in the central part of the state. . . . Whether this venture brings profit or loss depends on whether the cattle make satisfactory gains during the summer and whether prices remain reasonable or fall back to the level that most people would desire. We farmers here in the United States might as well recognize that we are a minority group, and that the prevailing interest of the nation as a whole is no longer agricultural. . . .

The day after we shipped the cattle, the long drouth was temporarily broken by the first effective moisture in many months—about one and one-quarter inches in two or three gentle rains. All hope of a wheat crop had been abandoned by March or April.

Contrary to many published reports, a good many people had left this country either temporarily or permanently before any rains came. And they were not merely "drifters," as is frequently alleged. In May a friend in the southwestern county of Kansas voluntarily sent me a list of the people who had already left their immediate neighborhood or were packed up and ready to go. The list included 109 persons in 26 families, substantial people, most of whom had been in that locality over ten years, and some as long as forty years. In these families there had been two deaths from dust pneumonia. Others in the neighborhood were ill at that time. Fewer actual residents have left our neighborhood, but on a sixty-mile trip yesterday to procure tractor repairs we saw many pitiful reminders of broken hopes and apparently wasted effort. Little abandoned homes where people had drilled deep wells for the precious water, had set trees and vines, built reservoirs, and fenced in gardens,—with everything now walled in or half buried by banks of drifted soil,—told a painful story of loss and disappointment. . . .

It might give you some notion of our great "open spaces" if I tell you that on the sixty-mile trip, going by a state road over which our mail comes from the railroad, and coming back by a Federal highway, we encountered only one car, and no other vehicles of any sort. And this was on Saturday, the farmers' marketing day!

The coming of the long-desired rain gave impetus to the Federal projects for erosion control. Plans were quickly made, submitted to groups of farmers in district gatherings, and put into operation without delay.

The proposition was that, in order to encourage the immediate listing of abandoned wheat ground and other acreage so as to cut down wind erosion, the Federal Government would contribute ten cents per acre toward the expense of fuel and oil for tractors or feed for horses, if the farmers would agree to list not less than one fourth of the acreage on contour lines. . . . The latest report states that within the few weeks since the programme was begun in our county 299,986 acres have been ploughed or listed on these contour lines—that is, according to the lay of the land instead of on straight lines with right-angled turns as has been the usual custom. . . .

. . . The primary intention of . . . contour listing is to distribute rainfall evenly over the fields and prevent its running off to one end of the field or down the road to some creek or drainage basin. It is hoped that the plan will indirectly tend to lessen wind erosion by promoting the growth of feed crops, restoration of humus to denuded surfaces, and some protection through standing stubbles and the natural coverage of weeds and unavoidable wastes. One great contributing cause of the terrible dust storms of the last two years has been the pitiful bareness of the fields resulting from the long drought.

I am not wise enough to forecast the result. We have had two most welcome rains in June—three quarters of an inch and one-half inch. . . . [But] the helpful effects of the rains have been for us and for other people largely destroyed by the drifting soil from abandoned, unworked lands around us. It fills the air and our eyes and noses and throats, and, worst of all, our furrows, where tender shoots are coming to the surface only to be buried by the smothering silt from the fields of rugged individualists who persist in their right to do nothing.

A fairly promising piece of barley has been destroyed for us by the merciless drift from the same field whose sands have practically buried the little mulberry hedge which has long sheltered our buildings from the northwest winds. Large spaces in our pastures are entirely bare in spite of the rains. Most of the green color, where there is any grazing, is due to the pestilent Russian thistles rather than to grass. . . .

Naturally you will wonder why we stay where conditions are so extremely disheartening. Why not pick up and leave as so many others have done? It is a fair question, but a hard one to answer.

. . . I cannot act or feel or think as if the experiences of our twenty-seven years of life together had never been. And they are all bound up with the little corner to which we have given our continued and united efforts. To leave voluntarily—to break all these closely knit ties for the sake of a possibly greater comfort elsewhere—seems like defaulting on our task. We may *have* to leave. We can't hold out indefinitely without some return from the land, some source of income, however small. But I think I can never go willingly or without pain that as yet seems unendurable.

There are also practical considerations that serve to hold us here, for the present. . . . We could realize nothing whatever from all our years of struggle with which to make a fresh start.

We long for the garden and little chickens, the trees and birds and wild flowers of the years gone by. Perhaps if we do our part these good things may return some day, for others if not for ourselves. . . .

August 11, 1935

My Dear Evelyn:

On this blistering Sunday afternoon I am, like Alexander Selkirk: *Monarch of all I survey; My right there is none to dispute.*[10] There is no one within a mile and a half, and all day I've seen just one person pass by in an old stripped-down Ford.

Will and Eleanor went early this morning with a family of neighbors to visit the dinosaur pit in the next county to the westward—about seventy miles from here—where the State University is engaged in excavating the bones of some of these ancient monsters, reminders of a time when there was plenty of water even in the Panhandle.

It seemed impossible for us all to leave home at once, so I stayed here to care for a new Shorthorn brother, to keep the chickens' pails filled with fresh water, to turn the cattle and horses in to water at noon, and to keep them from straying to the extremely poisonous drought-stricken cane. We spent the better part of a night during the week trying to save two of the best young cows from the effects of the prussic acid which develops in the stunted sorghum.[11] We thought they would die and I am not sure yet whether they recovered because of the liberal doses of melted lard and molasses. . . .

We cannot complain of laziness on the part of our citizens. Oklahoma is one of the first states to get away from direct relief. Official reports of the administrators here emphasize the eagerness with which people accept any sort of work to help themselves and to make unnecessary the acceptance of public aid.[12] . . .

This progress toward more nearly normal conditions of employment occurs in the face of the most critical farm situation that we have ever encountered. For over a month we have had *no* rain, and the two light local showers early in July had only a slight and temporary effect.

All hope of an adequate forage crop has now followed into oblivion the earlier hopes of wheat and maize production. We have no native or cultivated hay crops. The cattle stay alive thus far on weeds, but the pastures are destitute of grass. Many think it can never be restored. The heat is intense and the drying winds are practically continuous, with a real "duster" occurring every few days to keep us humble.

. . . Will has been working early and late with one of the county terracing machines, laying up ridges on contour lines for every foot of fall. He hopes to be ready tomorrow to turn the machine over to a neighbor who will also make the experiment. Later on he would like to run the terrace lines across the pasture lands, but the future for us is most uncertain.

Everything now depends on whether a definite change of moisture conditions occurs in time for people to sow wheat for 1936. The "suit-case farmers"—that is, insurance agents, preachers, real-estate men, and so forth, from cities near or far—have bet thousands of dollars upon *rain*, or, in other words, have hired the preparation of large areas of land all around us which no longer represent the idea of *homes* at all, but just parts of a potential factory for the low-cost production of wheat—*if it rains*.

A short time ago a big tractor . . . accidentally hooked on to the cornerstone of the original survey and dragged it off up the road. All these many years that stone has marked the corner of our home-stead. . . . It has suggested the beauty of the untouched prairie as it was when the surveyors set the stone, the luxuriant thick turf of native grasses,—grama grass, buffalo, and curly mesquite,—the pincushion cactuses, straw-color and rose, the other wide flowers which in their season fulfilled the thought of Shakespeare: — *The summer's flower is to the summer sweet, Though to itself it only live and die.*[13]

The cornerstone has also suggested the preparation for human occupation—the little homes that were so hopefully established here, of which so very few remain. After twenty-nine years, eight places in our township, out of the possible 136 (excluding the two school sec-tions), are still occupied by those who made the original homestead entry. And now the stone is gone and the manner of its removal seemed almost symbolic of the changes that appear inevitable.

. . . We feel rather proud that the proprietor of the Elkhart flour mill which we have patronized for many years has withdrawn from the group of Kansas millers suing the government for recovery of the pro-cessing tax. He explained his position by stating that, as the benefits derived from these taxes had been an actual lifesaver for farming and general business interests in this section, he would not seek to embarrass the government in its attempt to collect the tax. . . .

It's time to do the evening work, put the guinea pig to bed, and begin to watch for the return of our explorers. I do hope weather conditions are favoring the growth of your crops.

JANUARY 28, 1936

DEAR EVELYN:

As I have said before, our own problems seem of slight moment as compared with yours. Yet more than ever of late "the day's journey" has indeed seemed to "fill the whole long day." As yet there are no decisive changes, no clear light on our way. Late in the summer, before Eleanor returned to her work in the medical school, she drove the tractor for her father, and with the help of the old header they worried down the scattering, scanty crop of sorghum cane and Sudan grass which had made all the growth it could through the hot, dry summer. That there was anything at all to harvest we attribute to the new planting methods encouraged by the Soil Erosion Control Service,[14] of listing on contour lines and laying up terraces. . . . A shower the night they finished cutting and another about ten days later, conserved in the same way, gave us most fortunately a second cutting over the same fields, and a few loads of maize fodder from spots here and there on another part of the farm. These crops of roughage have little or no market value, but are indispensable if one plans to winter any cattle. The old, nutritious native grasses which used to provide winter pasturage are forever gone. Killing frosts happily came later than usual. In October, I drove the tractor myself and we two cut and hauled and put into the barn loft (including the earlier cutting) some twenty tons of fodder from two hundred acres, expensive feed when regarded as the entire outcome of a year's work and investment, yet essential to our attempt at carrying on.

As you know, however, wisely or otherwisely, this region has permitted wheat growing to become its main concern. The wheat situation around us is so varied and precarious as to be most difficult of appraisal. Our own acreage is fairly typical of the general condition. We have a little wheat that came up in September, made a fair start, and for a time furnished pasturage for the small calves. A part of it was early smothered out by the drift from near-by fields. Part of it would yet respond to abundant moisture if that were to come. . . .

After the four-to-six-inch snow of early January, the editor of our county paper was asked by the United Press [International] for a candid report of actual conditions. His estimate allowed the county as a whole a 25 per cent chance; not, if I understood him, a fair chance for a 25 per cent crop, but about one chance in four for anything at all. . . . And you must try to remember that a failure this year would mean five in succession for a large part of the high plains region. . . . You can readily see that the conditions I have so hastily outlined promise no protection against the ravages of dust storms if the spring winds rage as in previous years.

On the whole it is not surprising that here and there some bitterness should have been felt and expressed, perhaps immoderately, over the recent AAA decision in the Supreme Court. People here, business men as well as the farmers themselves, realize that the benefit payments under AAA and the wage payments from Federal work projects are all that have saved a large territory here from abandonment. A December statement by the Soil Conservation service reports an area in five states, including part of all of sixty-eight counties and 87,900 square miles of territory, as in need of active measures for protection and control of the dust-storm menace. Mr. [Hugh H.] Bennett, director of the service, regards this as the greatest "physical problem facing the country to-day." I was astonished to find by a little primary arithmetic that the area involved is equal to that of all the New England States, with New Jersey and Maryland and about half of Delaware added for good measure. . . .

Farmers are not asking for special favors. They ask only an even chance as compared with other workers. But people don't understand.

Perhaps the many books on pioneer life with the usual successful and happy outcome have helped to give a wrong impression and perpetuate the idea that country people live on wild game and fish and fruits and in general on the free bounty of heaven. Many people have no idea of the cash expense of operating a farm to-day, or the work and planning required to keep the wheels going round, to say nothing of a decent living or suitable education for the children. . . .

I think I told you of shipping our cattle to pasture. It proved to be a disastrous mistake. To keep in tune, I suppose we should blame Secretary Wallace or the broad-shouldered Mr. Tugwell, who likewise had nothing to do with it.[15] Really the source of trouble was our own erroneous impression that grass is grass, and that our cattle would gain if they could have ample pasturage. Evidently other factors of acclimatization must be considered. . . . I was quite alone here for a week while Will went after our little bunch.

That was November first, and most of our efforts and resources ever since have been devoted to trying to bring our cattle back to a normal condition. They are gaining slowly, but our homegrown feed is disappearing rapidly, and the grain feed of threshed maize which we must purchase . . . is piling up expenses. We have sold one mixed bunch of older cows and summer calves. . . . In general, there has been an improvement in farm prices, both absolutely and relatively, which has given us courage to keep on working, and has kept alive our hope for some definite change in weather conditions that may once more make our acres fruitful and restore to us some sense of accomplishment. . . .

Perhaps it is a sin to parody anything as beautiful as Ulysses. Yet as we gray, lonely old people sit here by the fire to-night, planning for the year's work, my thoughts seem bound to fall into that pattern. It may be that the dust will choke us down; It may be we shall wake some happy morn and look again on fields of waving grain.[16] So good night, dear friend, and a happier to-morrow.

MARCH 8, 1936

DEAR EVELYN:

Since I wrote to you, we have had several bad days of wind and dust. On the worst one recently, old sheets stretched over door and window openings, and sprayed with kerosene, quickly became black and helped a little to keep down the irritating dust in our living rooms. Nothing that you see or hear or read will be likely to exaggerate the physical discomfort or material losses due to these storms. Less emphasis is usually given to the mental effect, the confusion of mind resulting from the overthrow of all plans for improvement or normal farm work, and the difficulty of making other plans, even in a tentative way. To give just one specific example: the paint has been literally scoured from our buildings by the storms of this and previous years; we should by all means try to "save the surface;" but who knows when we might safely undertake such a project? The pleasantest morning may be a prelude to an afternoon when the "dust devils"[17] all unite in one hideous onslaught. The combination of fresh paint with a real dust storm is not pleasing to contemplate.

The prospects for a wheat crop in 1936 still remain extremely doubtful. There has been no moisture of any kind since the light snow of early January. On a seventy-mile drive yesterday . . . we saw more wheat that would still respond to immediate rainfall than I . . . had expected to see. A few fields were refreshingly green and beautiful to look upon. There seems no doubt that improved methods of tillage and protection are already yielding some results in reducing wind erosion. But rain must come soon to encourage growth even on the best fields if there is to be any wheat harvest. Interspersed with the more hopeful areas are other tracts apparently abandoned to their fate. A field dotted thickly with shoulder-high hummocks of sand and soil bound together by the inevitable Russian thistles presents little encouragement to the most ardent conservationist. My own verdict in regard to plans for the reclaiming of such land would be, "Too late." Yet such fields are a menace to all the cultivated land or pasture ground around them and present a most difficult problem.

The two extremes I have just suggested—that is, the slight hope even yet for some production on carefully tilled fields, and the practically hopeless conditions on abandoned land—are indicative of the two conflicting tendencies now evident through an extensive section of the high plains. On the one hand we note a disposition to recognize a mistake, to turn aside from the undertaking with the least possible loss and direct one's time and energy to some new purpose. On the other hand we observe that many seem determined to use even the hard experiences of the past, their own mistakes and other people's warning signals, pointing the way to changes of methods and more persistent and effective effort right where they stand.

The first attitude may be illustrated by an incident of the past week, the attempt of former neighbors to sell the pipe from the well on their now deserted homestead. This may not seem significant to you. But to old-timers in this deep-water country, so nearly destitute of flowing streams, the virtual destruction of a well of our excellent, life-nourishing water comes close to being the unpardonable sin against future generations.[18]

The same disintegrating tendency is shown in a larger and more alarming way by the extent to which land once owned and occupied by farm families is now passing into ownership of banks, mortgage companies, assurance societies, and investment partnerships or corporations. The legal notices published in our county paper for the past week include two notices of foreclosure proceedings and nine notices of sheriff's sales to satisfy judgments previously rendered. These eleven legal actions involve the ownership of 3520 acres of land, the equivalent of twenty-two quarter sections. . . .

I am not questioning the legal right of these companies to take over the title of the farms for their own security or that of the people whose money they have invested. . . . [But] this remote control stands in the way of constructive efforts toward recovery.

Yet there are numerous evidences of the persevering restoration of which I have written. The big road maintainers keep the highways in excellent condition. New license tags are appearing on cars and trucks. Churches, schools, and basket-ball tournaments continue much as usual. One village church reported forty people in attendance on one of the darkest and most dangerous of the recent dusty Sundays. The state agricultural college for this section has an increased enrollment this year. More people are managing in some way—we hardly see how—to keep in touch with the world of news and markets, politics and entertainment, through radio service. A local implement agency recently sent out invitations to a tractor entertainment with free moving pictures of factory operation and the like. The five hundred free lunches prepared for the occasion proved insufficient for the assembled crowd. Within a few succeeding days the company took orders for three tractors ranging in price from around $1200 to $1500. Some people must still have faith in the future!

More impressive to me was the Saturday rush of activity at the small produce house where we did our marketing. Cars kept driving up and people coming in with pails or crates or cases of eggs. Cream was delivered in containers of all sorts and sizes, including one heavy aluminum cooker! . . . In many cases the payments were pitifully small, but every such sale represents hard work and economy and the struggle to keep going.

At the hatchery they spoke of slow business through the extremely cold weather. The young man in charge also referred to the changes or postponements in people's plans because of their failure to receive the expected payments under the now extinct allotment plan. With spring in the dusty air, however, and renewed hope that the government contracts will later be fulfilled, orders were coming in encouragingly.

We plan ourselves for four hundred baby Leghorns about the middle of April. That will be an increase for us, but is about the safest small investment we can make to yield an all-the-year-round return. We shall have to put quite a bit of work and expense into the brooder house to keep out the dust, and the rain—if it ever comes. But we are happier to keep on trying.

This impressionistic account of conditions here and of our hope for the future would scarcely be complete without some mention of government assistance. We have had only slight contact with the Rehabilitation Service.[19] We know that the man in charge here is taking his work seriously, trying to give definite aid and encouragement to those who have reached the end of their small resources and have lost hope and courage. He stopped here the other morning to see whether we really meant it when we promised the use of our tractor and other equipment to a young man in the neighborhood who is trying to make a new start for himself and wife and small daughter through a rehabilitation loan. In spite of seriously adverse conditions, this agent, who meets many people, spoke of a rather surprising general spirit of optimism. I suppose there is something of the gambler in all of us. We instinctively feel that the longer we travel on a straight road, the nearer we must be coming to a turn. People here can't quite believe yet in a hopeless climatic change which would deprive them permanently of the gracious gift of rain.

To me the most interesting and forward-looking government undertaking in the dust bowl centers about the group of erosion control experiments scattered over a wide area. The Pony Creek project, fifteen miles east of our home, includes all of one congressional township and parts of three others, seventy square miles altogether, or something over 42,000 acres. This is a pretty seriously damaged area, principally devoted to wheat growing, and even now blowing badly. If the methods employed succeed in checking the drift and in restoring productivity, much will have been accomplished, both of intrinsic value and of use as a stimulating object lesson. We hope some day to drive over and see how they are progressing. . . .

Our personal plans—like those of all the rest—are entirely dependent on whether or not rain comes to save a little of our wheat, to give grass or even weeds for pasturage, to permit the growing of roughage for the winter, and provide some cover on the surface and promote the intertwining of rootlets in the soil to reduce wind damage. Our terraces are in good condition to distribute whatever moisture may come. We hope we have learned a little about protecting the soil which is the basis of our physical life. In the house the poinsettia and Christmas cactus are blooming a second time and the geraniums blossom in spite of the dust. Eleanor has just sent us budded hyacinth and daffodil bulbs in little moss-filled nests. They will help us to look forward for a time at least.

⇜

JAN. 19, 1936

DEAR ROSE:

Your Christmas letter found us at the same old place. We made two or three different plans for getting away to investigate other possibilities. Each time some unforeseen circumstance seemed to block the way. There has been no definite or reassuring change in weather conditions here. The hoped-for fall rains were very scanty, yet with even so slight encouragement, people have gone on and put in their wheat, hoping to accomplish a double purpose: that is, first to qualify for the benefits under the AAA—in reality the only thing that has saved the country side here from complete abandonment and the small towns from ruin; and second, to keep up the struggle to hold their land from blowing, even if the wheat didn't prosper as we hoped. Logically, I suppose I've got the two considerations in the wrong order. Yet, as an immediate hope, the AAA looked the more dependable. Now it is wrecked and only the uncertainties of the weather for the next few weeks can determine whether the other purpose may not be quite as illusory. Much of the wheat sown has never yet come up. . . .

I thought of you and Mabel the night of the Christmas Carol concert and it was pleasant to know that you could be together. Mabel also spoke of their anticipation of a happy evening. I am afraid I do not remember the Dr. Barnes you spoke of, but can understand your feeling about his little Testament. You may remember Grissell McLaren ('98). I had a letter from her also at Christmas time. . . . I am sorry to say that my young nephew (12 yrs. old) balked in public school work, so they put him into a military school, with a $105.00 uniform! Yet they are (politically) opposed to "regimentation," the bugbear of all good individualists.

Aren't we all funny folks anyway? I wonder if by chance you have seen the book "Man, the Unknown" by Dr. Alexis Carrel[20] and whether it is worth the price ($3.50). I have seen some very good reviews of it and it is apparently the kind of discussion that interests me. But I've hesitated about spending so much for one book which perhaps no one else would care for.

You may have heard of Eleanor's recent marriage as I sent a note and newspaper clipping to Neshanic [New Jersey]. . . . They came home for their vacation Dec. 22. We met them in Guymon and I was too happy to sleep that night. The next day we carried out a plan of many years' postponings—to drive out into New Mexico and bring home a Christmas tree. It was a <u>beautiful</u> Oklahoma winter day. On the way we found interest in visiting the dinosaur pit in the western edge of Oklahoma, where the State University is excavating quite successfully a very well-preserved accumulation of several types of those remote and peculiar creatures. They were working very carefully and patiently upon a large femur—over four feet long and nearly that much in circumference at the enlarged ends. It was pleasant to learn that the man in charge, crippled with arthritis, but with the most gentle and gracious personality, was a friend of a Mount Holyoke woman, Mrs. Margaret Morse Nice, whose husband used to be in Okla. University but is now in the University of Ohio. They had cooperated in bird studies of this western area. We cooked our dinner opposite a large striking bit of erosion called locally the Battle Ship and were near another still more interesting relic of ages gone by, called the Wedding Cake because of its almost perfect symmetry, cone-shaped summit, and distinct stratification in varying colors. The children wandered around, Will cut a <u>branch</u> from a pinon (I couldn't be willing in this barren land to sacrifice a whole tree) and we ate our dinner on a large flat rock facing the haze-filled valley leading on to the west-ward. It was a happy day for us to remember. . . .

It smells good tonight with bread just out of the oven and the narcissus bulbs that Eleanor brought home coming out in all their fragrance. Altogether I think your Christmas wish for us was pretty well fulfilled. Thanks and the same to you for every day.

～

January 1937

"Our Own Letter from the Dust Bowl," *American Chamber of Commerce Journal*

Dec. 8, 1936

Dear Neighbor—across the world: [Mr. Walter Robb]

I've just been reading again your friendly letter which brought to us so much stimulus and encouragement. I'm sorry that even after the long delay I cannot write the kind of "postscript" to my spring letter that we know you would be happy to receive. . . .

For 1936 we must record another year of failure. Yet that failure might so easily have been changed to moderate success by one good rain in late July or August that we do not altogether despair. As I write I can hear the tractor laboring along on the north field while Will is laying up a fresh set of terraces in the hope that next year may give us all a better chance. It seems impossible to dispense with that little word hope, even though at times we are conscious of the pain of hopes too long deferred.

Soon after my last letter was mailed, Will suffered a painful accident which might easily have proved a permanent handicap. While he was unloading a barrel of coal oil, it slipped and fell, bruising one ankle severely and, I still believe, fracturing some of the smaller bones. At that time the dust storms were at their worst. For a while it seemed that perhaps, regardless of desire, we could not go on. There were many days, as I struggled to care for the stock, when I could not see from one of the farm buildings to another through the blinding, choking clouds. Dust was piling up every where, filling gateways, burying machinery, drifting around the buildings, making the less traveled roads almost impassable. The mere matter of getting milk or even water to the house in a condition fit for use presented a difficult problem. Will improvised a crutch from a short length of pump rod and after the first few days helped all he could to direct and carry on the outdoor work, actually crawling on hands and knees the length of the barn loft to break open the bales of Colorado alfalfa and get it ready for me to drop into the mangers. In spite of his being almost compelled to do the things he shouldn't have done, the injured ankle slowly regained its shape and strength and the recovery is one thing to be grateful for as we look back over a difficult year.

The wind and dust continued without much abatement through March and April and early May. The first sign of any hopeful change came with a light rain on May 17 though the following week of high winds destroyed most of the benefit. By this time any lingering hope of wheat production in our vicinity had faded away, though limited areas in the extreme eastern part of the country returned small yields. The ground was too dry and hard to permit satisfactory preparation for spring planting, though Will had done some listing and "chiseling" as well as the condition of the soil would allow. On June 4 as if to confute all theories about the diversion of our moisture-bearing winds to Greenland and such attempted explanations of the long-protracted drought, we had one tremendous rain—a regular "gully-washer"— when two and a half inches poured down in half an hour. The unworked soil could not absorb it fast enough, especially as there is a strong tendency for the fine wind-ground silt to coat over the surface, closing the pores of the soil as if with a thin cement and preventing natural penetration. So much of this precious moisture proved ineffective for actual crop production, broke over contour and terrace lines and finally formed several "playa" lakes in the neighborhood in basins which have no outlet. One of our neighbors now plans to pump some of this still standing water back upon his fields.

During the fall these temporary lakes furnished sanctuary to immense flocks of seagulls, possibly driven inland by storms along some coast or attracted by the hosts of grasshoppers which had helped to complete the damage done by the drouth. It was a new and delightful interest to us to watch the strong, impetuous flight of these gulls as they skimmed low over our fields or massed in silvery shimmering clouds against the darkening horizon as they returned at nightfall to the sheltering lake. All at once they were gone and we saw them no more.

That heavy rain on June 4 before a seed was planted was our only source of moisture through the growing season aside from two or three drouth showers which scarcely dampened the surface. . . . Where our terrace lines remained unbroken and held the water back to soak slowly into the soil, the effect upon production was noticeably beneficial. From one small field where the water had stood, which was sowed to cane as soon as the ground was dry, we were able to save two fair cuttings in August and October. From still smaller areas of maize along the terrace lines we threshed out about forty-five bushels of grain for chicken feed. . . . On the other hand where our terraces broke in the swift onrush of the flowing water, there was slight penetration, the ground dried quickly and seed failed entirely to come up. . . .

A few families have removed from our neighborhood during the spring and summer but most of those who held out through the dust storms are still here, working along various lines toward their individual hopes for the future. There is no constraint and little agreement as to the best methods to pursue in attempts at recovery. The planners, however, might be divided into two large groups, those who would rely upon improved cultivation to conserve every bit of natural rainfall, and those who believe in the possibility of rather extensive irrigation by pumping from deep wells. The first group includes the adherents of contouring and terracing methods and also those who abhor the crooked lines and inconvenience of that type of farming but would seek to gain similar results while keeping their fields square and their rows straight. These people are placing much reliance upon the further development of the so-called "basin-type" lister, which has a special device for dumping little dams every ten or twelve feet across the furrows, thus preventing run-off of water in any ordinary rain.

Each irrigationist has his own pet plan but the great obstacle in all of them is the initial expense required for the deep wells and an effective pumping system. Some question the feasibility of irrigating comparatively small plots while the surrounding area might be up in the air or drifting in upon the watered field or garden. Others wonder whether even our apparently unfailing supply of deep ground water could stand the drain of continuous pumping. . . . I haven't myself any technical knowledge regarding either the water supply or the engineering required to make it available. . . . Some enthusiastic advocates of irrigation believe that eventually the supplies of gas under the Panhandle can be utilized to develop cheap power for pumping. Here again we come up against the hard fact that every material resource comes to an end unless constantly replenished. But at least these various possibilities provide subjects for discussion and some incentive to look forward to happier days.

So we work on caring for the house and the chickens, the horses and cattle, trying to make our scant supply of feed go as far as possible, filling the days with the innumerable tasks necessary on any farm, hoping somehow, as the passing years steal away our strength, to be able to provide easier, more convenient ways of accomplishing the essential tasks.

We were interested in what you said about Mr. Cordell Hull's foreign policies, for we regard him as one of our most useful and far-seeing public men. We hope he may be equal to the great responsibility he now has in the South American conference for strengthening and giving form and direction to the world's desire for peace. Mr. Hull is surely right in thinking of international peace as something not merely to be accepted but to be striven for actively and devotedly.[21] We might think of it as Edgar Lee Masters did of immortality, that it is "not a gift but an achievement."[22]

. . . Will joins in thanks for your letter and in the hope that 1937 may be for you a year of accomplishment and generous fulfillment. If ever you come back to look over those homesteads of earlier years, just take another step and look up ours too. We have set back that old cornerstone as you desired and shall probably not wander far away from it for any length of time.

So be sure of a welcome here from the Hendersons.

⌒≋⌒

DEC. 20, 1936

DEAR ROSE,

This paper was evidently not intended for correspondence, but perhaps you can make it out. I got up early to get the chicken roasted in the pressure cooker before we have to start on the thirty mile trip to Guymon to meet Eleanor who is expected at noon today. We had them both with us for a time in the late summer and enjoyed a few blessed days together out in New Mexico where we have before found rest and refreshment. Later we made a harder, but apparently necessary trip to the old farm home in Iowa, where we spent all our time making some of the most essential repairs. On the last afternoon Eleanor and I repaired the stepping stones at "The Ford" on the little stream where Susie and I spent so much of our time in the long summers of long ago. . . .

I wish I could write hopefully of the situation here. Even if we were "liquidated" there are a good many people still clinging to their little homes. It would need only "a quarter of a turn" in the weather, as Henry Wallace said of the world's heart and will to bring comfort and some sense of accomplishment. The very insufficient amount of forage and chicken feed that we did raise was due to the newer methods of tillage encouraged by the Soil Conservation Service. The scanty crop had no rain during the growing time and grew entirely on stored moisture.

Mr. Henderson's chronic cough is much worse this winter and he has become very hard of hearing and has no teeth, not even the factory sort. I have only a few with just two matching and show the wear and tear in many ways. So we see we aren't going to be young any more and must get what good we can from those whom we hope to see going on. . . .

I love to get your letters and hope to hear of yourself and the rest of the family.

⌒≋⌒

JUNE 1937

"SPRING IN THE DUST BOWL," *ATLANTIC MONTHLY*

APRIL 6, 1937

DEAR ATLANTIC:

The kindness of your letter brought us definite encouragement. It is difficult to appraise our present situation with any exactitude, but some incidents and observations from our daily life may help you to judge of the prospects for 1937.

On our bleak Easter morning a jack rabbit sat crouched in the kindling pile by the kitchen door. He was, however, no frolicsome Easter bunny, but a starved, trembling creature with one eye battered out by the terrific dust storms of the preceding week. He made no effort to escape. I bathed his eye and put him into shelter with our guinea pig, hoping that he would live until showers might bring some tinge of green upon our dust-covered wasteland. Another blinded rabbit picked up in the yard had just died in spite of all my care. When these wild creatures, ordinarily so well able to take care of themselves, come seeking protection, their necessity indicates a cruel crisis for man and beast.

After another dry summer in 1936, with only the scantiest production, hope was revived by light rains in late September. This moisture was barely sufficient to encourage the sowing of wheat for the possibility of spring pasturage. Our acreage, like that of our neighbors, was materially reduced. The seed sprouted, but again the hope of a crop has vanished with the dry winter and the raging winds of spring. We are now reluctantly feeding the last small remainder of the crop of 1931.

High winds and consequent dust storms began early this year and still continue at frequent intervals. While perhaps no more violent than the storms of previous years, their effects, being cumulative, seem more disastrous and overwhelming. On some days the limit of vision has been a row of little elms about thirty feet from the front windows. No eye could penetrate any farther the swirling, blinding clouds of dust which made noonday as dark as late twilight of a clear evening. The worst storm thus far in 1937 occurred immediately after a slight snowfall which again roused delusive hopes. That snow melted on a Tuesday. Wednesday morning, with a rising wind, the dust began to move again, and until late Friday night there was little respite.

Almost as distressing are the more frequent days when the northward-creeping sun shines faintly above the dizzying drift of silt, ground to a fine whitish powder, which gives a ghastly appearance of unreality to the most familiar landscapes. On such days we suffer from a painful sense of helplessness and utter frustration. We need no calendar to tell us that planting time is here again. The cranes went north some time ago. Our hyacinths bloom fragrantly in the windows, and the Easter lily has a bud ready to open. The hardy yellow roses are struggling to put out a few green leaves on the tips of twigs rising above the dust. The other morning a solitary shrike trilled his spring song from the windmill tower. Yet any attempt to proceed with planting under present conditions would be stubborn and expensive folly. . . .

The stripping of humus from the top soil is one of our most serious losses during these critical years. A striking evidence of this regrettable waste came to my notice last summer. I was herding our cattle near a temporary lake formed by the run-off in one rain which fell so fast that the unworked, wind-swept fields could not absorb more than a small portion of the precious moisture. Surrounding the lake were thick sheets of pure vegetable material, ground by the winds and washed away and deposited by the flowing waters. Both humus and rainfall should somehow have been saved to fill and fertilize the depleted subsoil. . . . Verily we are losing the "cream" of our land.

Seeds for field crops are scarce and expensive, and their purchase requires the closest planning. Forage crops are all-important, as we can go no further with cattle or poultry unless we can provide them with home-grown feed. Our seed supplies include cowpeas, pie melons (for winter greens for chickens), sweet clover and crested wheat grass for experimental purposes, Indian corn, cane seed of different types, Sudan grass, Kafir corn, hegari, broomcorn, and millet. If rains come even by the middle of June, we must somehow secure seed of milo maize, our most dependable grain crop, which, under normal conditions, could still mature before frost.

In attacking the problem of erosion control, one great handicap lies in the scarcity of people left to do the essential work. On a recent drive to our county seat thirty miles away, we could count only sixteen occupied homes, including those within half a mile on either side of the federal highway.

Yet experienced people with ample opportunity for knowing the difficulty of the struggle are advising against general abandonment. As the dirt ploughed up here by the unrelenting winds darkens the sky in cities hundreds of miles away, there is a growing realization that the problem is not simply that of a few unsuccessful farmers who might be as well off in one place as another. People are beginning to understand that such conditions, if left unchecked, are progressive and threaten the welfare not only of other agricultural areas but of towns and cities dependent upon rural prosperity.

I am almost ashamed to remember that some years ago, when we first saw the extreme desolation in parts of New Mexico, I thought that surely our own locality could never experience such tragedy. The answer to that mood of unintentional pride is all around us to-day in barren fields, ruined pastures, buried fences, dead trees, abandoned wells, desolated homes.

We can easily understand the skepticism of those who ask what the government can do to help, since obviously it has no power to rule the winds or grant the of blessing of rain. But other important things do come within its legitimate scope. In fact, to restore large areas to production and to prevent the increase of the seriously damaged acreage, rain alone no longer seems sufficient. We may say, as Robert Frost said to his young orchard trees, "Something must be left to God,"[23] and still recognize the need for human toil to counteract the damage already done. . . .

When the entire root system of the hardy yuccas may be seen in places of special exposure, with their thick woody roots writhing on the surface and the finer rootlets extending like guy wires for perhaps twenty feet in different directions, the indications of serious erosion are too plain to be ignored. Often, while trailing the cattle around for scattered grazing, I have been dismayed to notice how tracks of cattle, horses, or tractors, made some time on dampened surface, now project sharply several inches above the surrounding soil like rude cameos carved by the restless wind.

We cannot criticize the conservation plans of the Department of Agriculture. They embody many of the control measures that our own experience would recommend. They grant large individual liberty in working out contributions to the common welfare. The proposals seem practical and sufficiently generous. . . .

We personally hope for the gradual success of these methods, because for the past two years we have had cane on terraced land. Though the crop was lighter than in normal years, enough stubble and roots remained on the ground to prevent appreciable erosion. Moreover, that particular plot still holds subsoil moisture. Dirt brought up with a post auger from a depth of over three feet retains sufficient moisture to be packed into a solid ball.

Naturally, all these plans must fail, at least for this year, unless rains come soon to settle the soil and prepare a normal seed bed. For that we must trust a government established in the nature of things beyond our utmost reach. It is good to remember that the laws of the universe recognize no favorites and cherish no hostility or small vindictiveness; that before sun and rain, stormy winds, or summer's kind beneficence, we all stand upon one common level.

Your interest and that of other friends have been to us a very real and present help.

Chapter 5

Slow and Partial Recovery, 1938–1951

This chapter documents a period of slow recovery for the Hendersons and for the Great Plains generally. From 1938 to 1940, the region continued to experience damaging winds, but 17.64 inches of rain in 1938 and 15.77 and 16.32 inches in the next two years provided enough moisture to stimulate some recovery. Record-breaking rains in 1941 effectively ended the dust bowl, and agricultural prices rose sharply with the beginning of the Second World War in Europe. In 1948, the Hendersons reported their best year ever financially, but the hard years of pioneering and persistence through the Depression and dust bowl had exacted a human toll far more enduring than the damage to the land.

The spirit of optimism that had defined Caroline's early years had been replaced by a generalized sense of anxiety. Her physical deterioration paralleled the destruction of her hopes. She suffered from chronic asthma, undoubtedly exacerbated by the dust storms of the preceding decade, while other injuries and ailments continued apace. Even as the Hendersons celebrated more than a decade of largely favorable weather, Caroline lived in dread of the next disaster.

Something of Caroline's state of health and mind can be seen in her first expression of concern about aging. In 1935, a newspaper account of her visit with her sister Susie in Wichita had identified her as Susie's mother, and the accompanying photograph could well justify the writer's error. The picture presents her as a thin, wrinkled, and worn woman who stood in stark contrast to her much better dressed and sleeker sister.[1]

Caroline's letters from 1938 to 1951 include her continuing correspondence with Rose Alden plus two new correspondents: In

1939, she began writing to Eli Jaffe, the Communist organizer who had visited her earlier that year. She would write to Jaffe often in subsequent years, never agreeing with his convictions, but always communicating her respect and regard for him. A letter to Eleanor in December 1946 is the only known remnant of the early years of correspondence from mother to daughter. It includes Caroline's response to the pending birth of her first and only grandchild, David. Subsequent letters to Eleanor reveal the increasing importance that correspondence had for Caroline.

Caroline's references to "Robert" refer to Susie's son, Robert Putney, for whom the Hendersons had assumed responsibility with Susie's death in 1937. Robert, who had inherited a degree of financial security from his parents, proved an indifferent student and a continuing source of irritation to the Hendersons in later years. But the other development that followed Susie's death, Caroline's inheritance of her father's Iowa farm, brought a measure of financial security to the Hendersons.

Caroline's letters to Eleanor also contain frequent references to a variety of people in the Panhandle region. Caroline rarely identified these people by more than their names as they were well known to her daughter, and most of them remain otherwise unidentified.

≈

CA. DECEMBER 1938

DEAR ROSE:

I had hardly dared to hope for a Christmas note from you this year as my own negligence has been so great. So I was deeply moved by your message this morning and the beauty and significance of the card. Surely its gentle appeal was never more needed, for the world does indeed seem "weary and heavy laden."

I ought to have thanked you long ago for "The Years."[2] It interested me for I had never read a book written in just that manner and I thought the life of almost any family through so many years might make a story of similar texture, color, light and shade. Perhaps I felt a special interest become of the name of the one who seemed to me the central character—Eleanor—and because of its truthfulness in showing how inconclusive life is anyway. . . .

It is hard to sum up in a few words the ups and downs of this crowded confusing year. The winter and spring, until late May, were a blur of almost continuous dust. We had during that time a rather unusual guest for two weeks, a young New York writer of Lithuanian Jewish origin who through some strange throw back had developed a consuming interest in the special problems of the dust bowl and had come out to see for himself. He was a zealous communist, had been severely beaten up at Claremore, the home of our Will Rogers, and we had many fine friendly discussions and arguments. I only wish the proponents of democracy were as ardent and as willing to sacrifice for its success. In late May we had some light rains, enough to encourage planting, and tractors roared day and night. The crop started but soon came to a standstill because of a long summer drought, unbroken till September.

In the later summer August and Eleanor decided on the purchase of a home as Eleanor, especially, was terribly weary of living tucked up in a room or a small apartment. They were fortunate in finding a home not far from the Hospital and from August's work in the research laboratory of a bakery organization, which seemed almost ideal for their use. Nothing grand or imposing but home like and comfortable with the roses and fireplace that Eleanor considered indispensable, as well as other more commonplace necessities.

In early September we drove up to K[ansas] C[ity] to help them pack and move and get settled, as they are both tied up in their work day by day. We also took Robert, my sister's boy, along and arranged for his enrollment at a Polytechnic school, a part of the public school system there. He made passing grades at Elkhart but nothing to be proud of, as his whole interest is in mechanics or more especially electricity. From his report card and one letter from a teacher we feel that he is really gaining and we surely hope so, for dealing with other people's children is truly a heavy responsibility. It makes a lot of extra work for Eleanor in addition to the regular work of her home and the taxing work at the hospital. We have urged her to lighten the load wherever she can, especially as she now has a chance to do some special research work on blood chemistry following the use of a new anaesthetic—cyclopropane and to report the results at the AMA meeting in St. Louis in May.

While we were gone it actually rained over this dry, desolate region and when we returned our rain water lake was once more full to the brim. . . . It seemed quite impossible then that the so late rain could revive the dying crop in time for it to produce anything of importance. But I have never seen more astonishing growth and before frost checked it completely, we had the satisfaction of seeing a fair feed crop develop with some matured grain, though much of the maize and kafir corn was too late to reach its full maturity before the frost. The September rains encouraged a good deal of wheat sowing and some of it still looks very well and should be benefited by the fine covering of wet snow which surprised us this morning.

Through the actual harvesting we had to have hired help but since then we have been alone again and trying to do the threshing and feed hauling by ourselves. The snow has interrupted that work for the present.

This all seems so trifling. I wish there were some real achievement to record. We should love to know more of the European journey and are interested to know of your nephew's position in "Texis" as the radio announcers say. We make some infrequent use of Robert's radio and it makes one link with the world. Thanks for your forbearance and every friendly wish.

DEC. 20, 1938

DEAR MR. JAFFE

I never thought I should be so slow to reply to your letters but it has been a crowded, confusing year and much has been neglected or indefinitely postponed. I have often wished that we could have made it worth while for you to remain here for the season, for I feel that you would have found [much] interest in our varying hopes and fears, our efforts and disappointments and slight achievements. The end of the year is just about as inconclusive as most of life is, at least for the Hendersons and possibly for other people.

We all hoped, since it was obviously going to happen anyway, that you could be a witness to the rather spectacular dust storm that came rolling across from the north on a Friday evening, I think, soon after you left Eva. No doubt Mr. Baker of Boise City found some plausible explanation![3] The cloud, as it approached here with unusual slowness, was one of the most solid and terrifying in appearance that I have personally observed. In late May we had light rains which encouraged quite extensive cultivation. Tractors ran day and night getting in belated row crop. The rains were so light and so gentle in their fall that Mr. H. has never had any real test of his big terrace or dyke on which you saw him working. For once the rains have soaked in where they fell, but he is still faithful to the idea. The summer was again excessively dry and it seemed that we should again be disappointed in regard to even a feed crop. . . .

Robert, to our great surprise, received passing grades at the close of the year. I hardly dare to say he "made" them. [B]ut his interests remain so exclusively mechanical that small town high school courses are practically lost on him, though I felt that during the year there had been considerable gain in general attitudes and he put in a quite contented, busy summer about the place. . . .

While we were gone [to Kansas City] this whole section was favored with fine general rains and the rain water lake which formed then south of our house is still a pleasant resting place for perhaps 200 fine green-headed mallards who fly out at late dusk and fill up on our maize ricks. The rain was so late that it seemed impossible that the almost dead feed crops could revive sufficiently to amount to anything. But I have never seen more vigorous, enthusiastic growth. While much of the late setting grain was cut short by the frost in late October, some of it matured along with an abundance of roughage. So for the first time since 1931, I think we shall have enough feed for our stock and poultry. And of course we are thankful, even though it represents no immediate cash income and dollars are as scarce and elusive as ever. . . .

Don't believe all you may hear or read about any striking "comeback" of the dust bowl. Conditions in general are really somewhat better; there is more feed, better cover, and some fair looking wheat where it was sown immediately after the September rain. But the rich native grasses of our earlier days are gone forever, and we are, at best years removed from anything like a full recovery. Some cling to the idea that the dust-blowing is over, but I'd rather wait until March or April or early summer to make a prophecy. We know that there is all around us much bare, untilled land ready to blow whenever the wind rises. So we shall have to wait and see. . . .

We expect Robert home for his vacation Dec. 24 so we shall not be altogether solitary on Christmas. To me it will be a day of sad remembrance for in my home as a child much was made of the holiday time and all the significance it is supposed to have, and now I feel so terribly alone, the very last of my own family group. And world conditions are so very painful, almost overwhelming to a person of any sensitiveness. Hitler seems the embodiment of the evil spirit which causes the "hero" of Paradise Lost to say boldly—"Evil, be thou my good."[4] A complete repudiation of every decent, humane instinct! Sometimes I wonder whether there is any stopping place short of ultimate and complete wreckage for all that we have considered civilization.

I didn't send in the order slip for the worker's magazine, not because of a lack of interest but because, aside from the two inexpensive trips that we have taken, there has seemed to be nothing to spend except for the barest existence. I have not renewed subscriptions to several papers and magazines we have taken for years and have reduced expense wherever it seemed possible, as there seems no way of increasing income, and operating costs keep climbing up. I say sometimes we are sacrificing too much on the altar of modern improvements, or in other words we are spending more than we can for repairs and running expense for tractors, binder, header, combine, car and what not.

I have often thought of our pleasant conversations and have wondered whether you received any favorable response to any of the stories or articles you sent from here. I really hope you did and that even a postponement of success may not be too irksome if it must be endured. Meantime keep alight the flame of your love for humanity. You will find all sorts of places where just that gift is needed, not only at Christmas time but all the year around, and the warmth will be reflected back to you again. . . .

Come and see us if you ever come near the dust bowl again. Mr. H. joins me in all good wishes.

⌦

MARCH 28, 1939

DEAR MR. JAFFE:

If you were here tonight you could look out on an Arctic scene instead of the Sahara-like landscape with which you became familiar last spring. Today has brought low temperature and snow, following a deluge of rain and hail late yesterday. Water flooded in from the road and Mr. H. is gloating [over] the frozen pools of water along his terrace lines.

For ourselves the winter has been quite wearing and disappointing. Various causes, among them a quite painful accident to Mr. H. when he lost his balance and fell under a loaded wagon which passed over both feet, almost crushing them, have combined to delay our work. And now these recent wet storms, following upon the dry dust storms of previous weeks, render the task of getting in the remainder of our feed a difficult problem, about which at present we can do nothing. We are just getting too old and slow for the work which must be done.

I enjoyed particularly your fine friendly letter at Christmas time and sent it on to Eleanor as I thought she too would appreciate your sympathetic understanding of our problems. Since then we have received several papers, bulletins, etc, for which we thank you. I was especially glad to see that you are receiving some recognition as a correspondent and I hope such opportunities may continue.

The enclosures in this letter are from Eleanor. She and her husband had made a special effort to attend service at the Liberal Center (Unitarian) because Dr. Ise who made the address is a Professor at the University of Kansas and they both knew him in Lawrence.[5] I was particularly interested in the searching questions printed in the small church publication "the Liberal" and felt as if they would appeal to you. You need not return them but feel free to make any use you can of them. These are indeed awful days for all to whom liberty and human rights and ideals of justice and humanity all are precious. I am heart sick over Czechoslovakia and Lithuania and Spain and feel that Britain and France can never blot out the stain upon their honor, for permitting all these things to happen, with no effective protest. We too, as a nation are not quite free from blame. . . .

Robert seems contented and to be gaining in some ways. We recently had his piano sent to K.C. so that he can go on with his music. It is late and "time to retire" so I'll close with every good wish for yourself and your work, both personal and social. Your Sincere Friend

MAY 29, 1939

DEAR ROSE:

Your letter was most welcome and I was interested in all your employments and reflections. Just last night while waiting up to see whether a young heifer was going to need our special help, I filled in the time with the closing portion of <u>Reaching for the Stars</u>.[6] I too was impressed with the writer's complete sincerity and yearning love for all people. Her restraint and generosity in writing of the gross brutalities of the Hitler regime seem admirable and wise—considering her purpose—even though I couldn't duplicate them myself. (The young cow has a beautiful daughter this morning.)

If this attempt at an answer to your letter lacks any sort of coherence, perhaps you will be forbearing enough to lay part of the blame upon our restless cows. In the recent desperate years, our greatest loss has been the ruin of our native grass pastures. The soil conservation service now admits the sad fact, and in 1939 for the first time the sowing of grazing crops on denuded pasture lands is permitted. Heretofore, the theory had been that with normal rainfall the grass would come back. That too optimistic idea is now officially abandoned. So on this breezy morning with the dust resting for a time I am straying with the cattle among the dust filled hammocks of a once smooth field then thickly set with buffalo and grama grasses. They eat eagerly the Russian thistles which form a heavy mat among the masses of dried thistles remaining from last year's growth. I must try to keep them from wandering to our neighbor's withered wheat or to our own freshly planted furrows. Many small lizards go scurrying among the dust heaps, big brown crickets work industriously at digging underground shelters, and the bob-o-links fill the air with their cheerful music.

Across the road Will is planting Sudan grass in the old pasture for later grazing. The continuing noise of the tractor makes a kind of background for all lighter sounds. Though we are far away from normal conditions as yet, we are thankful for a <u>little</u> gain during the past year; for home-grown feed through the past winter; for some replenishment of subsoil moisture; for the possibility of a partial wheat crop, though it has been seriously damaged by the dry winds and frequent dust storms of the spring. These changes indicate some slight improvement but it will take years of favorable seasons and persistent effort to effect any real recovery.

We have both worn down fast during the years of extreme desolation since 1931. Every small accomplishment now seems to demand a greater output of energy and resolution than in the years that are gone. But perhaps that is common experience.

Aside from our own absorbing task, our supreme interest lies in our daughter, Eleanor, and her home in Kansas City, Kansas. She has found her year's work as anesthetist in the Kansas University Hospital professionally profitable and stimulating and is offered the same work again at a substantial increase of salary. . . .

I am glad you and Mabel are going to the reunion. It will be a happy experience to mingle again with those who in my mind at least, are endowed with the charm of perennial youth. Pictures or hints of change make no difference. I think of you all just as you were "when you and I were young."

Greeting to all and "quietness and confidence" for the years to come.

⌁

Dec. 14, 1939

Dear Mr. Jaffe:

I have just been reading again your friendly letter of away back in the summer. I should be ashamed to admit that I didn't do anything about your suggestion for some sort of cooperative movement for improved conditions for Oklahoma workers. I really didn't know what would be expected and distrusted completely my own value in such a project, which would require all the gifts that I conspicuously lack. But thanks anyway for your complimentary thought, even if it wasn't deserved.

This has been for the Hendersons a most laborious and disappointing year. The spring seemed more hopeful but summer conditions were unfavorable and we had more weeds than crops. We are just now trying to wind up the scattering tasks of the fall harvest, and have got the fodder in the barn or stack and the small amount of grain thrashed and stored away. We haven't sown any wheat this fall and doubt now whether we shall as conditions are all against any reasonable hopes for success.

I am enclosing a review which I thought might interest you. It is from the <u>Manchester</u> (England) <u>Guardian</u>, one of the leading liberal papers of Great Britain. I've never had a chance to read <u>The Grapes of Wrath</u>[7] but have seen many favorable comments. On the other hand a student at the Panhandle College at Goodwell (west of Guymon) said the English teacher there condemned it as giving a false impression of Oklahoma and its people.

We should like to know of your work and whether you still find time and inclination for literary work. I hope the increased feeling against Communism since Russian's ruthless purposes have been revealed has not caused you personal inconvenience or discomfort.[8] I feel that you are too good an American and too appreciative of whatever our imperfect democracy means to all of us to be able to rationalize the Soviet policy. As I think you know, I was sincerely sympathetic with their aims and while I couldn't see in out-and-out Communism the solution of our national problems, I was entirely willing and even glad to have them make the experiment, and ready to accept any phases of their system which promised social betterment for the under privileged groups, <u>provided they could be adopted by democratic procedure</u>. I am all against dictators where or whoever they may be. So I can't go along in mind with Stalin or Molotov anymore than with Franco, Mussolini, Hitler or the Japanese cut-throats. They all look alike to me now, however much I may previously have tried to distinguish among them.

Eleanor and August came in early September and took us for a delightful vacation in New Mexico and Colorado. . . . The real climax of our trip was the night and day we spent in Mesa Verde Park in south western Colorado among the ancient homes of the cliff dwellers. Don't miss it if you are ever anywhere near, for it seems to me of surpassing interest and charm, both for scenery and for human appeal. . . .

You may be tempted to say, "The struggle naught availeth; The effort and the wounds are varied."[9] But don't give up. There is much need for constructive thought and work and above all for human sympathy with which to weave "the garment of praise for the spirit of heaviness,"[10] which does at times afflict us all. So good cheer and all friendly hopes from the Hendersons.

CA. 1940

DEAR MR. JAFFE:

I was deeply touched by your letter and expressions of loyal friendship when I know your mind must regard us as hopeless "Kulaks" or worse. We have been plodding along through heavy going since the storm of Dec 23. Roads have been blocked and everything difficult. I've done my share of ploughing back and forth through the drifts to see what might be going on at the "maternity ward" as Mr. H. expresses it. We have nine very pretty little calves now and you would enjoy the "moving picture" when they get out and frolic in the snow!

I respect the constancy of your faith in Russia, even though I can no longer share it. You may think me a miserable opportunist or compromiser, but I can't see why a person might not be sincerely convinced of the merits of socialism as a method of distributing the wealth created by all working together and at the same time condemn utterly Russia's foreign policy in Poland, Finland, and the other Baltic states.

I realize that argument accomplishes little and I didn't mean that the "Guardian" should be interpreted that way, but I did want you to know that we are some what familiar with your own point of view and that of the pamphlet you sent. (I'll return it soon). In spite of all I have read and heard and thought, my own conclusions are substantially on p. 442 of the "Guardian." Lest you think this is merely another capitalistic paper, I must say that for years I have found it the most sincerely fair and impartial of anything we read: (they were as heartily disgusted with Chamberlain's deal with Hitler at Munich as they are with Stalin's). I think as Americans we should try to give more vigorous life to the basic principles of our own democracy. Let's go!

APRIL 25, 1941

DEAR FRIEND ELI [JAFFE]

For some obscure reason I am strangely moved this morning toward fulfilling my Christmas promise of "a letter soon." We were distressed by the uncomfortable tidings of your card at that time but grateful for the good wishes and glad for your hopeful spirit of better days to come.

It would be pleasant if I could give you good news of ourselves and our undertakings, but the winter has brought only increased anxiety and misfortune after a season of practically complete failure in farming—a combination of unfavorable weather, old worn-out machinery and some mistakes in judgment and planning on our own part. Naturally little could be expected in such circumstances. Still we might have pulled through had not illness intervened.

A relapse from a serious case of flu just at Christmas time for Mr. H. resulted in a general weakening and a condition of the heart arteries which Eleanor and the Elkhart doctor agreed was coronary occlusion—failure of the arteries to supply sufficient blood to the heart muscle itself. He has rallied more than at the time seemed possible to any of us, but still think you would notice a considerable difference in vigor and vitality. So far we have been unable to secure any permanent help and there seems no clear way to lighten the load. I do all I can but have been handicapped myself by a recurrence of the old asthma. Trouble which I thought I had out grown. It slipped up on me again with the outbreak of the spring dust storms, less violent and persistent than in previous years, but still distressing and ruinous to our crop hopes for the late sown wheat. And now our spring work is belated by various untoward circumstances and conditions.

During the winter and spring one by one we had to give up the three beloved horses that formed the last link with a happier day, when we were all together and had some hope of accomplishment and the building of a home, with something of grace and power to lift on the sad world's burden. Perhaps you would involuntarily reproach me for grieving about the horses but they were very precious to me and we owed to them the little means of comfort and continued activity that we still possess.

Eleanor and her husband are still in K.C. He goes on with his work in cereal chemistry for a bakers organization. Seems to be doing well in that line. Eleanor now has a responsible position as head of the anaesthetics work at the K.C. [Kansas] General Hospital. . . . The children are very considerate and generous to us, do much more than we wish them to do. Last September they took us for a most happy vacation out in the picturesque Red River Valley of northern New Mexico. . . . At Christmas time Eleanor surprised me with a fine power washing machine which is indeed a wonderful help. This year they plan, as much as any one can in these uncertain days, to take their vacation in the Yellowstone National Park and want us to go along, but the future looks quite dark and doubtful. More than at any-time in my life, I am living from day to day.

You did not need to think of our possibly having harsh feeling toward you. We respect the sincerity of your desire to improve the opportunities for the Joads[11] and others for a fuller, more satisfying life. I do not know your present convictions as to the international situation. From our point of view the forward march of the dictators can mean only contempt and oppression and destruction of liberty for the world's common people—those like ourselves who like Thomas Hardy's old peasant in his poem "In the time of the breaking of nations" keep plodding on, perhaps as in his picture, harrowing the clods of the unsown field with the patient labor of the old white horse.[12] But liberty—like life itself—is hard to crush completely. I do not despair even yet of "a new birth of freedom" and a more vital passionate translation into everyday life of the basic principles of our American democracy in the world around. . . .

⟵⟶

MAY 3, 1941

DEAR ELI:

You will easily believe that I am deeply distressed by the news of the trial which concerns you and your future career so importantly.[13] It is no wonder that I felt an urgency about my long delayed letter even though I had <u>no</u> hint of any such tragic threats to your peace of mind. You see, with the appearance of the little paper and your name as managing editor, I took it for granted that you were free to go on with your work for humanity in your own way.

I considered writing to the County Attorney, but we have been beleaguered now for several days by very heavy rains—a relief at least from dust. I am hoping Mr. H. can get out on the road tomorrow but am not sure. I realize that anything I might write in a general way of our interest in your literary endeavors and social ideals would be, as they say of our aid thus far to Britain, "too little and too late." I am handicapped moreover by lack of any definite knowledge of what a person would have to do to become a "criminal syndicalist."[14] I have tried to look it up in dictionary and encyclopedia but with very little satisfaction.

You might remember telling me that some of your friends called you "the bourgeois humanitarian." Certainly I am not able to imagine you in acts of violence against our government. You always assured me that your desires for better conditions, the more abundant life for the oft-mentioned "third of the nation"[15] were to be brought about by democratic procedures. And as you know, I am in sympathy with every such sincere attempt to "bind up the nation's wounds" as Lincoln expressed it. Unfortunately war is not the only source of wounds, physical, mental, spiritual; and I have hoped with an agonized longing that these days of trial might cause us all to reappraise the value of our American System, and dedicate ourselves anew to its continuance and a more perfect expression of its possibilities.

Undoubtedly the trial is over before this. I wish you would let me know the outcome. It is quite impossible for me to imagine a court depriving you of liberty and the pursuit of happiness just because of political opinions with which they might not agree. There are a good many of us who don't agree with Colonel Lindbergh, but we are letting him go on talking to do all the harm he can. That as I understand it is the American way, not German, Italian, Russian or Japanese. I thought of you when I read the paragraphs about Archibald McLeish. I remember your admiration for him. I'd like to know too about your brother and sister and how they do. With sincere hopes for some good news.

～⊜～

MAY 26, 1941

DEAR ELI:

This can not be an answer to your fine-spirited letter which awaited our return from K.C., where Mr. Henderson had a general checking over and among other things a tonsil operation from which he is recovering, though rather slowly.

I am much burdened but must not let you think I am indifferent to your personal difficulties or to what looks like a definite threat to fundamental American principles. I am trying to learn all I can of this incredible situation. Meantime if you like you may use the small "scrap of paper" toward the defense fund for appeal to the higher court.[16] I assume that you will have some way to collect it or endorse it and turn it over wherever it can do you the most service.

If I should collect my mind sufficiently to write to your defense attorney or to the Judge of the Court of Appeals, would you mind my quoting from a letter to us dated April 13, 1940 in which at the close you gave a sort of summing up of your basic and dynamic faith? I was much moved by it, however much we might disagree as to details of method by which to reach the goal. I am sure we both desire liberty, justice, the beckoning of opportunity for all our people. . . .

Yes, we should welcome you whenever you might visit this part of the U.S.A. again. Could find much to talk about.

You might be surprised to know that Eleanor said she had been thinking of you at the very time when I felt so urgently moved to write, knowing not of the immediate situation. She may have heard of Mr. Woods' disturbing experience in K.C. but did not mention it.[17] Glad to hear good news of your family. Try not to be downcast. I can still not accept the verdict of the jury as valid and feel that a higher court must correct the injustice.

CA. WINTER 1941–1942

Dear Eli:

This will be a sort of "night letter." I feel so uncertain whether this will find you that it seems not worth while to go into detail about all our endeavors and perplexities. We were sincerely glad for your last letter. When I heard, through clippings from Eleanor that your appeal was before the court, I wrote to Judge Barefoot, adding my own protest, enclosing your letter as witness of your own ideals, and also a stirring editorial from The Christian Leader of Boston, condemning the "Oklahoma Witch Hunt." I had no reply and have heard nothing of the outcome of the appeal.

We are, now more than ever secluded. Have had no help throughout the year and must make up for slower pace by longer hours. In late August, Mr. H. joined the children in a refreshing camping trip in the Rocky Mt. Natl Park near Denver. I took my turn at looking after the farm family. Robert has been working in Chicago since graduating from Manual Training H.S. in K.C. So possibly in the Naval Reserve by now unless this latest change has prevented enlistment. Won't you send your present address?

May I quote the most eloquent word I have heard today referring to December 7? It was from a Jewish Rabbi, "Deep in the heart of Texas." Here is his promise; "The lamplighters of democracy will dispel the darkness and rekindle the eternal light of freedom."[18] May we all do our part in hastening this time.

~⧾~

FEB. 6, 1944

DEAR ELI JAFFE:

First of all I must thank you heartily for letting us have an advance reading of your book.[19] We have both read it and been grateful for your sincere interest in farm life and difficulties. I hesitate to send my attempt at criticism, even now that I have spent so much time trying to note down my impressions. I feel as if pointing out possible defects in a young writer's first novel would be a good deal like finding fault with a new mother's baby.

In any case, please do not conclude that I thought the writing hopeless. In that case, I would have said so and spared you the more specific criticisms. There is so much that is wholesome and helpful that it should be possible to cure some of the blemishes. . . .

It would hurt me deeply if I thought my frank criticism would cause any break in the friendly feelings we have cherished since the spring of 1938. We shall be glad to learn more of your military training. I should think with your keen relish for humanity you might gather material that would be useful later on. . . .

We have had a most difficult winter ever since the big snow of Dec. 8. A later one just as that was beginning to clear up was followed by a still worse blizzard on Jan. 7, some said the worst storm in 50 years. The yards have been almost impassible ever since for mud and slop. This last snow was disappearing when a heavy rain fell and refilled all the pools and made the roads practically bottomless, as soon as we got away from the paving. Never have had a chance to finish up our fall maize threshing. Now we have to haul fodder for the cattle as our stacked feed is exhausted. This is all the [worse] because a hernia which Mr. H. has developed recently is growing more troublesome. We have tried vainly to get help, but so far there is no chance for him to get away for repairs. So the people in your book are not the only ones whose struggles overshadow everything. . . .

~⧾~

DEC. 13, 1944

DEAR ROSE:

Thanks so much for both of your 1944 letters and for the card to remind us that Peace on Earth has at least been proclaimed as an ideal to be striven for. I was indeed glad to have news of Mabel's family and of your own people, just now as widely separated. . . . Surely we hope it may not take too many more tragic years before the children may have a chance to get acquainted with their daddies, now so far away. But I am not a renowned <u>optimist</u> and have never been able to visualize any sudden end for this destructive conflict. I think it will have to be <u>fought</u> through to some bitter end.

It would be hard to find two people anywhere so little touched outwardly by the world's turmoil. Our nearest contact is with the young pilots of the Liberators or Flying Fortresses from the training field at Liberal, Kansas. We are hardly conceited enough to suppose that our little spot of earth and trees and buildings can give them any guidance. But so habitually they pass directly overhead that we think we must be, as they say, "on the [team]" between Liberal and probably Dalhart, Texas. I wave an apron or dish towel to them and the dogs bark but we get no response. Once in a while, mostly at night, there seems to be either a transfer or mass training for night flying, and the darkness is resonant with the distant murmur or the near-by roar of the motors. I have even seen three Lightnings (P. 38's) and at first could hardly believe my eyes, not then having heard of "any such animal." And we hear often from Robert but he tells very little of training or prospects. . . .

Our greatest privations are apples which we can't afford to buy, elastic for hose supporters, and gasoline, too limited to carry on even our most necessary travel with any convenience. One of the little country stores folded up; the other stopped buying eggs and it has been a problem to get them marketed 15 miles away with only an A card to roll around with.[20] Now that production is slowed down we can hardly afford the trip, though eggs at 31 cents per dozen are still a good price for here and have provided our living and quite a bit of the farm expense.

We had an all-too-short glimpse of the children on their return from a vacation in Arizona. They seemed to be fascinated with the strangeness of the desert scenery and may decide to locate there a little later if Eleanor cannot get relief from the asthma and nasal trouble which are so aggravated through the winters by the damp, smoke laden air of Kansas City. She seems successful professionally and financially, but works under a heavy day and night strain.

California could produce nothing more "unusual" in the way of climate than Oklahoma did in 1944. We had for once a super-abundance of rain and already three snows, one a heavy blizzard with violent winds and road-blocking drifts. Wheat was a fair crop. We saved most of it between rains. I worked on combine or tractor through both harvests. But much of the nice barley was lost by the overwhelming growth of sunflowers. . . .

For some obscure, subconscious reason I still retain title to the old [Iowa] farm home. After I am gone, Eleanor will receive a life interest in it. But unless there should be a child or children, which now seems quite improbable, it will later go to the University of Kansas Medical School, to support, so far as possible, a research fellowship in any line of work they might choose. I think this would suit my father whose boyhood ambition, never of course realized, was to be a skillful surgeon. . . .

It would hardly have seemed possible that I could miss Mabel so much as I do considering the very tenuous nature of our association for over forty years. I am sure I wish well to all her family, but, perhaps mistakenly, decided against a Christmas greeting, feeling their interests all to be so different from ours that an attempt on my part to continue the old custom might be burdensome to them. I liked your idea about the "thought waves." May Christmas bring you peace of mind, strength of heart.

⤝⤞

DEC. 17, 1944

DEAR ELI:

You can hardly know how pleased we were to receive your V. mail greeting card.[21] I hope this will find you somewhere. I had saved your last message and had been wondering rather despairingly whether it would be any use to mail a letter to the address. Thanks indeed for the clever card and for your remembrance of us. We should be happy to hear from you anytime and to know anything you are permitted to tell about the nature of your service and the strange surroundings, wherever you may be.

Under war time conditions we are more than ever solitary and I rarely leave the place at all. Even when Mr. H. goes to town for essential marketing or supplies, there always seems to be something I must watch or guard, and I feel as if I have suffered the penalty for "all work and no play."

We have had a most toilsome year all by ourselves with not a bit of help for anything. It seemed rather a surprising coincidence that after the late sowing and alternating hope and despair about the wheat, there should have been at last a fair harvest as in your story, and just as <u>wet</u> a harvest period as you portrayed. I worked on [either] combine or tractor all through both summer and fall harvests. By the utmost effort we saved eventually nearly all the wheat, but much of the good barley was sacrificed to the overwhelming growth of sunflowers while only some amphibious "critter" could have navigated the saturated fields. All alone we erected a partly fabricated CCC granary west of the barn and it is full of wheat for bread for the world, so far as it will go.

We had ample pasturage with the increased rainfall and cattle have done reasonably well. The Leghorns have paid house bills and a good part of the farm expenses, and we had a nice garden with most of our winter's living stored away in one form or another. So it might be worse but I am unable to carry out any of my plans for improvements about the home that might make our work lighter and living more comfortable.

Mr. H. is in poor condition. Has never found a chance to let go to have the hernia repaired and suffers a good deal from what is probably some type of arthritis. So he doesn't feel like undertaking anything extra and everything moves slowly. We were working hard to save the fall feed crop and had just combined the last of the maize when winter set in with a violent blizzard on Dec. 4 and since then we have been shut in by snow drifts or mud. . . .

I may have told you that Robert is in the signal division of the Army Air Force but so far not been sent over seas. We have not seen him for over three years, but in a recent photograph he looks very well and hearty and I think has benefitted in some ways from the rigorous training. I need hardly say that we are grateful to <u>all</u> regardless of race or rank or religion—or no—religion, who are defending our American principles.[22] Our earnest hope is that all this sorrow and sacrifice may not be in vain. But I think we might say of Peace as Edgar Lee Masters did of immortality: "Immortality is not a gift. Immortality is an achievement and only they who strive mightily shall possess it."[23] For that better world we all desire much depends on the leaders in every nation, but more, I think, upon the followers, great masses of humble people, and a determination on their part to establish justice and peace and brotherhood everywhere.

Mr. Henderson says to be a good soldier and that he wishes he could be there to help. With best wishes for yourself personally and for all who are dear to you.

～

May 1945

. . . As to the suggestion about the letters of years gone by, my first (and still enduring) conviction was that they could not have any possible value for any one that would justify their taking up space in a library. Two considerations serve to modify my attitude just a little. I had got for Eleanor's Western Collection Bernard De Voto's <u>Year of Decision</u>[24] (1846), and as I read the long detailed story, I realized how very much of it must have come from old letters, journals, and personal recollections. And while we were so bedeviled by the "dust bowl" situation Victor Murdock, a friend of my sister's and long editor of the <u>Wichita Eagle</u> was generous enough to say that my accounts of that distressing period might at some time serve as source material to social historians of this portion of our nation.

So I finally relented to the extent of suggesting "passing the buck" on to Miss Blakely and letting her decide.[25] As I see you have already consulted her, I'll just leave it to your judgment and hers. I think anything before 1907, when I ventured to start here on this homestead, should be destroyed. And as far as I am personally concerned, the material might as well be made available any time. But I'll leave that also to your decision, as there might be personal messages. . . .

So the world goes on, but I resent bitterly the waste of this war, which I shall always feel ought to have been avoided by keener intelligence and some capacity for international co-operation after 1918. The clipping from a Kansas City paper (sent by Eleanor) expresses our feeling about the loss of our Commander-in-Chief at this critical time.[26] It is hard for us to think that his work was done.

Spring here is cold and late. Recent rains have given a fresh start to the wheat held back by the drying winds of March and April. We have at last assembled most of the materials for piping water into the house with a [sink] in the kitchen and indoor toilet in the bathroom. But we need a Superman to do the work.

～

CA. Sept. 1945

Dear Eli Jaffe:

Our thanks for your kind words of encouragement. We have thought of you often, especially since Aug. 14. If you are already at home or on the way, that is all the better. Yes, do try to make a detour by Eva, if at all possible. You could tell much that would be of extreme interest to us. Robert was here for a furlough in Aug. but didn't have much to say. He and his bomber crew barely got into combat before the German surrender.

We are thankful for the end of the shooting but realize that <u>Peace</u> doesn't come automatically but must be striven for with intelligence and courage by all men of good will. We have had a rather wearing year and we both show the effects of "attrition." The wheat harvest crops were just about the 10 year average for us, though some had heavier yields. Have had favorable conditions for sowing this fall and once more the fields are green with promise for 1946. Have cut down considerably on cattle and chickens, though they continue to pay most of the running expenses. The garden has provided a great part of our living. Have put in considerable time and expense on the water and drainage system but it is still far from completion. If you could pick up any bits of foreign currency of small or no value, I know Mr. H. would appreciate them for his collection. Best wishes to you and yours,

DECEMBER 1946

DEAR ELEANOR:

Your tidings of great joy have really been a sort of bombshell in my mind, and I still feel rather dazed. Have tried earnestly to restrain both hope and anxiety until we hear from you again, as I realize you and the doctor <u>could</u> be mistaken. Usually I can find release of a sort from worry by some kind of activity, but in this situation, there seems nothing I can do. I haven't even unburdened the little walnut bed of its collection of junk! There will be time for that if you want it, as I hope and pray you may, in good time.

It is harder in some ways for men to readjust themselves to new conditions. For August's sake as well as for your own and all the rest of us, do take every possible care of yourself, to bring this bright promise to fruition. I wish some of you would tell Dad when you feel reasonably sure, for in a way it would mean even more to him than to me, and that is saying a lot. Mrs. D. and Elmer came late yesterday. I could do no less than ask them to stay for the night. They seemed anxious about us all and I appreciate their visit but see I can't now finish up the small package for Christmas Eve. When Dad comes send the curtain cloth with measurements and I'll do my best. Love every moment, every day,

⌒

CA. JAN. 1947

DEAR ELI:

Here, though belated are our sincere thanks for your generous for-bearance and the beautiful greeting card at Christmas time. If you have thought of us during these difficult days, you must have con-cluded that I wasn't glad to hear of your return to our own good land, or that perhaps I had left it permanently and gone on across Deep River. Either conclusion would be a mistake for we are still here, grop-ing along, and we surely hope that by this time the keen edge of unhappy memories begins to dull some what and that you are making a place for yourself in your chosen work. We should be so glad to hear all about it—good or bad—just anytime when the typewriter isn't too busy with other things.

For ourselves I can now do little more than list a partial "table of contents" for 1946, one of our most upsetting and disappointing years since the dust began to settle. In January Mr. H. [had his eyes checked because of] the advance of the cataracts, of which I may have written. Apparently the doctors' advice was OK and the eyes do not seem to have grown any worse during the year.

Late in February Robert got his discharge at Scott Field, Illinois. He had purchased a second-hand V8 and drove out here before enter-ing upon his work in Chicago. He went back to the same electrical company he had worked for before being drafted. . . .

Against all the rules I fell quite seriously ill later in May. Some type of flu which left me quite weak. Mr. H. had to sleep with the baby chicks for 12 nights! Our wheat was light because of the very dry winter and spring. Harvest delayed and [our problems] increased by a badly sprained wrist for Mr. H. while cranking the combine motor. After harvest our sweet Eleanor was stricken with the dreaded polio which was almost an epidemic in K.C. I was with her a short time and as it proved came home too soon, for she had a relapse later and was even more seriously affected. We hope in time she may make a complete recovery but it is slow. Late in Nov. Mr. H. went to K.C. for a too long delayed operation for a hernia. He came home New Years Eve and is gradually regaining strength. I was alone for the month with much responsibility and heavy work. So nothing was done about Christmas. And now—after 11 years—it seems that at this most inopportune time, with Eleanor's vitality so greatly diminished there is just a chance that we may be grandpa and grandma about mid summer! . . .

We do not want to lose track of you, so do write when you can.

DEAR [JAFFES]:

This is a stingy return for your forbearance and several notes clippings etc., during the year, all of which have been of much interest. I feel honored to have been shown samples of your writing and feel that you are gaining a surer command in your handling of material. I do hope you can derive tangible benefit as well as experience from your persistent efforts. It might not impress you but years ago I read a small book, Beyond Life, an extended essay by James Cabell.[27] I often think of the conclusions of the two friends who talked the night through on literary subjects. They decided that we desire in literature the same qualities we desire for our individual lives. So here they are, perhaps not in the logical order: distinction and clarity; beauty and symmetry; tenderness, truth, and urbanity. At least an ideal to strive for!

I was especially interested in the article from the N.Y. <u>Times</u> about weather wind, and dust conditions here on the great plains. I think not at all exaggerated, taking into consideration the entire area[,] though right here, while serious enough, [is] not quite so bad as in part of Texas and Missouri. I sent the article to friends in Kansas and they were acquainted with some of the papers mentioned. So you will not be surprised to know that this had been an all tough year for the Hendersons. No wheat; only a scattering of maize; and a scanty forage crop for the small bunch of cattle we can hardly afford to sell at the prevailing low prices.

We have encountered not only the crop failure but a series of over lapping disasters, most of which seemed as unavoidable as the small tornado which leveled the hen house, causing a lot of extra work and expense. Mr. H. still has a weak right shoulder as the result of a fall while loading some of the emergency hay in G[uymon] last February. I was laid low—very low—by a cow and the results threatened to be serious, apparently a slight brain hemorrhage or "cerebral spasm" as one doctor called it. But gradually the hard painful lump on my neck, apparently caused by drainage from some injury to the tissues, was absorbed and I have fortunately been able to keep going and do my part; even drove the tractor again for our small harvest of feed crops. . . .

I suffer tortures from the state of this troubled world, unable or unwilling to follow what light we have. I could face the dark valley for myself with greater courage if I could see any hope of abiding peace to men of good will. We don't deserve it but should welcome a word to let us know how you all do at the close of another year. Best wishes always,

[P.S.] In my haste and extreme weariness last night I omitted to mention that the wheat prospect for 1947 is now just about average, I would say. We need it to do well, for much against my own judgement we have sold off nearly all the shorthorns that have been our main stay for so long.

The meadow lark [on the stationery] is to remind you and Wilma that Oklahoma has some good qualities in spite of all her faults. I surely meant to tell you that if either or both of you return to Okla either temporarily or permanently we should be most happy to welcome you here. We could make you more comfortable now, as we did manage in 1946 to get water piped into the house a small kitchen sink and bathroom filled up with all necessities even a heater for hot water!

~

DEC. 31, 1947

DEAR FRIENDS: [THE JAFFES]

Health and hope and achievement for 1948! Our thanks for the remembrance and the unusual card. All our own plans were set aside to take care of our grandbaby—David Eugene—Dec. 16–24, while his parents took a brief vacation in Arizona. I'm sure you would think he is a nice baby, strong and active, with a friendly smile for every one. Mr. H. is very busy with [ploughing?] postponed because of the extremely dry weather and soil of the usual seeding time. We had fair wheat this year, some forage, but no maize. I made two trips to K.C. on account of the baby so altogether a rather broken year. I wish we might have seen you as you took the long flight eastward. I feel that by now you are as discouraged as we are by Russia's foreign policy. . . .

~

OCTOBER 3, 1949

DEAR ELEANOR

Dad is ready to go to Eva for lumber to finish the windmill tower on the south place (I feel it is all a waste for I learned recently that in all these years of idleness he never even covered the pipe so I suppose it is blown full of surface soil and the good well lost!) But anyway it is a way to get rid of our last small reserves.

I shouldn't write this cry of distress but am not very well and fear giving way before I can get anything settled up. There seems to be a partial recurrence of the stiffening or tightening of muscles in the same shoulder and knee and an irritating (not so bad as in 1948) quivering of eyelids beyond my conscious control. But the worst is that I'm so very anxious about all of Dad's infirmities, the early coughing setting in so soon for the winter, that muscle-bound condition in right shoulder and all the groaning and of course the ever-present deafness much worse. . . . I have worked beyond all reason to try to give him free time. Even wrote to Robert about some time here this winter as I thought I could manage with him better than with high priced strangers. He replied favorably at first as he seemed bent on leaving Chicago anyway but hasn't answered yet a more definite proposition.

I thought I was getting things headed at least in the right direction. Then yesterday Dad kicked the whole thing over (though he had agreed previously). Said he wasn't going anywhere this winter. Said he had told me plainly that he would not change eye doctors (which he absolutely never hinted at before). When I said OK, if he would really rather go back to Dr. L[emoine] we would plan for the K.C. trip, he said wherever he went he would <u>drive through</u>. Well, I simply collapsed with all this load of anxiety. He had an accident on one of his recent trips to Eva. . . . I don't know yet what it will cost. . . . But day or night even if he thinks he is being careful, the wrong side of the road attracts him like a powerful magnet and all these expensive trimmings won't do a bit of good. So you can imagine how I would feel about his starting out alone either east or west. . . .

I don't know whether you can think up anything that would help. I've always known that sooner or later he would drive me over the edge of sanity and maybe this is it. Just about a year ago he saw Dr. LeMoine. Perhaps you could talk with the eye doctor there; find out whether he would make use of any data Dr. L. could supply to judge changes in condition. . . . Just anything you might think of to suggest we will consider, but the more wrong he is, the more set in his opinion it now seems. He is ready so must let him go. No eggs to send this time which seems more dreary. Love always,—Don't write to Dad as if I had appealed for help.

⊰⊱

CA. DEC. 1949

DEAR CHILDREN [ELEANOR AND FAMILY]:

May this find you both well and able to enjoy whatever of Christmas cheer this sad world can provide at this fateful time. May you find in your hearts and in your home a refuge for the inner peace essential to useful, triumphant living.

We have not had yesterday's or today's mail so this can not be an answer to whatever might have come. Dad will be going on to Elkhart as soon as he gets back with another load of maize fodder. We hope that Robert got my letter in time to climb aboard last night so that we shall not have to make the trip again tomorrow. If the present bright weather could only last a few days, he could give quite definite help by taking the cattle to water, etc., leaving Father more free to go ahead with other things. He thinks he could go on with the drilling by Monday unless it storms again. So many are anxious now to sow their wheat that no one is voting for snow just now, but we shall have to take what comes, as always.

You won't need to hurry about reading the notes on our happy vacation. Some of it I wrote on the spot; the penciled part, while I was herding the cattle. It is very incomplete, but perhaps sometime may serve as a framework on which to hang your own perhaps more vivid memories.

I thought the card showing the winter trees—parable of life—so very lovely that you ought to have it back. Of course if you wish to pass it on to someone else, that is all right, so I haven't marked on it in any way. I used to enjoy so much the . . . elms in New England and also the variety of form in the trees at Lawrence. We often wonder how Red River Valley looks now. Earlier we heard of a good deal of snow in that region.

I'm using the <u>last</u> of our Christmas seals to enclose a stamp for Eleanor's collection. The man at Guymon said the 1¢ education stamp has a picture of Horace Mann, but unfortunately they did not have one, either there or at Elkhart. I wonder if you ever listen to the stamp collector's program on Saturday at 12:15 from WDAF.

We have had many cheering messages from friends near and far and perhaps later I shall share them with you. We think of you <u>all the time</u>

⟜⟜

JANUARY 5, 1950

DEAR GIRLIE [ELEANOR]:

. . . We are worrying through the storm period as well as possible. A little better today. It was +7° this morning at sunrise instead of that -8° of Wed. a.m., almost as low as we have ever seen it here. It must have been about correct for Guymon had reported -7° a short time before. It makes lots of extra work for stock, etc. It is doubtful whether I could have pulled through by myself with only part-time or indifferent help. Naturally the gas bottle for [?] heater burned out yesterday but we fortunately had a second one to turn unto. For the first time too, the Kohler motor [for the family electrical system] refused absolutely to start Tues. eve. That reprobate Henry has never turned up though Mr. C. was profuse in apologies and assured us he would get him out here before New Years. . . .

In regard to the stranger pig, honesty proved the worst of all possible policies. If we had hauled him off to market instead of penning him up when dragging him away (as far as 1–½ miles) proved utterly useless, we should have done OK for ourselves and everybody. But supposed one must advertise and did so at considerable expense. Now if the wretch brought 2 bits over actual expense, the 25¢ would have to go into the county road fund. We have not yet received the books you spoke of sending. May come today. I have a very favorable impression of <u>The Way West</u>[28] from various reviews I have read.

⟜⟜

JANUARY 28, 1950

DEAR ELEANOR:

Your good letter (with enclosures) came on Thurs. Also the envelope of magazines etc. Our thanks for all. Glad to hear of Mrs. Backus again; also from Christine. I wish you might see them again. A distance of 100 miles ought not to be prohibitive in these days of lavish spending.

. . . The bond issue for the new school house etc. carried: 140 to 71. More opposition than we had anticipated. A switch of 14 votes, about 7%, would have given the necessary 41% to block the levy. There were too many renters (with their "soak the landlord" policy), too many hired men (with nothing) and probably quite a few land owners (with just one ¼ of a homestead exemption and a free ride at other people's expense).

We think you should be congratulated upon the successful year. You have done better than would have seemed possible with the complete change and readjustment.[29] Congratulations. I know our own report would seem discouraging to you and I agree that it is nothing to boast of. Still we could have sold around $3,000 worth more in wheat if it had seemed advisable. That could have been done with only a small increase in expense, that is the cost of marketing and would have shown a lower proportional expense. However you are perhaps influenced in your opinions by what you remember of the pre-gasoline or "<u>Ann</u>-diluvian" age, when it didn't cost so much to turn around. Not very long ago I read in some of the farm papers or bulletins that on the average, one year with another, one can count that his farming expense will take about ½ his farm income. The aim is to beat that ratio if possible. A young energetic farmer with good buildings and new equipment in a favorable year can do better. (We did ourselves in 1948 with <u>gross</u> farm profits of $9,430.13 and expenses 2,301.87 with calculated depreciation of 621.93). This left Net Farm Profit at $6,506.33. Not too good but better than many of our age are doing. Actual <u>operating</u> expense only about ¼ of the gross return. Am making no forecast for 1950 but will do the best we can. . . .

<hr/>

APRIL 28, 1950

DEAR ELEANOR:

. . . Father is itching to get at the usual spring time task of ploughing out wheat. Some are already at it. He got the plough reassembled (<u>without</u> the hoped-for repairs) and ploughed the garden yesterday. I can't do a lot but will try a little. He is going to Guymon today to try to straighten out a mix-up . . . apparently the result of leaving one piece of volunteer [wheat?] to fill out our allotted 303 Acres. It seemed to be understood at the time by the young man who did the measuring but now they charge us with replanting and consequent penalties. He will also try to see Henry L. about the Kohler. I finally got out the book and found a point we had not known—that by disconnecting the magnet's ground wire from its terminal one can start the motor with the hand crank, regardless of batteries. (There seems some obstruction to prevent the charge coming through for the automatic starting, but have been able to use the lights in this make shift way and to do a big ironing yesterday.) Of course it isn't satisfactory to have to go out to the wash house each time for starting. . . . We would like to go on without much more expense if we can for they set stakes for the R[ural] E[lectrification] A[uthority] installation. . . . That is another of around 2 more things we should have backed out of while it was allowable. . . . Too late now. We shall have to spend several hundred dollars for installation, rewiring according to REA specifications and $5.00 a month minimum charges for one year at least, whether anyone ever turned on a light from it or not. They have agreed to get service to Eva elevators etc. by harvest time. (There will probably be <u>some</u> poor to fair crops here and there.) Our wheat on summer fallow on south place looks fair (better than Ramsey's east or Forrest's north) but will need more rain of course for any crop. Will try to get Dad to leave it for a while. He is ready so will let him go. . . .

Father is charmed, as I am myself, with the marvelous shells of such a variety of form and coloring. Incredible the multitude and beauty of the forms in which the <u>elan vitale</u> becomes manifest.

. . . The check is for the telegrams and thanks besides. If any left get some fast-growing shrubs or vines or whatever you most want to begin on the beautification program. I fear it is now too late about the roses and trumpet vines unless I got a break immediately and pulled out regardless. Of course if Gabriel gave an extra loud call I suppose I'd have to try to answer "Ad Sum" like the old man in one of Thackeray's novels whose mind drifts back to his school boy days where they answered the roll call with the Latin expression. Wish I could do better to help you understand the situation here. You have been too long away. Much love, . . .

━━━

(Nov. 27) ca. 1950

Dear Eleanor:

. . . The vacation still up in the sky over Dreamland. However I have decided we <u>must</u> call it all off unless we can get someone to live here while Dad would be gone—approximately Dec. 21–29. There are just too many things to be done or watched to depend on the hit-or-miss care. We have thought of Cecil and Ann but they are going—or have already gone—to Texas for a visit with her folks.[30] . . . So I'm really quite helpless and unable to suggest any other possibilities. Harvest is over. The country [is] pretty well cleared of drifters and they couldn't be trusted anyway. The permanent residents all have their own homes and family gatherings and responsibility of their own work. As the main objective was to be one more Christmas for us all together, it would be quite futile for me to come alone and leave Dad here alone. . . . But will keep watching for any possible chance.

. . . Dad is almost ready so must stop here.

⸻

JAN. 13, 1951(?)

DEAR ELEANOR:

We have plenty of writing paper but this is nice and smooth and I thought I might manage it better than typing paper if I had to take to writing in bed, as might be possible.[31]

This may seem rather "cut and dried." There was so much in your long letter that required answer or comment. I was afraid I would forget, so went back and noted especial points I should mention. We thought your upholstering material very well suited to the purpose. I hope it will wear well to pay for all the careful work. If you really have no use for the 2' X 6' strip, I could probably make a tie-on or tack-on flat upholstering for the very old rocking chair (born in 1908) which would improve its appearance and comfort. But don't send it if you could use it in any way. . . .

The <u>washing</u> has become a critical problem here as well as there. . . . I spent most of this evening cobbling up one more set of underwear for Dad and we do hope to tackle the awful mess tomorrow if the weather is favorable and nobody any worse. I couldn't find anything useful for myself!

. . . I have worked most of today on our accounting again having finally finished the polka dot dress late yesterday. Our report is very disheartening though it could "of" been worse. Really I rather expected a definite loss on farm operations considering the absence of a wheat crop and the greatly increased expenses for the combining ($660), seed ($107) and ground maize ($672) because of the combined failure of the 1950 maize and of our faithful little grinder. REA costs a little more too and apparently we spent something over $100 for car and truck tires. As it figured out there was about $500 margin between farm income and actual cash outlay but the allowable depreciation took up more of this. They seem still to grant the double exemption to the old has beens, so outside income of something over 1,600 won't be enough to put us into the tax-paying group this time. (Should have to have a clear margin of $2,675 to be eligible.)

Actually the situation is not as hopeless as it would appear from the figures. We must have on hand, untouched, in the form of "advanced buying" which is legitimate and advocated by farm advisors, from $100–$150 worth of essential farm supplies—paint, oil, hardware, time, mill feeds, oyster shell, bind weed dope, etc.[32] Moreover, we have on hand in the two granaries around 500 bu. of 1950 wheat, about 1,200 of maize (threshed) and [surely] 100 in two large stacks. This in addition to four steers that could go any time and a nice heifer I suppose I'll have to let go, as she was ruined (by the bull) while still a calf, on one of the very rare days when I ever leave the place and relax my watchfulness. . . . They could have been sold late last year for around $600 but I thought it better to hold down the income which we could possibly scrape along without.

Eggs came to $466+. I figure (like all these other things very conservatively) that <u>if</u> ½ of that was return on my work, I did earn our grocery bills and that is something in these dark days.

Monday noon—We have just finished up the outrageous washing. Bright but windy and at first thought too unpropitious. But decided we might do worse by waiting so pitched in and washed steady almost 2 hrs. which is unusual, and am so glad to get all the rags and tags pinned up on the line. Dad will go for the mail. We may get the package. I will send this—incomplete as it is for fear we are in some way prevented from going to Guymon tomorrow to wind up the Income Tax report. It would mean a great release to me to get it off my mind.

. . . As to the poem, I shouldn't know any place to look for it. I have one "little girl" poem about snowflakes in my scrapbook.[33] I suppose it must have been as Walt Whitman said about the letters from God along his path. He didn't always pick them up for he felt sure they would keep coming![34] . . .

FEB. 5, 1951

DEAR ELEANOR:

A pleasant day with the meadow-larks singing, so glad that the storm is past, though they may not know that another cold spell is supposed to set in tomorrow. We hope the rain in Arizona will make at least a start toward replenishing the springs and streams and perhaps a little mud behind the great Coolidge Dam. Hard for greenhorns like ourselves to see why the disheartening process should be repeated . . . and that many more false hopes raised and that many more millions thrown away. What happens to these supposedly "self-liquidating" projects when everybody is left high and dry? I feel as if our new Senator Monroney is to be commended for courage at least in daring to set forth his plans in Guymon and telling them to forget about their long cherished Optima Dam. He told them if ever advisable, the time is not now. It hardly looks as if anyone should need to be told that, but a small group has been working over time to try to keep the idea alive.[35] We are always grateful to get a letter or even cards on Sat. as Sunday is always a bad day to drag through and it is pleasant to hear of your more varied experiences.

As my sadly depleted judgment had foreseen, it proved impossible to get the radiator [for the Kohler electric system] mended, so we are in the dark again indefinitely and right back, as I said before, where we started in 42 years ago. I've taken it pretty hard, for the little period of reading at bed-time and the light to get around by had been of the greatest help to me. But Dad never wanted it at all. I shouldn't have put it over. He can go back now to the old smoky lamps and be better satisfied. But it was a terribly expensive lesson.

He got back in fair time on Sat. with 2,680 [pounds] of coal and has been reveling in the heat. He had it up to 106° here yesterday p.m. and said it was just about right and sat with his feet up on the stove at that! He is working on the east bin in the granary, trying to seal up the cracks around the edge of the floor with metal stripping. May go for the mail presently. . . .

FEB. 6, CA. 1951

DEAR ELI:

In these hurrying days I always feel honored if anyone takes the time and makes the effort to write us a real letter. So sincere thanks for yours recently received. Looking it over again I feel pretty sure that you intended to give us further information about the new American citizen in your home. You spoke of an enclosure, but I think you must have forgotten it after all. So, we don't know Baby's name or birthday but are happy to know that all is well with "you all." We thought, in spite of desperately hard conditions, that we were rich with one little daughter. You are doubly rich with two. I could not wish anything better for you and Wilma than that they should always be the stimulus and comfort to you that our Eleanor has been to us.

I'm afraid my suggestions about possible literary openings or opportunities would be of little value. . . . You might try the <u>Atlantic's Accent on Living</u>—perhaps a sketch of aged Kulaks like ourselves (when we have been "liberated") and we see the ancestral lilac bush being bulldozed away, the home built with loving care being remodeled for a collective pig pen or cow shed, etc. I have no ability in creating characters or situations but think such a tragedy, in your hands, might make a vivid impression. . . .

The things you spoke of desiring in your letter are the same things we and our widely scattered friends desire. Your paragraph reminded me of the enclosed sermon summary on Human Rights. I <u>can't</u> see why the Russians and their servants should be hostile or indifferent or why they should make it so hard for their friends to apologize for them. In fact I don't attempt that anymore, though I still long for freedom for the great masses of those long suffering people.

I am reading a rather terrifying book received from Eleanor, <u>Behind Closed Doors</u>.[36] I know of course from my memory of Niagara Falls that if you have carelessly let your little boat drift to the brink, there is no point then in starting a frantic paddling. We easy going Americans may be now too late to save our heritage of liberty. If so, I still have faith that somewhere, sometime that sturdy plant will spring up to new life. . . .

I hope you have heard that at the U. of Okla. they have taken down the silly little fences that separate the one or two Negroes from the other students![37] For ourselves we are having a tough winter. Four spells of zero weather, almost unknown here. The last cold wave pushed the thermometer down to -14 degrees and knocked out our Kohler electric system which had been such a help and comfort. So we are back in the dark again and so far no prospect of repairs, even after two trips to Guymon and all the floundering around that we can manage. I have never been able to throw off entirely the effects of my "Arizona cold" and dread the long dark nights of difficult breathing. The wheat prospects are very poor after the dry fall and winter so, with Mr. H's deafness and other infirmities, we are a pretty silent gloomy house hold, but thankful for the younger people and hope that some how <u>they</u> may have the peaceful world we now see is denied to ourselves. . . .

⌒

MARCH 5, 1951

DEAR ELEANOR:

It has been a wearing broken day so I'll have to postpone a little my usual "early to bed" so as to have a letter ready, though not much to tell.

I hardly finished my financial discussion on Sat. but simply meant that we wouldn't have <u>income</u> enough to live on [if we retired]. . . . It is all very baffling and tormenting, but the one clear thing is that some way we ought to earn our way as long as we possibly can.

The last few days, including today, of wind and dust have finished any lingering hope of wheat for us and I feel myself that we simply threw away the carefully hoarded barley seed. Hardly any hope that it had time to sprout or could survive if it had under present "dust bowl" conditions. I always said I was the only one who could remember those dreadful days—for any practical purpose. People have simply assumed it couldn't happen again. . . .

Ever since a girl in Professor Hopkins class mentioned . . . <u>Of Human Bondage</u>,[38] I have hoped to read it. I think the title rather fascinated me, and I had no slightest hint of the story. I must confess that while I found it absorbing and spent more than I should of sleep time in reading it, I also found it terribly depressing. I believe it was partly because I kept comparing this worthless Philip to Robert and wondered whether he would <u>ever</u> amount to anything. Of course the end of the book still left the question unanswered. . . . The one point of relief was the belated declaration that the unspeakable Mildred would appear no more. I had assumed she would hang like a millstone around his neck to the bitter end. . . .

Father has read <u>American Guerilla</u> and is now reading <u>She</u>, which came out first when I was just a young girl and made a considerable sensation.[39] I have never read it. Mr. Farnsworth noticed it and said it appeared as a serial in some paper his father took when he himself was just a youngster. . . .

I'll leave a space for another word before this goes. —I almost forgot to mention the beautiful catalog of roses etc. We can enjoy the pictures but could have no hope of anything of the sort surviving here. So good night. . . .

～

DEAR ELEANOR:

It is planned for Father to go to Eva in the morning for marketing 48 dozen eggs etc., and to take in the annual school meeting at the far-famed Yarbrough school on the way home.[40] . . .

Not much going on here. Another day of high wind and cloudy damp air but I fear the hoped-for showers will not arrive. With our everlasting longing for rain, it seems ironical that the heaviest rain fall we ever had in one year should be followed by a complete failure. Lillian[41] . . . says the destruction is more nearly complete than I—here at home always—had realized. Some fields show spots or streaks of green yet here and there, but—hardly enough to be worth harvesting. The worms devoured their oats before they ever got out of the ground and no doubt the same is true of our barley. . . .

. . . I planted several of the myrtle berries after Christmas and just now the living plants are punching up. I thought they were smart to find their way out of the fruit and up toward the light. . . .

Phoebe has three lovely long-haired kittens today and is so very happy with them. They are black, blue and dark tiger striped. Today I was astonished to find one belated bloom but, fairly well started—on the Christmas cactus!

I had a large quantity of hollyhock seed here, descending from seed I brought from Canada some 50 years ago. But it has simply disappeared. . . . I'll have to make a new start if I ever have any again and am so sad about it. It couldn't have done any harm to let me keep a few of the flowers and plants that have been such a comfort to me.

I'll have to sleep for tonight and read up a little on that absurd book, Ruggles of Red Gap, before I try to go to sleep.[42] So good-night.

Tues. a.m.—Father is preparing for his trip to Eva. Since Sunday when he did an unnecessary amount of spade work, he has complained more of his rupture and I suppose that situation must be faced, sooner or later.

The air was fresh and pleasant with a touch of dampness before sunrise, but nothing of the desired moisture. People hardly know what to do to substitute for the lost wheat crop. When I returned from Arizona an old railway engineer sat in front of me as we crossed the Texas Panhandle. He was so exhilarated by the beautiful fields of new spring wheat everywhere, just making the ground green but still showing the drill-furrows. He said that in 29 years of going back and forth over that run he had never seen anything like it. I wonder how it looks now and of course hope it doesn't share our own complete desolation. . . . Our love and thoughts will be going with you.

~

APRIL 4, 1951

DEAR ELEANOR:

Father got back from Eva quite early. He brought your last three cards and a big envelope of interesting clippings. If you don't mind I think I'll paste a few more pictures in the darling <u>cat</u>-a-log and send it on to Eli's little girl. The Robert Wood, recently kicked out of the Communist party (picture and paragraph in the last <u>Time</u>) was a one time friend and associate of Eli's at Oklahoma City.

. . . By the way, I have finished that horrifying book <u>1984</u>.[43] I think the author must have been glad to get it out of his system before his recent death. One might think he was diseased in mind as well as body, if one didn't know that just such horrors as it relates had been, and perhaps are still, common practice in Germany and Russia. I'll have to remark, however, that I still can't conceive of the bulldog <u>English</u> being reduced to such depths of ignominy—even in another generation, say 30 years from now. It would have seemed more real to me if it had not been localized but established in some never-never land of the imagination. Anyway I'm glad to have had the chance to read it and think there are points in it worthy of our careful consideration.

. . . Certain circumstances throw doubt upon our dating for our nice Jersey milk cow and we were not sure just when to look for the calf, though appearances seemed in favor of the earlier date. So I've been patrolling the barn from three to four times a night for quite a while. . . . Mon. night I felt would be a crisis; went out at 8:00 (Dad about 10:00, then I again at 1:00). Nothing definite but still uneasy. So finished <u>1984</u> and went back at 3:00. Was sure then the time had come. To my surprise Father did reluctantly drag himself out but so slow that by the time we got back to the barn the baby was already there and trying to get on her feet. A lovely little heifer, the picture of her dad, even to the markings and Dad said this morning she was the nicest <u>Shorthorn</u> we had had. Such a playful little scamp. Could hardly suck for wanting to jump and frolic. The cow has a terrible bag, pretty badly caked so that will give me more work and anxiety. . . . We have 4 more marked down for the next four weeks. . . . So I'll have to begin my night prowling again in a few days. . . .

⤙⤚

MAY 18, 1951

DEAR ELEANOR:

It is good to have sunshine today in this area, especially Texas. They reported from there this morning rainfall at various points from 4+" up to 11.93" at Panhandle! Many places around 7–9." For a time late on Wednesday practically this entire farm was submerged; all the south side still, and lake is brim full. The flood backed in from the east and into the yard and garden. For a time it looked as if the basement would be full again but began to recede as the crest was about 1" below the basement window on the west. . . .

⤙⤚

JUNE 16, 1951

DEAR ELEANOR:

. . . Thurs. in late p.m. we worked over the little boy pigs and yesterday one of the purchased calves so there's no lack of variety. I judge the cattlemen haven't got anywhere with all their fuss. Really I believe it comes the hardest on small folks like ourselves who had hoped to make a little on home raised or purchased calves by utilizing weeds and grass through the summer. . . . The price reduction just about balances any possible gain in that way but wouldn't make a fuss if they would only hold other things to some proportional level. I resent it when the greedy farmers are represented as trying to deprive the poor and needy of <u>beef</u> which all at once seems to have become an essential of life—though I don't remember when we ever had any!

Dad looks very thin but weighed 147 in Eva Thurs. which is actually a gain of 9# since the last time.

I guess I didn't tell you that Governor Murray[44] vetoed the cooperative telephone measure on the ground that it would be unfair to private companies not being subject to the rules of the state corporation commission. So our $5.00 membership proved a total loss. . . .

. . . We have set out . . . 76 tomato plants of four varieties and most look fairly well.

Father has just returned from looking over the north place. Sudan grass showing up better now; millet only in streaks here and there which is a great loss and disappointment; maize about 40–50% of a stand but too little for replanting; truck crops, melons, citrons, pumpkins; corn a good start but late. . . .

Chapter 6

When Hope Has Gone, 1952–1966

A tragic element dominated Caroline Henderson's last years on her farm. She was unable to resolve either her sense of failure or her fears about the future. She had not attained the goals she sought and seemed to be searching for a graceful exit that was ultimately denied her. If Caroline had any hope of regaining her sense of accomplishment, it was destroyed by the resumption of near dust bowl conditions in 1952. Most of her letters from that time seem to have been lost in one of Eleanor's moves, but enough remain to give a picture of her deepening despair. Severe drought and blowing dust ended in 1956, but the great blizzard of 1957 and another drought in 1963 were only the most notable of the environmental challenges the Hendersons would face in their sixth decade in the Oklahoma Panhandle.

As seen primarily in her letters to Eleanor, Caroline still found moments of respite and enjoyment despite frequent threats to her sense of well-being. Though most of her letters reflect her fears and frustrations, they also reveal her continuing search for the pleasures afforded by her books, flowers, and pets. Similarly, she regularly returned to her hopes for Eleanor and David to balance her own sense of failure. Her daily letters and cards to Eleanor were the vehicle she used to vent her frustrations and to remind herself of her pleasures and commitments. Together, these assured that she would not quit what she saw as her appointed task. Will persisted in his work as well, plowing his fields for the last time shortly before he and Caroline left Oklahoma to join Eleanor in Arizona in December 1965.

Caroline was now 88 years old. Her fading eyesight had caused her to lose the ability to read extensively, her handwriting had deteriorated, and she showed increasing inability to focus long on a subject. Yet she remained in charge of her own life as long as her mind permitted. Her last letter shows all of the signs of her deterioration, but the final paragraph is much bolder and more assertive than the rest. After facing the bitter fact that an abdominal tumor assured that she might never see her "beloved home" again, she took a firmer grasp on her faculties and pen, asserting that there would be "*no operating*" or any nitrogen treatments.

The final letter in this chapter contains Eleanor's account of her parents' final months. Eleanor was still drawing inspiration from Caroline long after her death, completing a Master's degree in literature at the age of seventy-eight, in part because she thought of it as honoring her mother.[1] Interestingly, Eleanor wrote her Master's thesis on Willa Cather, the writer that Eli Jaffe equated with Caroline because of her "fusion of farm and literature, as well as her innate belief in American democracy."[2] That comparison points to Caroline Henderson's enduring contributions to plains literature. It also reminds us of the courage she embodied throughout her life, persisting until the very end against adversity and loving nature, the world of ideas, her family, and the land.

꒰꒱

FEB. 3, 1952

DEAR ELEANOR:

So many "enclosures" won't leave me much space, but there really isn't much to tell. Your Tombstone card with its striking confession came yesterday. It makes me think of the "Ox-bow Incident."[3]. . . . Today has been very bad, after a raging hurricane all night. We got off on the wrong foot and the whole day has been a headache of one sort or another. . . . I did manage this morning to apply a fresh layer of outside patching (including one of August's canvas sampler flour bags from K.C.!) to Dad's old chore coat in the rather desperate hope of holding the lower layers of patches together till spring. It is a truly fantastic sight! He really intended to grind maize today but the weather was just too violent. We did winnow and hand-pick and wash and set to drying another mess of wheat to grind for cereal but it doesn't go down very well without milk. . . .

꒰꒱

FEB. 6, 1952

DEAR ELEANOR:

Yesterday proved to be one of our worst days so far. A cold north wind lowered temperatures and raised dust till we were shut in as by a circling red-brown wall. They said visibility at a.m. was reduced to ¾ mile, but for part of the time in the p.m. we could not see half way across the place. I was so glad Father had done his grinding on Mon. and I had sorted laundry and prepared for the washing early in the a.m. No chance yet to see what it has done to our fields but Dad will try to look tomorrow. They are urging people to take any measures they can to hold the ground. Fortunate for the country as a whole that the emergency maize crop has left an increased amount of stubble and better protection over considerable areas.[4] . . .

꒰꒱

MARCH 9, 1952

DEAR ELEANOR:

. . . Dad put in quite a bit of time yesterday on the combine. I tended to the usual outdoor tasks, rearranged pictures etc. in the north room to display Dad's shadow box to better advantage, cleaned up the house and the wash house which was in bad shape and potted some various slips I have been rooting in water.

Today has been a dreary lonesome day. . . . It has been rather a lost day so far as progress is concerned. I seemed to feel unusually tired and have tried to rest a little for the week to come and have gone on with the Dobie books—now almost done.[5] Dad is reading one of the other books and seems quite absorbed in it. . . .

We had quite a scare here last night about little Wagtail. We had some of the back bone waste for supper and I gave him a nice section to take out on the porch as often before. . . . Later when Dad went to the door he came in and I saw at once something was wrong. . . . He wouldn't let us look into his mouth and threatened to bite, but I got the screwdriver and pliers and finally we forced his jaws open and fortunately Dad discovered the trouble. A flat piece of bone about 1" x 2" was wedged across the top of his mouth, firmly set between his teeth. We managed to get it loose and I put the Terramycin ointment on his lips. He seems all right except that he is quite delicate about eating. . . .

Monday, 10:00 a.m.—The evening drizzle changed to heavy mist by bed-time and to snow during the night. David would be wild with excitement if he could see the heavily-laden trees and shrubs. Still snowing when I got up at 6:30 but checked about 8:00. Apparently about 2" and some must have melted into the soil on the wet ground. So we still wonder whether these light snows and showers may not yet prove "too little and too late." We can't get enough at one time to give any real encouragement. . . .

I will try to do the ironing today, though cautious about the electricity. The blanket takes about ½ point a night and an ironing around 2 points. Lights around 1—1-½ a day. So we have enough with the 65 kilowatt hours to get in at the minimum rate, unless there should be some emergency calling for extra use.

The recent stamps have reminded me of how many changes I have seen. I didn't exactly see the <u>first</u> railroads but can well remember how I used to watch from our upstairs windows in Clinton, Iowa, and see the trains passing far down on the river bank, their funny old cone-shaped smoke stacks puffing out the white smoke rings which were so fascinating to me. Our little Diesel train trekked by this a.m. in the storm.

As for automobiles, there were a few odd-looking contraptions at the Columbian Exp[osition] in Chicago in 1893 but the first one I ever saw in motion was downtown in Des Moines, about 1901 and looked a lot like the toy affair on the stamp. . . .

It seems almost like sacrilege to parody the Gettysburg oration, but if done it all, <u>Time</u> has a good one; p. 27.[6]

Tues. a.m.—The road was too slick yesterday to try to get the mail. I see cars and the school bus on the roads west so perhaps with sun and a brisk wind our road will be passable sometime today.

I carelessly left the Dobie book around and Dad got hold of it this morning so suppose nothing more can be done in "the foreseeable future." Of late he has taken up a discouraging habit. As soon as he is through breakfast he piles up on the corner couch and reads or sleeps the morning away. He is snoring now for the best part of the day. I don't see how he can <u>think</u> of farming and have asked more than once if we hadn't better rent the crop land. He says he will try to hold out for me(!) this one more year and rent it for 1953. . . .

APRIL 23, 1952

DEAR ELEANOR:

It is disconcerting to note that another year is almost ⅓ gone— and nothing done! . . .

The sun is shining today and it looks like more settled weather. He will try to get out to go to Eva. Eggs already kept too long and no chance to send for bread or other groceries for an even two weeks! . . .

. . . I have finished now <u>The Water and the Power</u>,[7] and found it most interesting and informative. . . . I'm not so sure as he seems to be of the wisdom of complete Federal control of all water resources, but perhaps it is the only way. Nor could I yet accept so unreservedly the feasibility of the rain-making projects. Haven't heard yet to whom we owe this late series of rains, but as you will remember, we have had our pond full time and again when <u>rain making</u> was on about as scientific a basis as the Hopi's Snake Dance, which I believe is quite often followed by rainfall! They are to hold a meeting in Guymon this week to try to convince the skeptics and get them to throw in the $10,000 yet unpledged for the renewal of the contract on May 15.[8] . . .

MAY 8, 1952

DEAR ELEANOR:

Our 44th milestone [wedding anniversary] was not mentioned here. The roses as usual but see there is one out for each of us this morning. . . . Sad for the almost complete loss of the little mulberry thicket which made a pleasant spot of shade. I don't know whether I shall always have to look at the bared dead trees but probably so, as Dad has more than he can do anyway. He is planting Sudan yesterday and today, double-rowing with the old worn-out lister, as he seemed to think he could get it in deeper with the chisels than with the drill.

Every day seems to bring some new sorrow in these last years of fruitless effort and disappointment. Now another of my small group of cats has gone, we suppose destroyed by the cruel coyotes. This time the very handsome corn-striped Persian, one of dear Pusnella's last little family. I thought the world of him and all these small creatures have become so much a part of my life it seems hard to go on without them. I see that I must soon give up my little Puffer as he is weaker this morning and not calling for his improvised diet of millers, flies and angle worms.[9] . . .

I discovered late yesterday that the basement light was also a casualty of the first electrical storm. It wouldn't seem that these various break-downs should make so much difference, but really they seem . . . most essential, . . . especially the . . . electric iron. I must go back to the old primitive method today to smooth out a few things until Dad can take part of a half-day to help with another washing. He will have to go to Eva tomorrow with the eggs.

Wagtail is cute this morning. He has piled up that hand-made rag rug Dad wove while we were at Lawrence and is asleep on the top of the pile. He too is failing; quite gray on the top of his head now and has coughed all winter. . . .

. . . I think we shall have to give the larkspurs . . . the prize for perseverance. Most of the other blooms quite withered now but they are still opening new and smaller single blooms toward the top of their stalks! Perhaps a lesson for us to try to keep doing what little we can.

JUNE 11, 1952

DEAR ELEANOR:

It is hard to write under such depressing conditions when we see our living disappearing before our eyes and the little things that might make life worth living fast fading away. This is the fourth successive day of extreme heat—98⁰–100⁰—and uninterrupted blasting winds. It is a wonder that anything remains alive. I tried to put water on parts of the garden this morning but couldn't keep up with the furnace blast of the wind and the most I could do was to keep chasing my truck driver's cap which Dad picked up in our lake after one of our big floods. They say no hope of moisture while the upper levels of the air also remain hot. . . .

I always try to look over the Arizona Farmer to see what I can quarrel with. I observe that the editor has for the Wellton-Mohawk project[10] all the enthusiasm that I so conspicuously lack. So short a time since everybody, except the reclamation engineers, agreed there were too many farmers anyway and that all marginal lands and lands requiring excessive cost for production should be <u>withdrawn</u> from cultivation. Now here we go pouring out millions upon millions to raise more cotton at almost prohibitive expense so as to keep up the price and make $4 overalls an almost unattainable luxury. Someone ought to tell that editor that his immense <u>75,000</u> acres is a very small spot. Roughly a strip just over 3 miles wide across Texas Co. which could sink to the central fires and never be missed. Approximately ⅔ the area of our <u>school district</u>!

I suppose if it seemed desirable and enough millions were spent to transport sand and water one <u>could</u> raise a small garden on the Pyramid of Cheops, but as the Romans put it neatly, Cui Bono. Or in more modern language, So What? It's time to go to work. . . . Keep cool and be careful.

~

JULY 11, 1952

DEAR ELEANOR:

I don't know how far I can get. Dad is likely to come just any time and I would have to dust out of here[11] into the heat and wind and dust again. He couldn't get a new screen to fit the very old combine, so bought a short length of 1 x 4" material and laboriously built a new frame and pounded out the old mangled metal screening as well as possible and nailed it on. We were able to use it yesterday to salvage about 10 bu. of wheat, clogged up in the machine after the last breakdown.

Later we made one round on the barley. It <u>looks</u> fair but is really very poor because of the lack of moisture at the critical time. Mr.

Angle would hardly recognize the shriveled grains. But we hate to lose it all after the double expense of the spraying to try to save it [from bugs]. This was not as effective as I had hoped, though we probably could not have cut it at all if it hadn't been done. . . .

Father has gone down to grease the machine all over again for one more trial. A good deal of trouble yesterday with one of the elevator chains halting as if caught on some obstruction. It takes all my horse power to pull backwards or forwards on the pulley belt while Dad does the tinkering overhead. No time for anything around here and wonder if we shall really starve before we can get through. The present plan is to combine the better part (on summer fallow) and cut the rest with the header with considerable green Johnson grass mixed in for emergency hay. No feed crop is now possible, though some did get a good stand of maize and it is holding out remarkably. . . . The one little rain of June 18 (the very last) was just enough to wash out or cover up what little we had coming up in the lister furrows. . . .

We still don't know just how much wheat was saved. We've stored in our west granary 580 bu. by a very close accounting and have the elevator weigh bills for 552 hauled from the field. That still leaves the comparatively small quantity from the north and south places. . . .

. . . I must try to finish up. We worked hard all the rest of the morning and in spite of many delays were making some headway and saving a little barley. But about 12:30 the final "irreversible disaster" occurred. Some part of the wooden frame work underneath the body of the machine gave way completely. It would take several days for rebuilding if possible at all. So we reluctantly gave up about ⅔ of our stint, including the best part of the field. Dad <u>said</u> he would fit up the old header once more and we would head that portion along with what we had hoped to save for hay. . . . It is a grievous disappointment to me for I had earnestly hoped to get this harvesting done this week, and now perhaps never. The thought of going through it all again in 1953 is more than I can endure. Yet I suppose there is no hope of escape unless through a final discharge. After all the hard work he has done here, it looks heartless to try to rent the land out from under his feet and probably impossible. . . .

I am cooking dried corn for our supper and it smells good. We can't have any roasting ears this year unless it rains as the small plot approaches the tasseling stage. . . .

SEPT. 10, 1952

DEAR ELEANOR:

. . . It is sad to have to tell you that my gloomiest forebodings about the wheat coming were completely justified. I have looked over the 60 acres on this place pretty carefully. Dad insisted there was fair moisture in the soil when he drilled but now one can find only dry seed in dry ground and scarcely any moisture even at a greater depth. . . .

The loss of the work and seed and hope of wheat pasture makes our prospects a little darker then ever, but Dad is still ploughing, even though I feel he is just fixing the land to blow in the winter and spring. I am making a fight to save the stubble and volunteer wheat on the home place for protection and pasturage, but probably a losing struggle. . . . Ploughing and the never-ceasing wind have dissipated the scanty moisture so that we hardly know what is fertilized. Our own drilling postponed for now but Dad seems to think most people will go ahead anyway and gamble their wheat seed in the dirt. Sometimes it looks as if the folks who have the nerve to sow at the right time, regardless of conditions are the ones that win out. And sometimes the worms in the soil destroy the germs if the wheat lies long in dry ground. . . .

. . . Mrs. W.[12] said she had had no income from her place (except the gas money) for 3 yrs. So decided to sell it to Alford Myers for $2000.00 which seems low as land has been valued lately. . . .

I still cling to my bright little flowers, cosmos, zinnias, asters, morning glories and of late a few portulacas also to the small spots of native grass which came out so surprisingly after the rain.

I wonder if you have anywhere the inscription on that bronze tablet marking the "Prairie Acre" at K.U. I'd be glad to have a copy of it if you do, but if no, never mind. And do you have the Hardy poem, Afterwards? "She was one to notice such things."[13] I once had it and liked it but it has escaped me. Almost time to follow the auto home. So all for now.

⟞⟝

CA. JAN. 1954

DEAR ELI:

A word of appreciation for your friendly holiday greeting. I wrote my own under such extreme pressure that I don't remember how much I told you of the disasters of 1953. One [phase?] is suggested by the fact that (with our double exemption, after 65) we do not have to pay any income tax this year! Must try to do better. I know you are always busy but if you have a moment to spare, I believe you would find the little bulletins from Indianapolis expressing much of your own desires. We agree regarding Sen. McCarthy.[14] I think most people outside of Wisconsin feel the same. Enjoyed your portrayal of the small girls. I feel that our privileges as American citizens have been bought by great sacrifices. Most earnestly I hope that nothing would ever happen to cause you to cast aside that citizenship as of no value. c.f. Acts 22:27–29.

A lonely world this morning. A study in gray and black and white with every smallest twig rimmed with hoar frost. I wish Alice and Bonnie could see our eight baby calves run and play in the snow drifts like a bunch of small children. Every good wish for the play[15] and for all of yours.

⟨⁓⟩

CA. DECEMBER, 1954

DEAR FRIENDS [THE JAFFES]:

It really takes the children to make Christmas and I can imagine how your little girls look forward to the great day. I hope it has been a good year for all of you. A very bad one for us, measured by any material standard. I am not even sure that heavy losses and reduced resources will permit us even to try again.

At present I am quite by myself "on the lone prairie." Mr. H. left on Dec. 3 for Phoenix, accompanying a neighbor who was driving through. We are hoping that Arizona sunshine and medicines Eleanor had ready will give some relief from his bothersome joint pains. He and David (7) are having fine times and he is building the little boy a greatly desired "work bench." You can tell the children that Grandpa Henderson saw a lot of the little bright-eyed papooses on their cradle boards at an Indian Fair he enjoyed out there.

Complete lack of grass compelled the sacrifice of our cattle so it's very quiet and desolate here. But I try to be thankful for reasonable health and for our home and "America the Beautiful."

⟨⁓⟩

JUNE 29, 1955

DEAR ELI AND WILMA:

We appreciated your thought for us and the clipping from the <u>Times</u>, one of the most comprehensive and understanding reports I have seen on the 1954–1955 "dust bowl" conditions.

I hope you can use the very small gift, though I am no baby specialist and am not even sure that up to date babies even wear shirts! I always thought they were most engaging and Eleanor let me get a full set for our dear little David. . . . I only wish I knew that all the little children coming into this difficult world would be as welcome and tenderly cared for as your own.

The Lippmann[16] clipping reminded me of your own thought and does express a rising breath of hope that the hopes and dreams of the world's plain people may eventually enter into decisions "at the summit" or on any level. I wish I could report something hopeful for ourselves but, though we have had considerable rain fall since around the middle of May, the benefits were largely nullified by destructive hail storms on June 16 and 18, so that the already poor wheat prospects were reduced in varying proportions. Our own suffered I judge from about 35% to 75% damage in different fields. Really very little left. In some areas a total loss. I have even rather desperately tried writing for a small income but no good so far. We need to remember R.L. Stevenson: "To travel hopefully is better than to arrive and the true success is to labor."[17] Our fond wishes to you <u>all</u>.

⟨≈⟩

CA. DECEMBER 1955

DEAR FRIENDS: [THE JAFFES]

I am attempting to combine our Christmas greeting with sincere congratulations to you about the new member of your family, but I think most especially to Wilma. I can imagine what this small son means to her. May he always be a source of help and comfort to you and to the friends he will gather as the years pass by. It is good that you gave him a substantial and significant name. Paul was a man of sufficient courage to admit his own mistakes. In his own words he was "not disobedient to the heavenly vision"[18] and it changed his whole life. So our thanks for the clever announcement card and the accompanying letter. I was interested in the variety of your reading. . . .

No one could resent more than I do the determination of some of the southern states to defy the Supreme Court decision.[19] I think eventually they will have to surrender. Really it isn't the young people in the schools that are making the trouble. It is the older people still clinging to their doctrine of states rights and white supremacy. But I sincerely believe that except for that minority group the drift or tendency now is in favor of justice and equal rights for all our citizens. I realize that they can yet make a lot of trouble. . . .

For ourselves the year has been a terror. Not only a practically complete failure of crops and absence of all farm income but like Job we have been stricken in body as well as in family resources. Even now when we should like to be peaceful our sweet Eleanor is trying to fight of[f] the third recurrence of undulant fever during this year. Mr. H. had a light "stroke" in May. Was left speechless through paralysis of the vocal cords. Hearing gone. It is hard to get on. I am supposed to be indestructible. . . .

~

MAY 16, 1956

DEAR ELEANOR:

Here they are at last, the green stamps I thought were lost forever. I found them yesterday in an envelope I had obviously meant to send to you. . . .

Dad has given good care and lots of water to the little cherry trees. They bloomed nicely and, as all else had failed, we hoped for a little fruit. He looked pretty sick last night when he went out to locate the [?] again and found the tiny green fruits all blighted and shriveled by the 5-day blow of last week; more especially I presume by the electrical conditions on Thursday, the day when I got several shocks, touching the stove or some bit of metal at the brooder.[20] I almost perished of clear terror as I sat hour after hour thinking the light building might roll over at any moment, chickens, stove, grandma and all.

Much of the foliage, trees and shrubs looks as if a fire had passed over it; iris buds blighted and small plants destroyed. It seems that we can't be allowed to have any <u>little</u> thing. We did dig out a small mess of asparagus Sunday though most had to be discarded as it had grown too tough trying to reach the surface. . . .

On the tip-top of the small locust that developed from a sprout here in the yard, there is one spray of fragrant bloom. I am reminded of the sweet air over on locust grove corner when we came home from Rolla after your graduation in 1926. Now with so many changes and losses we are still here alone, but it seems sometimes with little to cling to. Dad has started his protective plant listing out west on this place. Working on the contour. Ground is like a concrete pavement and he was badly shaken up last night. Today is bad again and I hardly thought he ought to go out, but he had almost caught up with the blowing spots, so felt as if he should put in the half day at least. . . .

⋙

FEB. 17, 1957

DEAR ELI:

Your letters are always very welcome because of their understanding sympathy with our problems and their kindly encouragement. So I must not delay longer to thank you for your after Christmas note and the picture of your beautiful children. Surely the truly wise men of every generation must bow in reverence before the innocence and the unlimited possibilities for each new life. You and Wilma have every reason to be proud and happy in your family and I earnestly hope they may always be a comfort and support to you (spiritually) as our daughter is to us.

Thus far the winter has brought no moisture to our section of the desolate Great Plains. And so we have no promise of a seed time for 1957. Only continued and abnormal rain fall could make a start at restoring subsoil moisture, without which there is hardly one chance in a thousand of raising any significant crop. There just isn't, even in a normal year, enough spring and summer rainfall to produce crops here without the reserve underneath. So more than at anytime in our common life, we live from day to day, busy with small tasks, thankful that we can still get about and that for the present at least, Eleanor seems better than for some time.

There is much discussion and criticism of the elementary schools, but judging by our David's progress, one could hardly expect anything better. . . .

I fear you think I was indifferent to your request for possible suggestions of conflict in the inner life of supposed spiritual leaders. But I have been trying to think of such examples without much success. I have drifted too far away from any constructive efforts. If I last a few more weeks I shall complete the "four score" which do indeed bring much of "labor and sorrow." Psalm 90:10. I suppose Martin Luther (whom I do not particularly admire) would be one outstanding example. You may have seen the film?[21]

Tolstoy appeals to me more with his long struggle between the claims of his family, his workers and estate, and the stern injunction: "Let him deny himself and take up his cross and follow me." . . . I

believe <u>The Nun's Story</u> is classed as non-fiction. A friend whose judgment I have a great confidence spoke of it as one of the finest things
she had ever read. Here I think the choice is between continued sub-
servience to some artificial ecclesiastical hierarchy and the demands
of simple humanity. . . . I had wondered about <u>Keys of the
Kingdom</u>[22] (Cronin) but am afraid I may have confused it with some
other book. . . .

I must stop or you will regret having written. . . .

MARCH 8, 1957

DEAR ELEANOR:

You may have seen the enclosures. I don't know how this "citizens
committee" got our name. The Clearwater Dam problem is new to
me, but they do present an appealing case. The Wichita Mountain
give away comes closer to home.[23] Did you read in a recent <u>Harpers</u>
the pathetic story of the two Indian graves? I'm not superstitious about
any graves, only it does look as if once in a while for a change they
could honor a firm promise given to the Indian people. It is absurd to
claim that the area coveted by the Army is worthless for recreation
purposes and inaccessible; for we spent one quiet restful night at one
of the camping places. And I'll never forget how the mother buffalo
pushed her baby away from the fence and got between him and our
old car, Henry II. There too I saw the only wild turkeys I have ever
seen.

There is no necessity for the change and it looks like a clear case of
blackmailing the support of our Senators and Representatives through
a threat that if this spot is retained for all the people as at present, then
the Army will abandon all the expensive buildings and equipment at
Fort Sill and so deprive that portion of the state of whatever economic
advantages may accrue from the military installation. I am convinced
this is only a threat, but if they were permitted to carry it out, then
Lawton etc. could doubtless learn to get along without the soldiers at
least as well as our own part of the state has always done. I know you
have a lot on your mind, but perhaps even a posted card to your
people in Congress would register a protest. Senator Goldwater is at
least independent. I see he is one of the 5 Republicans who voted
against the Eisenhower resolution about the Middle East.[24]

I didn't oppose a warning to the Russians to watch their step, but

I do begrudge $200,000,000 held out as a lure to any nations that ask for it! And never a dollar to apply to payment of our own staggering national indebtedness. And more and more of our public domain and national resources being dissected for private exploitation. So I think I'll try to write my brief words cursing the S[ocial] S[ecurity] for farmers, protesting against 5 cent letter postage and urging them not to be intimidated by threats, either by the Army or by political hay-makers. . . .

Today I cooked up the last 2 citrons which grew all by themselves down among the hegira. I also soaked out and cooked dried apples for flavoring and so made 4 kinds of really pretty good apple butter. Dad thinks it is good and it's a lot better than no fruit at all with bread and butter.

He has finished a quick cleaning of the hen house yesterday and today. I suppose is pretty tired but relaxing with a Western that Mrs. Grable brought in this morning on their way to Guymon. . . . The young man from Guymon representing the loan company I mentioned turned up again today. He seemed quite anxious for us to make some investment and we do need more present income.[25] . . .

⤜⤛

MARCH 26, 1957

DEAR ELEANOR:

We are so stunned and bewildered by the conditions of recent days and the realization that the worst is yet to come that I don't know whether I can write anything intelligible.

The storm I mentioned on my Fri., Sat. card raged on until nearly noon on Monday, though at the last the blowing snow was more from the drifts than from the clouds.

On Sat. Dad was able to give partial care to the cattle and chickens. No water for the cattle as the tank was under about 10" of packed snow. The electricity held out through Sat. until nearly dark. Went off then until around 10:00 p.m. on Sunday. A wonder that it could be restored in the midst of the storm and for a while they were quite anxious about the five boys out in the pick-up; but they made it through some way. Another young man went on horseback and took food to them and later a rescue team got to them and I suppose helped them get in.

Sun. was even worse. Dad put out feed once for the cattle but never got to the hen house at all. Three hens apparently drifted from the barn and perished near the hen house, a bitter pang to me. (We have on hand around 70 doz. eggs which we shall have eventually to cook for the cats and chickens. I see no hope of any getting out of here for weeks to come.) Monday the temperature began to rise and some melting on the surface began to check the drift to some extent. The chickens were about crazy from hunger and Dad managed to shovel a path to one door and they piled all over him for feed. He brought in 2 pails of eggs for the two days. Several dented but I think none frozen as I feared.

That has been the one redeeming feature of the worst storm we have ever seen. If the temperature had gone down as low as it might have done, there would undoubtedly have been much more acute suffering and loss of life. So far we have heard of (5) five deaths in the Panhandle Counties. . . .

Both of our doors were blocked solid on Sun. morning. Dad had to drop out of the north bedroom window! Everything in the room covered by snow before I could clear the frame and get the window down again. So damp I didn't dare take the risk of anyone's sleeping there—without the electric heat—so we dragged the old couch back into the dining room and camped there for 2 nights but will try bedrooms again tonight.

. . . Contrary to any previous storm every building on the place has a solid mass of snow banked against the south side and extending indefinitely toward the south-east. I estimate that there is enough snow banked on all sides around us (from 4' to 15' or 18') to fill the basement and the first floor to a depth of 3'–4'! So that is why I say the worse is still to come. No place at all for all these drifts to go.

Between the house and hen house is a small white mountain which rises above the REA wires and extends into the pasture, probably about 30–40 rods altogether. Another nearly as high through the space east of the house yard. . . . Cattle are all over the country, crossing the covered fences as if they weren't there. One bunch of Herefords corralled on a front lawn in Guymon. I fear heavy losses when the snow is melted and people can see what has happened. It had to be this way when my nice heifer Jill was to bring her calf. Tomorrow is the day and no fit place to put her because the barn is just a filthy mud hole. . . .

A great curving cliff like wall of snow extends from north of the barn around nearly to the corner of the pasture. . . . We are thankful that conditions in the house are not as bad as they might have been. So far we have food and fuel and propane gas and have managed to keep reasonably comfortable. . . . The drift that blocks the south end of the house reaches to the middle of the south (upstairs) window.

Now noon on Wed. The sun is shining. Sun. Temperature—6o degrees. The drifts are slowly settling but the yard south of the house, to wind mill and wash house is still packed solid about 8' deep from ground level. Highest point . . . still just about level with the eaves of the barn. Our only hope for not being flooded out completely is that the snow will melt very gradually and drain slowly away from the house and yards.

I am sad beyond expression over cattle losses all over the plains country. At Guymon this morning they estimated roughly 20% of the cattle population gone. Some had lost into hundreds or even thousands. Tough luck for people who had endured these recent lean years, perhaps put borrowed money into cattle and feed, hoping they could pull out on enough feed and pasturage. I feel the worst about the darling little innocent calves, but of course the growing loss of human lives is the worst of all. . . .

I am heartsick with anxiety over the impossibility of getting any word to you to reassure you of our safety. . . . It may of course be several days yet before side roads are passable. So I don't see what I can do—aside from telepathy which isn't so dependable. I'll have to stop and try to have something for Dad to eat whenever he comes in. I dare not urge him to do extra miles of walking, for he is getting run down with all the mountain climbing, shoveling, etc., and I feel as if his hip and bad leg may not hold out. . . .

Thursday 10 a.m. . . . Ralph has come in and will take this to go to Eva via Riley's so will finish some other time. Love,

⤙≋⤚

APRIL 14, 1957

DEAR ROSE:

I'd like to have this reach you by Easter but it may be impossible, especially if next week again no mail is delivered on Saturday. It seems that you and Eleanor must have joined in a plan—or conspiracy—for April 7 which worked out very nicely and brought me much support at a very difficult time. The "April Showers" reached me from East and West and were indeed appreciated. Besides your own greeting came cards and notes or letters from Ethelyn, Annabel, *Gertrude*, Margaret Wheeler, <u>Grace Bacon</u>, Lavinia Rose Wilson and finally one from Mount Holyoke, signed by a Miss Mills. So with cards and gifts from Eleanor and David, also from former students of days long gone and from the neighborhood, I really had quite a birthday.[26]

As it turned out I needed all the help I could get, for Sunday April 7, proved a day of extreme anxiety. The weather men at Amarillo, Texas, began early and insistently to warn of <u>another</u> storm, possibly as bad as the blizzard we were still hoping to survive. The new storm was then centered near Albuquerque and expected here during the afternoon. It came just about the appointed time but had lost force and, while adding to our difficulties while it lasted, was not as violent a storm as they had feared. A little more snow on the still mountainous drifts and a high wind, which caused the REA wires to writhe and thresh around alarmingly. We had spent much of the day in preparation for another siege, both for ourselves and the hens and cattle. But the thought of the heart-warming letters helped me through the day.

. . . I have seen the storms of fifty winters now in this particular spot but nothing approaching the fury and persistence of the blizzard of March 22 through March 25. . . .

It was exactly three weeks before Will could get out for marketing or replenishing any supplies, so a good thing that we are used to <u>austerity</u>! Excepting of course our sadness about actual loss of human lives (4 in this county) the most painful part to me personally has been the crushing and destruction of so many of the young trees and shrubs we had tried so hard to save through the long drought; and the heartbreaking suffering and death of the innocent creatures that no one could save. Not only cattle and sheep but the wild creatures that are so dear to me. I suppose whoever wrote the tender verses about the "sparrow's fall"[27] had not seen the fields littered with the little migrant birds that will never come again and the rabbits that I have always loved to see running and playing together. A wonder if any survive. Meadow larks stay here through the winter, but I've not seen or heard one since the storm.

Through the kindness of neighbors who had access to a telephone, we were able to get word to Eleanor of our safety by March 27, but she had been extremely anxious.

A little brother calf arrived on March 30 and I named him Stormy. You wished for us a "blossoming Easter" and so you will be glad that —incredibly—one daffodil and six hyacinth buds remained alive under a 5-foot drift and are now coming into bloom in yellow, pink, blue and purple. I'm sure you are exhausted so I must stop with sincere thanks for your letters a kind effort for me.

⟜≋⟞

JUNE 20, 1957

DEAR ELEANOR:

. . . A pang to see the old <u>horse collars</u> hanging in the stable, as here at home. I have begged Dad to burn them up but he doesn't do it. Every such thing <u>hurts</u> me so now and I miss unspeakably, the earlier days while we still had hope and "forward-looking thoughts." The brave little flowers bring some comfort. The first morning-glory yesterday—a deep lovely purple; today is bringing out the first cosmos, from volunteer plants—a dark, beautiful rose color. Dad brought home from the pasture a small blooming wild verbena and set it here by the south gate. I hope it will take root and go on blooming. I always admired the vivid purple color; a little different from those of your area. . . .

⟜≋⟞

MAY 8, 1958

DEAR ELEANOR:

. . . Our anniversary passed very uneventfully. We had for dinner stewed (frozen) chicken, I think one of those you dressed; mashed potatoes; the first asparagus; chopped raw carrots, citron butter and frozen custard ice cream—all home grown except the potatoes which Dad thinks must go with chicken gravy. In the p.m. Dad ploughed the stubble ground along the south road. I planted . . . mixed carrot and radish seed; also zinnias and marigolds; showered the lettuce, beets and carrots—already planted to break a heavy crust and weeded out the very few Porter plants in one row.[28] Ann came for eggs. She seemed pleased to have heard from you. She brought an arm load of the loveliest tulips many colors and types including several double ones a lot like peonies. . . .

For May 7 supper we went back to May of 1908 and had crackers, cheese and oranges in memory of our way side supper on our way <u>home</u> from Guymon. Only Dad wouldn't eat his orange! He liked the night shirts.

⤝⤞

NOV. 18, 1958

DEAR ELEANOR:

Stopping in the midst of things—pinto beans, baked apples, pumpkin pies and corn bread—to start a word to you on the very poor chance of mailing it to reach you on Saturday. You have no doubt heard of the High Plains "cyclonic" system which burst in here late on Sunday and continued through most of Monday, though snow actually began to check about noon. Much high wind and drifting till nearly night. The snow was preceded by thunder, lightning, sleet, and rain—about .60" of moisture altogether, which should promote rooting for the wheat.

Being warned of the advancing storm we undertook—too late—to get the upper barn door back in place. For once we failed of our purpose. The wind was to a high gale and raised the dirt around the barn till we could hardly see what we were trying to do or avoid or endure the chilling. We got the door anchored to cover about ⅔ of the vacant space which was of course not enough but may have cut off a little of the wind and drifting snow.

Probably about a 4" snow but as usual much piled up to make the most trouble. It seems remarkable that since Sunday we haven't seen *one* car or truck on any of the near roads, for usually that's the time everybody feels the urge to go somewhere! . . .

We are doing the best we can and trying not to grieve too much over the maize and hegira covered by the snow. Only the future can tell whether any more can be salvaged; at least Dad had his own way about it and did as he was determined to do. He has a delusion that some way the almost exhausted supply of threshing grain will be replenished for my chickens but I am more realistic. . . .

It seemed to me one of the most direct sources of comfort for [August's] parents within your control would be to arrange for David to write them a letter or card at least once a month, perhaps oftener. He is so mature and sensible in many ways. I think he could understand that his writing to them would help to fill in for the letters his Daddy used to write and give them courage and a motive for trying to go on without their dearly beloved.[29] . . .

. . . We had 9 degrees here and it will be cold again tonight with so much snow on the ground, things above freezing now in the p.m. and a little melting around small bare spots. We put the old lantern out under the storage tank last night and I will try to hitch up Father's electric blanket for tonight. . . .

⤜⤛

MAY 1, 1959

DEAR ELEANOR:

This is certainly a mild day for the first of May and of the Pioneer Day celebration; continuing through tomorrow.[30] I was up early and before sunrise a weird sort of salmon-colored light over everything. However the morning was endurable but the wind has been rising all day and now at mid-afternoon has developed into a howling dust storm not so good for the "revelry" at Guymon. I'm thankful to be at home. Occasionally the wind slackens almost entirely in an unnatural calm and then whoops it up again worse than ever.

I've just run out to shut off the wind-mill because I feared all the gusts and flopping around would snap the sucker-rod. Earlier in the day I was glad to have it pumping to water the little cherry trees. Trying now to bloom—so very late—but one seemed so slow I feared it would not develop its blossoms without the push of extra watering.

Mr. and Mrs. Grable were here late yesterday and into the evening. They too begin to realize the need of more moisture for the wheat. . . . They said the wheat is failing at least as far as they went.

I don't know whether you will be glad or sorry to hear that the threshing in the field is done, even if not finished. We put in a day of quite steady work on Wednesday and surpassed any previous record, by [?] out 48 shocks and filling out one more load. For the first time I began to wonder if just possibly we might be allowed to finish the long (3-months) and weary effort. But I didn't wait long for the answer. Just at the last it began kicking off the auger chain faster than Dad could put it back. He found that the sprocket he had had rebuilt at Eva was stripped on one side again and no hope of its working, though he did try to make another tightener and gave it one more chance Thursday a.m. with no better luck. So we hauled the 29 Baldwin home to our growing junk yard. . . . I estimated about 80–90 shocks left when we had to quit—probably 7–8 loads. Too heavy work for him. I meant to help by going along to tear out the bundles from the piled up dust and shake out what I could. . . .

⤜⤛

SEPT. 8, 1959

DEAR ELEANOR:

. . . Really not much to record. A very small break-through from the general inertia of many weeks. We did eventually pick up the Sudan from the wind rows in 25 nice shocks and I sickled down—for appearance sake—the small fringes of uncut grass here and there.

Dad couldn't think of any more excuses—with the chicken grain at the vanishing point—so said he would thresh on Labor Day. But we didn't accomplish much beyond a bare beginning. Several changes had to be made. . . . Just made a small start in the p.m. when a key dropped out of the cylinder and it took nearly all the rest of the afternoon to get that righted up. We did start up then for perhaps half an hour but slow heavy work and small return. So much to handle for so little grain. Incredible that we should hold out to do the four stacks by such an awkward method, but can perhaps get a little more chicken feed, while they last. Father grows more erratic and contradictory and ungovernable all the time. . . . He says he wants more cattle. In the next breath he says will wipe the place clean of every living thing before he leaves for his three months vacation during the winter. . . .

I often think of a remark in some of Mr. DeVoto's writings.[31] I wondered at the time how so young a man could have such insight. He spoke of the <u>character</u> required at the end of a long life when there is no chance to redeem one's mistakes and one realizes—too late—the utter <u>failure</u> of all he has hoped and striven for, the sturdy tenacity of purpose needed to keep on trying anyway in the face of inevitable failure, compounded with each days' lost effort. I "very fear" I don't have that much character or perseverance.

Yesterday was a bitter day for me. I remembered early that on Sept. of 1891, Mother and I rose extra early and made the long slow drive to LeMars [Iowa] (15 miles) in time for me to enter the High School there. I can realize better now how much they sacrificed to give me the chance for an education and a broader life than would have been possible on the farm of that period. And so it is painfully humiliating to realize how little use I made of it and that now there are no fragments worth picking up. You and David and what you may yet accomplish are my only hope and comfort. No wonder that I am perhaps over-anxious about his future work and the influences that might shape his course. . . .

I am sending <u>Time</u>. For some reason Dad wanted to keep the cover picture of Eisenhower from a painting by A[ndrew] Wyeth.

More serious and like the Eisenhower many people must have thought they were voting for.[32] . . .

⟨～⟩

JAN. [?] 1960

DEAR ELEANOR:

We haven't heard about Arizona weather but rough and threatening here tonight and we probably can't go to Guymon tomorrow as intended. . . .

We received your letter and card yesterday. . . . We also received a nice friendly letter from Eli, whom I had really given up, with a picture of his three quite beautiful children. They didn't move to Ohio as planned but he commutes occasionally to Cincinnati and does publicity for the Jewish theological training school there doubtless Rabbi Myerberg's alma mater. Apparently his one-time communist principles have worn out. He admits that now, instead of knowing all the answers, he hardly knows the questions. Perhaps some time I'll send the letter and let you judge whether people under life's discipline can change very tenaciously held beliefs. . . .

⟨～⟩

JAN. 18, 1960

DEAR ELEANOR:

Truly a scene of Arctic desolation here this morning. . . . They said 8" of snow . . . at Guymon and Dad thinks about the same here though hard to find a level place for any accurate measurement. . . .

. . . They look for zero temperatures tonight and most unhappily I can't get Father even to look at the car to see if radiator is frozen like the cup of tea on my bedside table! . . .

. . . I have finally got the preliminary figures for the tax report together. Am stalled because from what they say about purchase of automobiles, machinery etc. and about "depreciation", I can't decide whether—as always here before—I am allowed to try to recover the $655 purchase price of the car. . . . I need all the depreciation and legitimate expenses I can figure up because it looks as if the tax will clean us out for a new start—after 52 years!

. . . You can discard the Rickover article on the "Uneducated" if of no interest. I found it quite absorbing, especially as I can't imagine any of the Yarbrough graduates for instance ever discussing any thing more abstract than girls (or boys), games, plays, etc.[33] . . .

Tues. a.m. Not much change so far. . . .

. . . No guessing when we could get out of the yard. Truck practically covered by the granary and car blocked in the garage. Most serious factor in the situation is the dwindling of stored fodder in the barn and impossibility for moving any from the stacks. They expect more <u>snow</u> tonight or tomorrow! J. F. finally came to get his cattle home (yesterday) from the quarter with us and came on over to see if we were OK. No other sign of life in the whole area around us. . . .

⌐⇒

FEB. 4, 1960

DEAR [JAFFES]

I have thought of you so often since your very brief visit in the summer time. So I was especially glad to find your cheerful note in the Christmas mail. . . .

I was interested in the enclosure about the Eleanor Roosevelt cancer research institute and feel that it is an honor, both to the very talented lady and to the institution. Surely we all feel the need of swifter progress toward the eradication of that gruesome scourge of mankind.

I have just completed today our 1959 [Fed. Income] tax report. If this coming year should demand a payment again, so disproportionate to any comfort we can hope to attain, I think now I shall try to find some way to <u>give</u> enough to health or educational projects to reduce the payments to a more reasonable amount. I could at least <u>hope</u> the money would accomplish some small useful purpose.

We had a pleasant Christmas with our dear ones from Arizona. David (12) took charge of the <u>tree</u>, improvised from branches of our own evergreens and arranged a pleasant program of the familiar carols, readings, and a little original talk about the history of the great day. . . . One enjoyable feature of their visit was listening to sermons or addresses Eleanor had taken the trouble to record with their new tape recorder. I liked particularly lectures on Gandhi and Dr. [Albert] Schweitzer from a series Eleanor had attended at the YMCA. The speaker was a very learned and inspirational Rabbi.[34] . . . One could feel instinctively his enthusiasm for his subject. A most moving and memorable experience. . . .

I am now re-reading a book Eleanor gave me long ago—<u>This</u>

<u>Believing World</u>.[35] The author is a Lewis Browne of whom I know nothing. But, he has something of the same quality. It is rather astonishing to find how many of the ideas often represented as fundamental to Christianity appear in the teachings of other religious leaders or in their legendary origins.

There isn't much new to tell of ourselves. We are just plodding on from one severe storm period into another. It seems now that we made a serious mistake in holding a bunch of calves to gain what we could from pasturing the luxuriant fall-sown wheat. For several weeks now we, and the cattle, have been storm bound. The work of caring for them under existing conditions is far too great. We did plan to take a load to the community sales during this week. But again we are blocked by rain, snow, mud and impassable roads. So must keep on and try to find some way through. This present storm has put our much prized electrical system—REA—out of use. If they don't get it going by night it will mean cold sleeping, as we depend so much on our electric blankets. Still worse, it could mean the loss of our precious supply of frozen meals etc. We keep hoping for the light to flash on. Our best wishes to each and all of you for your chosen useful work.

[P.S.] Fri. a.m.—Sunny but cold. The electricity came back just before midnight to my great relief.

⟨⁓⟩

JULY 25, 1960

DEAR ELEANOR:

. . . We are now in the so-common after-harvest doldrums when it becomes hard to keep up a water supply—not to speak of building one up from nothing. On Sat. p.m. a very light breeze sprang up briefly. The windmill started to pump water, very . . . rusty, but still wet. [After a few] strokes it cut off completely, with the wind still blowing and the mill turning. No recovery, so later Dad disconnected the rod and let it go down with a splash. Apparently some small bit of gravel or flake of rust had lodged under the little plunger and prevented any water from coming up. Barely enough wind to start it pumping again before it sank away until afternoon on Sunday. Then very fitful; about 2 minutes pumping to 20–30 minutes standing still, so made no progress toward stock or irrigation water. Today (Monday) a light surface breeze but not enough to run the mill, so of course no certainty that the same obstruction may not occur all over again.

To make things a little worse, a peculiar accident for myself which makes me helpless for any useful work. We have a very mean rooster whom Dad calls Napoleon. He has attacked both of us repeatedly and my leg and back are all scarred up [by his] spurs. . . . But while doing my evening work yesterday he slipped up on me by the barn and injured my right wrist very badly. . . . The wrist is badly swollen and <u>hurts</u>. I swabbed it with Merthiolate and soaked in hot Epsom salt water with no perceptible effect. Even the writing is painful so must finish this up. . . .

⥱

JULY 2, 1962

DEAR ELEANOR:

It seems very quiet and empty here. Cecil and Ann [Grable] came for eggs to take to Hooker, and Mr. McNee gave us a wave as he set out for church. That was all our human companionship until nearly night when Johnnie F. started ploughing across the north road.[36]

I am very grateful for the telephone call, as we could have had no mail before tomorrow and there is always anxiety about the long dangerous trip. We are getting back on the old lonely trail. I have put away nearly all of the extra bedding, silver, dishes etc. Catching up on the first-of-the month's checks for various expenses and have brought the book-keeping up to date—a painful process since Dad determined, as he ought, to learn the process himself. But as I keep the records by the month, and he keeps his by topic (i.e. the various types of expenditures) it is always a dreaded task to [reconcile] and no hope of balancing such accounting.

I go on with the usual routine, doling out the medicine, burning trash, gathering and cleaning eggs, carrying things to the wash house in hope of some lucky week to get them laundered some time. . . .

I am getting more familiar with the electric stove. The hardest thing now seems to be to adjust the heat of the burners to cook without wasting electricity. . . . A few more flowers this morning and I want to get out to do some weeding and cultivating. Dad has reploughed the clover patch and saved a little barley. . . . We looked over all the planted feed crop yesterday. I advised taking what we got, even though an imperfect stand, rather than ploughing it again and starting all over so late. . . .

⋘≋⋙

DEC. 31, 1962

DEAR FRIENDS FROM LONG AGO [THE JAFFES]:

Just a brief word to bring the record up to date. We hope in these troubled times your home is a refuge and inspiration to all who enter its door. Have we ever needed any more than now the gospel of peace and good will justice and mercy and humility, not only between the covers of a book but translated into dedicated human lives?

A bad year for the Hendersons in all ways but still—rather literally—creeping along. Crops were poor, Season too dry, though dust storms not started yet. An accident in October among the cattle left Will with a broken hip, weeks of good care and treatment in hospital at Amarillo, Texas and Elkhart, Kansas. As good progress as we can expect but will be on crutches a long time. Forced to sell the cattle and the place looks bleak and barren, but are glad to be together again. I broke under the overload of work and anxiety and sorrow (about the cattle) and had to go to the hospital myself for nine days. Now I am going on as well as I can with nursing, house work, reduced to lowest terms, and out-of-door work, from chickens to saving fire wood for the old heater!! No oil wells for the Hendersons.

Hope you can look back on a better year and forward to one even more near to your own desires. Love to Wilma and your young people—hardly children, I suspect, any more.

⋘≋⋙

JUNE 21, 1964

DEAR ELEANOR:

Thanks for the pretty violet stationery, the emblem of my native state. We received your letter with enclosures on Sat., and very glad to hear that David had made his trip in safety and apparent comfort. . . .

. . . I am sitting in the shade of the south driveway trying to fight away the swarms of flies, watch the chicks, mostly now out in their little yard, and watch to see the attitude of the cats to these new members of our farm family. So far have shown little interest but it might be tragically different if we were to go away. The babes made it through the last night without watching or fire, though I took a peep at 2:00 a.m. and got up just as they began to stir at 4:45.

We put the cows and bull calves out on the pasture weeds today hoping the farm might thus contribute a meager portion of our living.

The June tamarix is quite lovely now. The earlier one bloomed weeks ago and is making a surprising growth. To our surprise after the burial by the blowing dust the tree and walking stick cactus produced a few lovely rose colored blooms but on the whole flowers are in very short supply.

I've been meaning to tell you of how I spent part of the birthday and Mother's Day money and hope you won't think it too frivolous. . . . I gave to Dad as a family relic, my Uncle William Boa's very heavy old-time Elgin watch. I used it only to time the washing machine. One day it stopped for no apparent reason. . . . The young man in Eva . . . [e]ventually . . . got it put together again and I think took pride in giving it an extra fine cleaning and polishing. But sadly it cost $9.50, really too much for a non-essential expense, and more than I would have felt like spending, with no farm income even in prospect. . . . I would like it if David could have it sometime. . . . For David it could only be a keep sake and a reminder of an earlier day when men put conscience into their work and production and "planned obsolescence" was still in the future. . . .

Dad worked on the pasture fence this morning. Intended to harrow more ground ready for planting this p.m. but afraid to have him attempt it in the heat.

I guess I can't stand the torment of the flies any longer so will bring this disjointed letter to a close. It looks as if your summer is pretty full so won't urge you to try to change your own plans on our account but always longing to see you and talk with you and lately often a strange feeling that you really are here. Love for all the days.

⚬⚬

AUGUST 17, 1964

DEAR ELEANOR:

Dad started out with the old mower to see if he can prevent a small part of the outrageous crop of weed seed from maturing. (Some weeds still in the flowering stage.) An odd feature of the 1964 weed growth is a large . . . basin-like area of old fashioned . . . ("hog persley" to old timers of long ago). It was never common here but plenty of it now.

I don't know how far he will get for the old mower, like the "one-hoss shay" is likely to disintegrate completely at any moment. . . .

Please notice, both of you if possible, the clipping from [Mount Holyoke College] Alumnae Quarterly in <u>Time</u>. I think this Dr. Holmes[37] has been a professor of Psychology for a long time, but seems to have a very sensible, humane point of view and I am in sympathy with much that he wrote 25 years ago and still believe.

This would apply to what he wrote about grading and the danger of too early specialization, and the value of so-called "humanities" as a part of liberal education. . . .

Still guarding the chickens, to the exclusion of about every thing else. . . .

Feed and cover crop would yet respond to an immediate rain—<u>but</u> no rain comes.

The morning glories are pretty every morning though fewer than in days gone by; several volunteer portulacas in different colors have withstood the violence of the spring and heat of summer. One plant is partly draped in a clear bright gold. A few zinnias are beginning to bloom though rather small as yet. Four o clocks look as if they would be blossoming soon. I have to try to be appreciative of what very little we have left. . . .

<hr />

Sept. 5, 1964

Dear Eleanor:

Perhaps I can get in a few words while Dad lingers about getting up for his breakfast. . . .

We have been working hard on the roosters. Have now [dressed and frozen] 28 but have about twice that many yet to do. However it seemed best to interrupt the work for 2–3 days as the canning peaches and other fruits are now in Eva, we hear, and I hate to miss the chance to replenish our dwindling supply. . . .

Everything is getting worse day by day. Scarcely one day passes without some disaster, break down, or hopeless loss. Yesterday Dad undertook to loosen the drain under the sink which has been slow or clogged for a long time and required frequent pumping out. All he accomplished was to break one sealed joint so now it leaks whenever used!

We also discovered the loss at some indefinite time of the small nozzle for the hand spraying outfit—we hoped to use in some small bind weed spots. So it goes.

The one cheerful note is that the red cow, Busybody, found a handsome, smart little calf one night during the week but alas! "She's a boy" when I had hoped so much for a little sister.

Quite a bit of trouble so far as the cow is very jealous of her baby and wants to keep him in the jungle weed growth in the pasture where the coyotes might find him.

The first night we looked about 2 hours and surely 2 miles before I found him in a fringe of weeds in a spot where it seemed no use to look! Last night for the first time the cow brought him home so perhaps the trouble will grow less as he learns to follow his mother. . . .

Must break off here. Try not to be too anxious. There must come "respite and release" sooner or later. . . .

~

JAN. 31, 1965

DEAR ELEANOR:

Thanks for the variety of stationery.

I like this spirited picture of the running horses. I couldn't trust anybody who professes to see beauty or significance in what passes for "Modern Art." A relief or refreshment to find even in <u>Time</u> this week examples of Peter Hurd's work.[38] I think you have one yourself. The little girl with the candle is exquisite. . . .

We pass from one crisis to another. The latest knock down blow is the practical loss of the pick-up which seemed so essential to our work and welfare. We finally got Leonard yesterday to help drag it up to town and the diagnosis was that the crank shaft is "ruined." . . .

. . . I see I can't take much more and Dad is increasingly unreasonable about just everything. Can't seem to face up to disheartening facts. Perhaps he has met too many of them.

Mr. Cole sent out the tax forms and we spent most of the morning on final completion. Will try to mail tomorrow. It cost $25.00 for Fed. and State accounting but I believe was worth it. No income tax but did decide to go on sheltering under the Social Security roof. . . .

Time so soon to get out and care for the chickens again. I get around 5 doz. eggs per day and so far have had a pretty good market but hardly a drop in the bucket as compared with expenses. . . .

~≈~

MARCH 3, 1965

DEAR ELEANOR:

Not much to write about. Just more wind and dirt, though the wind is coming in gusts with intervals of partial clearing between the highest waves of dust. Very upsetting and it has become impossible to make or execute plans. Dad has postponed a trip with eggs to 4 Corners, hoping the early morning may not involve heading right into an almost solid wall of gritty poisonous dust. It is just as hard as ever on hands and they feel like rasps. . . .

Mr. Strothman came home yesterday and is much improved but will need to be careful. The same for Jim Jordan.[39] . . .

Later: It's now evening and we have just finished up the day's work. The wind settled toward nightfall and Dad went for the mail as I was anxious to get the electric bill. Was surprised to find that the promised reduction in rates had gone into effect. For an increased consumption of electric current we were billed for [$]9.15 instead of about [$]12.00 as I expected. They figure the lower rate will encourage increased use and permit a lower rate per KWH.

I have finished the book about discoverers of America and Man Against Nature.[40] I really liked the latter better than the first which required too much conjecture and fanciful imagination. Still it was interesting and represented untold research and opened up many unfamiliar pathways. From the second book one gets a great variety of examples of courageous action in the face of heavy odds. I will send both soon as David may want to refer to them. I have now started "No Room in the Ark"[41] and am enjoying it.

Within the last few days our cat family has been again reduced. "Little Tiger," the handsome but wild tiger kitten disappeared. Probably a coyote was the murderer. The strange cat, Big Buster Blue is also gone so we are down to barely 3 cats. . . .

Friday a.m.: It now looks as if Dad might as well have gone on his round yesterday. Visibility still about a mile so I think he will try to get around before it gets worse.

Pretty cold at 20 degrees; was 16 degrees when I got up. . . .

~≈~

MAY 11, 1965

DEAR ELEANOR:

I've tried so hard (with no success) to think up something special for David's graduation that maybe I'm doing the wrong thing now. I'm sending the Iowa check to protect our Elkhart checking account, as this looks now like another lost year. However, whatever you do with it can be credited to Grandpa as well as to myself. . . .

I'm sorry to be so helpless and can hardly make anyone understand how bad things in general have become. We are both failing fast and may not be able to keep up much longer even the pretense of taking care of ourselves, but still trying. Father seems worse because of his practically total deafness so that I can no longer discuss anything with him and have to let them drift. . . .

The yellow roses, what few are left, are now a mass of fragrant blooms, very large and full. . . .

I want to make a start today on sorting for disposal the masses of old damaged or useless jars in the basement. Those 2–3 days of dipping and lifting were hard on both of us and it seems to me Dad's cough grows daily worse. Aside from the usual digitalis and [?] and Listerine as a mouth wash, we aren't doing any thing, following your example of <u>ignoring</u> the discomforts for both of us as much as we can. But it doesn't bring much relief. . . .

JUNE 17, 1965

DEAR ELEANOR:

Another droopy disappointing day. We surely hoped to get to the field work (ploughing and planting) during this week. But we had another good brief shower (perhaps .50") early Tuesday morning so everything soaked up again and the bathroom drainage drowned out again! We hoped for some progress today but still the surface soil very sticky and it creates a difficult problem if worked too wet by practically turning into concrete! . . .

The ground has been too wet and my joints too painful to get down to business on my few little seedlings but they will have to be weeded and thinned out if they come to anything. Can't get down through the pools and puddles to examine the wheat so do not know whether any of it withstood the excess of moisture. . . .

We have tried to do a little cleaning while waiting for the ground today. Have given so far a sort of half-hearted cleaning to the upstairs room, front porch, bathroom and a start on the living room. . . . I'm trying as we go along to sort out what are definitely your books, photographs etc. and put them in your room upstairs. I should tell you and must tell Mrs. Williams not to feel any obligation to send reading material. My eyes have failed so fast that I've had to cut down on reading to little more than the leading articles and <u>Essay</u> in <u>Time</u>. And Dad has given up the long hours of night reading and we still have mountains of magazines that I may never be able to read. . . .

. . . So everything is quite uncertain when I long for peace and quietness and stability. I do hope Father will feel better in the morning. I couldn't get him to use any aspirin for relief. . . .

. . . Looking for some word from David and hope he fits in <u>OK</u> to the college classes. They may seem harder than at High School.

Wish he could have a Saturday <u>outdoor</u> job to earn what he can.

AUG. 1, 1965

DEAR ELEANOR:

Another hot and desolate day—all to our lonely selves. When we don't hear from you it is hard to find material for a letter, but I know you are having a trying time. . . .

Nothing very good here either. We are both quite weakened by our struggles, either with asthma or a desperate cough,—I believe largely the result of working with the dusty wheat—sometimes moldy and unfit for use, . . . but perhaps can be used cautiously in chicken feed. . . . Am still quite weak and don't gain strength as I'd like to, but manage to carry out the routine work of the home and help as I can with outdoor tasks.

My little zinnia bed is quite a show with a large variety of colors and types. So far have had 3 kinds of gladiolus all very lovely, and have discovered two more small buds emerging.

I am writing with the new glasses in action, but not sure they help very much. And they are almost useless for reading except for one book, <u>Wild America</u>,[42] which seems to have type that fits my eyes and the lenses OK. Very different with <u>Time</u> which I can hardly read at all. . . .

We had reason to hope for a good rain for the feed crop—just now in need of encouragement, but the moisture was cut off with only a light shower.

We have two baffling tasks, hardly suitable for people in our condition. One is to spray several bind weed spots in the prospective wheat fields (for 1966); the other is to clean out the basement from the ravages of the May flooding. Plenty more but those are the worst. Do write when you can. You can't think how we have missed the letters!

Monday, 8:00 a.m.—Cool this morning at 42 degrees. Dad is taking his after breakfast treatment of heating pad and hot water bottle for his asthma. . . .

You might like to know that Dad had a lot of coarse rough baling twine from the last hay and he took it and <u>wove</u> a nice solid bottom for the old <u>chaise lounge</u>r you brought for our front porch. Have not used it yet as need to fit in some softer padding to make it comfortable. . . .

⇌

Oct. 13, 1965

Dear Eleanor:

We received your letter on Sat. after getting the later card on Friday! . . . Superficially I'd say Father is a good deal better with more rest and home treatments and less dust. But at times he goes back to the strong, <u>puffing outward</u> of his breath, whether from necessity or the desire to keep me stirred up. He rests very well at night—so far as we can judge. But he never admits that anything does him any good, yet will not consider kicking over the whole apple cart as possibly we should do and join the camps of the <u>retired</u>.

Of course everything at a dead halt. He got his shop work done on Sat. but when he got it together again he found the elevator canvas in such bad shape it was useless to try to start. So Sunday was wasted on that. We debated whether to try cutting this a.m. or start for town but wind came up early so hoped it might subside during the p.m. . . .

⇌

Dec. 12, 1965

Dear Eleanor:

Again I must try the almost impossible task of writing. The letter of Friday quickly became out of date and I was ashamed of its bitterness so I burned it up.

The check is intended to cover at least partially, Lee's offered help in our time of harvest necessity, that is getting in the baled hay. One can't be blamed for failure where the task is plainly <u>impossible</u>. . . .

I have had no chance for a face-to-face agreement regarding payment for the care-taking work here, in the present crisis. But I think you know we aim to be fair and reasonable. With much of the food and all fuel provided he should be able to save all he earns. If he should prefer to go to Four Corners three times a day for meals it would make some difference in our figuring but could not find fault as our need is so urgent. Lee would feel proud if he knew how welcome this decision is to the neighborhood. One nice woman called it "Perfect" and I do hope it will work out satisfactorily.[43]

I have a very dim hope of ever coming back to my long beloved home and have the burden of believing that the diagnosis was too long delayed and faulty, but that is over now and cannot be compensated for.

Thanks for the cards and letter recently received. The maple leaf is lovely, though I still don't understand the technique. Christmas cards are drifting in like early snowflakes.

Mr. and Mrs. H. will take us to the train.[44] Be sure to verify my own memories. <u>For Jan, 3, 1966</u> "Limited"—westward through Guymon at 6:30 a.m. Arrive at Phoenix around 11:00 p.m. Know nothing about management of tickets, reservations, etc.

There is really now very little in the way of actual heavy farm work. The payments, on Lee's own terms, will be for taking responsibility and for dependability about watering plants, care of gas, electric and wood fires; . . . four head of cattle and always our dearly beloved Jack; if Lee will pet him a little at the start, I think Jack will respond. He is very affectionate. Lee should allow about two days before we start to get used to the routine. . . .

P.S. I feel as if I must remind you that the only thing that caused me to consent to this search for renewed health was your firm agreement there should be <u>no operating</u>, and I believe the nitrogen injection would be as bad.

⤙⥲⤚

FORM LETTER FROM DR. ELEANOR GRANDSTAFF TO VARIED CORRESPONDENTS OF CAROLINE HENDERSON

DEC. 1966

DEAR FRIENDS:

It has taken me a long time to bring myself to write to my parents' old friends and break to them the sorrowful news that Caroline and

Wilhelmine (Will) Henderson have both passed away during 1966. When I was in Oklahoma in September 1965, things seemed about as usual, my mother more frail and complaining of some abdominal pain but going about her work about as usual. We tried to get her to go to the doctor while I was there but she refused. Later she became worse and consulted the doctor, [who] diagnosed an abdominal tumor and strongly advised that she come to me. December 15 they abandoned their home and came by train, expecting to be gone only a little while. However she was then so frail and confused I saw they could not make it alone in Oklahoma so kept them here for the winter. She apparently had a very large tumor of the spleen, felt inadvisable to operate. My father felt fine, very alert, got to go out on several little trips, and this was probably the best time he had ever had. Mother failed completely, both physically and mentally, very rapidly. In March I took them to Oklahoma briefly to attend to some of their business. Father finally made up his mind to stay with me permanently, was very happy after he made up his mind, anticipating much pleasure here with me, rode off without a backward glance. Three days later he passed away suddenly on March 17 of a massive coronary thrombosis. My mother realized only briefly that he was gone, we did not think it advisable to attend the funeral on her part, and she never remembered again that he was gone, finally no longer knew where she was or recognized her friends, sometimes did not recognize me. I was then unable to care for her, she passed peaceful away in a rest home on August 4, had wasted away terrifically even though she had had good care.

For my part, . . . I have had a rather difficult time alone here, my only comforts my pride in a fine son, and my memories of a wonderful and inspiring pair of parents. "Death is not extinguishing the light: It is putting out the lamp because the dawn has come."[45] Tagore

Best of wishes to you for the New Year as we join our memories of those wonderful ones who have gone before.

Epilogue

The house, the barn, and a few sheds still stand where Caroline Henderson spent most of her life. The now abandoned buildings bear mute testimony to her and Will's efforts but also to the power of the elements, which will eventually wear away the remaining evidence of the Henderson's presence on the land. The homestead has been placed in trust, ensuring that it will never again be plowed. Thus, those who visit that setting will always see something more akin to the deserted Colorado village Caroline described in her master's thesis than the prosperous farm she had envisioned. Indeed, a visit to Caroline's homestead can lead us back to her thoughts on those villagers' vain efforts and from there to her thoughts about the meaning of her own life.

Working on her thesis while the dust storms threatened an immediate end to her own dreams, Caroline wrote feelingly about the village: "It still seems impossible not to feel regret for the unfruitful toil, the disappointed dreams, the forced, abandonment of plans which had called forth so much of human effort." She then cited a historian who argued that the villagers' efforts should not be counted failures, as they had been pathfinders, paving the way for the future. She qualified her endorsement of that view, however, with a revealing "perhaps."[1]

Much of the sense of defeat that dominated the last years of Caroline's life echoed the ambivalence she felt about the efforts of homesteading an unforgiving land. Even though her published writing assured that she left much more than an eroding physical record of her presence on the land, her conclusions about her own life's work were pessimistic, even harsh. Yet we must heed her assessment, for one cannot casually dismiss the conclusions of a person with the qualities of mind Caroline Henderson demonstrated throughout her life. The same woman who was able to ponder Nazi totalitarianism while await-ing the birth of a calf also seemed to conclude that either she herself had failed, the Jeffersonian vision had failed her, or both.[2] She also indicated that her education, which she so treasured, had not served her well in the life she chose.

There are probably no final answers to the questions inherent in the doubts Caroline expressed. Certainly, the Great Plains have proven hostile to many aspects of the Jeffersonian vision. The dust bowl was only the most conspicuous of the regular challenges to creating and preserving the quality of life that nineteenth-century pioneers envi-sioned. Moreover, the economic forces of the twentieth century have destroyed the hopes of the vast majority of those people who have sought to build a way of life in agriculture. Thus, it is easy to under-stand why Caroline might conclude that her education did not pro-vide the tools she needed for such circumstances.

Instead of answers, then, we are left with two measurements of success that might add dimensions of meaning to Caroline's life that she was unable to see. First, she persisted where countless others failed, maintaining throughout her life an active and curious mind, a keen appreciation for beauty, and an undying thirst for justice. Much more than a pathfinder who prepared the way for others, she managed to fulfill the spirit of the Jeffersonian ideal that had shaped her. She demonstrated that education, ideas, and literature could remain sources of joy, just as the scent "of new ploughed ground" continued to inspire her long after her youth had vanished and its dreams had died. That enduring achievement provides far more meaning than would have any ultimate success measured in yields or profits. For those values have been preserved in the words she left behind and in her example, which is an enduring testimony to human integrity in the face of adversity.

Caroline could have found a second measure of success in her faith. Even though she largely withdrew from most of the comforts of conventional religion, she never left it completely behind. And she retained a broader faith in the meaning of life; besides the numerous examples that could be cited from her writing included herein, she also preserved three college papers that addressed that belief. Written between October 1930 and April 1931, each questioned the meaning of life when its promise does not seem fulfilled.[3] Her firmest answer to such questions came in the last paper, entitled "Things Not Seen." Here she asked, "Is it in vain that the flowers bloom by the edge of alpine glaciers or on the Siberian meadows, where no one sees their color or enjoys their fragrance?" She first averred that the value of beauty and goodness may extend far beyond our sight. She then concluded that "we should be grateful for all such flowerings of the spirit of man, both for their own sake, and for what they suggest of a beauty unrealized, of even fairer flowers growing abundantly on the higher uplands of the individual life." I can think of no more fitting words to summarize the meaning of Caroline Henderson's life.

Notes

Introduction

1. Henderson, "Bringing in the Sheaves" (see page 96); Henderson and Harris, "Letters of Two Women Farmers I" (see page 106); Henderson and Harris, "Letters of Two Women Farmers II" (see page 113); Henderson, "Letters from the Dust Bowl," *Atlantic Monthly,* (see page 147); Henderson, "Letters from the Dust Bowl," *Reader's Digest* (not included herein); Henderson, "Our Own Letter from the Dust Bowl," (see page 159); Henderson, "Spring in the Dust Bowl," (see page 163).

2. Henry A. Wallace to Caroline A. Henderson, May 1, 1936, Grandstaff Collection; Caroline A. Henderson to Eleanor Grandstaff, September 15, 1959 (not included herein), Grandstaff Collection, (hereinafter cited as Henderson to Grandstaff); Johnson, *Heaven's Table Land*, 189–91; Worster, *Dust Bowl*, 110 n, 22, 130 n; Rister, *No Man's Land*, 184–85, 188; Bonnifield, *The Dust Bowl*, 60, 87, 89, 160, 169, 187; Hurt, *The Dust Bowl*, 66; Watkins, *The Great Depression*, 189, 192.

3. For a discussion of this see Lookinbill, "Likely Stories."

4. Morgan and Strickland, *Oklahoma Memories*, 223.

5. Wallace to Henderson, May 1, 1936, Grandstaff Collection.

6. Smith, *Virgin Land*, 126–32, 156–57, 215.

7. Grandstaff, interview; Henderson, edited and introduced by Purdy, "Dust To Eat," 440–42; *The History of Plymouth and Woodbury Counties [Iowa]*, 916.

8. Ibid; "The Third Class Letter," March 1909, Caroline A. Henderson Papers.

9. Smith, *Virgin Land*, 126–32, 156–57, 215.

10. Grandstaff, interview.

11. Ibid; Henderson to Rose Alden, August 17, 1908, (see page 35), Caroline A. Henderson Papers (hereinafter cited as Henderson to Rose Alden).

12. Grandstaff, interview.

13. Henderson to Grandstaff, January 13, 1951 (see page 196).

14. Henderson, "The Day When The Well Runs Dry," March 13, 1931 (see page 100).

15. Henderson, "What I Read Last Year," 369.

16. Henderson to Grandstaff, January 1 and January 16, 1952 (not included herein).

17. Henderson, "The Love of the Soil," 5, 49–50, 90.

18. Ibid.; see also Henderson to Rose Alden, August 17, 1908 (see page 35).

19. Henderson to Grandstaff, November 8, 1957 (not included herein); Walter Prescott Webb, "The American West," 37–38.

20. Rainey, *No Man's Land*, 121–34, 214–27; Oklahoma Department of Commerce Web site, "Demographic Forum, C: City Population Estimates, Historical Census Population—City by County, 1890–1990." Available at: http://www.odoc.state.ok.us/osdc.htm.

21. Ibid.

22. Henderson to Ways and Means Editor, July 16, 1913, as printed in *Ladies' World*, February 1914, 14 (see page 50).

23. Ways and Means Editor to Henderson, July 29, 1913, and October 7, 1913, as printed in *Ladies' World*, February 1914, 14.

24. Henderson, "A Little Turkey Talk," "Turkeys for Profit," and four untitled pieces, *Practical Farmer*. Broomcorn is a grass producing stalks as high as twelve feet tall, with a flowering head, called the brush, that is used in the manufacture of brooms.

25. Apparently, *Ladies' World* paid ten to fifteen dollars for Caroline's initial submissions and probably more once she gained status as a columnist.

26. See, for example, the columns published in September 1914, June 1916, April 1917, November 1917, and January 1918 (see pages 68, 79, 81, 83, 84). Other such references may be found in columns published in August 1914, December 1914, February 1916, May 1917, and July 1917.

27. Rose Alden, "Dusty September—An Oklahoma Memory," unpublished manuscript, Henderson Papers; Grandstaff, interview.

28. Grandstaff, interview. One local informant assured me in 1997 that he was absolutely certain that the Hendersons had never married, though available records in the Texas County Courthouse disagreed; his statement reflects continuing local distancing from the Hendersons.

29. Henderson, "The Love of the Soil," 46; Matthew 25:40, King James Version (KJV). See another example of her concern with the issue (as early as 1918) in Henderson, "The Homestead Lady's Scribbling Pad," *Ladies' World*, January 1918 (see page 84).

30. Henderson, "The Woman Who Raised Her Hand," (see page 87).

31. Grandstaff, interview. Caroline's letters to Rev. Peabody were not available for inclusion herein.

32. See Henderson to Rose Alden, January 20 and December 22, 1912 (see pages 41, 47); Grevstad's father was Nicolay A. Grevstad, editor of the leading Scandinavian newspaper in the United States at the time and ambassador to Uruguay and Paraguay in 1911. Her husband, Anders L. Mordt,

promoted Norse Colonies in Oklahoma and Texas. Her move from Guymon about 1911 undoubtedly was in connection with her husband's promotion efforts in Hansford County, Texas; see Peter L. Petersen, "A New Oslo on the Plains."

33. See, for example, Henderson to Rose Alden, August 11, 1912 (see page 45).

34. For examples of Caroline's views on education, see *Ladies' World*, Spring 1914 and June 1916 (see pages 66, 79).

35. Grandstaff, interview.

36. Ibid; Henderson, assorted unpublished graduate papers, Grandstaff Collection.

37. Henderson, "Bringing in the Sheaves." Between 1929 and 1932, farm prices declined by 53 percent, resulting in a 70 percent decline in net farm income; see Green, "Great Depression," 162–66.

38. Henderson and Harris, "Letters of Two Women Farmers I" and "Letters of Two Women Farmers II" (see pages 106, 113); assorted clippings from unidentified publication, July 29, 1934, May 17, 1941, March 6, 1944, July 30, 1952, and November 10, 1954, Evelyn Harris file; *New York Times*, August 5, 1934. Harris would later publish *The Barter Lady;* see also Henderson to Rose Alden, December 12, 1932 (see page 119).

39. The annual amounts during these years were as follows: 1933: 12.89 inches; 1934: 13.05 inches; 1935: 14.05 inches; 1936: 12.49 inches; 1937: 12.37 inches.

40. Worster, *Dust Bowl,* 11–30; Rosenberg, ed., *North American Droughts,* 11–12, 20.

41. Henderson, edited and introduced by Purdy, "Dust To Eat," 440–42.

42. Henderson, "Spring in the Dust Bowl," *Atlantic Monthly,* June 1937 (see page 163).

43. Oklahoma Department of Commerce Web site, "Demographic Forum, C: City Population Estimates, Historical Census Population— City by County, 1890–1990." Available at: *http://www.odoc.state.ok.us/osdc.htm.*

44. Henderson to Harris, June 10, 1932, as printed in "Letters of Two Women Farmers I" (see page 109).

45. Henderson, "Letters from the Dust Bowl," *Atlantic Monthly,* May 1936 (see page 147); Henderson, "Letters from the Dust Bowl," *Reader's Digest,* 19–21 (not included herein); Henderson, "Our Own Letter from the Dust Bowl," (see page 159) 14–15, 45; Henderson, "Spring in the Dust Bowl," (see page 163).

46. Henderson, "The Love of the Soil," 59.

47. Ibid., 68.

48. Ibid., 4.

49. Henderson to Rose Alden, December 20, 1936 (see page 163); Henderson, "The Love of the Soil," 54.

50. Undated clipping, *Wichita Eagle*, ca. 1936, Grandstaff Collection.

51. Jaffe, *Oklahoma Odyssey*, 60–61.

52. Ibid, 15–29.

53. Ibid, 96–106, 145–57. See also Henderson to Jaffe, May 3, 1941; May 26, 1941; ca. winter 1941–1942, (see pages 179–81), Eli Jaffe Collection (hereafter cited as Henderson to Jaffe).

54. Grandstaff, interview; Henderson to Grandstaff, October 7, 1959 (not included herein).

55. Henderson to Grandstaff, January 28, 1950 (see page 193); miscellaneous Henderson financial records, Grandstaff Collection.

56. Henderson to Grandstaff, June 18, 1952 (not included herein).

57. Henderson to Grandstaff, ca. July 1950 (not included herein).

58. Henderson, "Bubbles," *Ladies' World*, ca. Spring 1914 (not included herein); see also Henderson, "Relaxation," Ladies' World (see page 66).

59. Will Henderson to Grandstaff, ca. March 1950, Grandstaff Collection.

60. Henderson to Grandstaff, November 28, 1958 (not included herein).

61. Henderson to Grandstaff, October 13, 1965 (not included herein).

62. Miscellaneous Henderson financial records, Grandstaff Collection.

63. Henderson to Grandstaff, April 28, 1950 (see page 194), August 9, 1951 (not included herein), March 9, 1952 (see page 207), March 1, 1959 (not included herein); Henderson to Jaffe, June 29, 1955 (not included herein).

64. Robinson, *The Unitarians and the Universalists*, 149–50, 174–81; Henderson to Grandstaff, ca. September 1951 , February 17, 1952, and March 31, 1959 (not included herein); c.f. her comments on religious explanations for the dust bowl in "Dust to Eat," July 26, 1935 (see page 140) and her expression of concern about the blizzard's impact on wildlife in her April 14, 1957, letter to Rose Alden (see page 221).

65. Henderson to Grandstaff, October 15, 1951, November 3, 1951, March 3, 1952 (not included herein), April 23, 1952 (see page 209), and March 11, 1957 (not included herein).

66. Miscellaneous Henderson financial records, Grandstaff Collection; Henderson, "The Love of the Soil," 64; Henderson to Jaffe, February 6, ca. 1951 (see page 198), and ca. 1955 (not included herein); see also Henderson to Grandstaff, March 8, 1957 (see page 218).

67. Henderson to Grandstaff, May 6, 1958.

68. Henderson to Grandstaff, December 12, 1965 (see page 238); Grandstaff to assorted Henderson correspondents, December 1966 (see page 239), Jaffe Collection.

Chapter 1: Beginnings, 1908–1914

1. Henderson, "A Little Turkey Talk," "Turkeys for Profit," and, four untitled pieces, *Practical Farmer*.

2. Henderson, "What I Read Last Year," 369 (see page 44); Henderson, "Our Homestead" (see page 51).

3. Rose Alden materials, Alumni Files.

4. Ibid.; Henderson to Rose Alden as excerpted by Rose Alden, May 1945.

5. Caroline usually wrote at least one letter every year to both Rose and Mrs. Alden. Her last letters to each were written in 1957 and 1932, respectively.

6. Unidentified reference.

7. Besides broomcorn, the primary feed source for bisons at that time, the Hendersons and their neighbors raised a wide variety of crops. Hegira, maize, and kafir (often erroneously referred to as Kafir corn) were all raised as livestock and poultry feed. Corn and cane were raised primarily for that purpose as well, but each was also regularly consumed by humans. Corn was probably the most versatile of the crops, and cane could be used to make syrup. The evolution from such agricultural diversity to wheat monoculture probably intensified the impact of the dust bowl.

8. Grisell McLaren was a Mount Holyoke classmate of Caroline and Rose's; she had graduated in 1898.

9. Alice Browne was possibly another classmate of Caroline and Rose's; I was not able to discover her "sad story."

10. Probably Mabel Gilbert, Mount Holyoke class of 1901.

11. "Cave" is an archaic term for cellar.

12. Unidentified; probably a child from Caroline and Rose's hometown of Kinsley, Iowa.

13. Mount Holyoke graduate, class of 1903.

14. Here Caroline refers to Robert Louis Stevenson, *Child's Garden of Verses* (New York: Charles Scribner's Sons, 1905) and probably Sam F. Woolard, *Pictures of Memory* (Wichita, Kans.: Goldsmith-Woolard, 1908).

15. These were all popular periodicals in the time Caroline was writing.

16. Isaiah 40:29, KJV.

17. *Outlook Magazine* was a popular periodical of the era.

18. The *Century Magazine* was a widely circulated magazine that generally dealt with literary, political, and similar content.

19. Dried cow manure was a regular source of fuel for pioneers and was used by some families to supplement coal through the 1930s.

20. Caroline's father had died earlier that year; see letter of August 11, 1912.

21. Pie-plant or pie-melon is rhubarb, often used as pie filling or made into jellies, jams, butters, etc. in much the same process as the better-known apple butter.

22. Unidentified reference (but see Matthew 6:34).

23. Homesteaders gained title to their lands after five years of possession by establishing their compliance with related legal provisions, including

proven residence and improvements to the property. Part of this process, referred to as "proving up," required a sequence of notices in newspapers to inform those who might wish to challenge the homesteader's claim.

24. Romans 5:3, KJV.

25. Unidentified reference.

26. Maria Montessori, *The Montessori Method* (New York: Frederick A. Stokes, 1912). Caroline's letter was written from Ponca City, where she was visiting her mother and earning extra income working for a physician, apparently as a clerk, in the time before beginning her regular columns for *Ladies' World*.

27. Marguerite Audoux, *Marie-Claire* (New York: Grossett & Dunlap, 1911); Mary Antin, *The Promised Land* (Boston: Houghton-Mifflin, 1912). *Marie-Claire* was the first in a series of popular novels featuring the title character, Marie Claire.

Chapter 2: Hopeful Years, 1914–1928

1. Several of these columns are found in the Henderson Scrapbook, Grandstaff Collection.

2. Walt Whitman, "Carol of Words," from *Leaves of Grass* (n.p.: T. Y. Crowell & Co., 1902).

3. Richard Henry Dana, Jr. *Two Years Before the Mast* (New York: P.F. Collier & Son, 1909), 38.

4. Ecclesiastes 11:4, KJV.

5. Psalm 19:1 and Isaiah 30:15, KJV.

6. Thomas Carlyle, unidentified passage.

7. Jacob Riis, *The Making of an American* (New York: Macmillan, 1901); Booker T. Washington, *Up From Slavery* (New York: Doubleday-Pope & Co., 1903).

8. Isaiah 55:2, KJV.

9. The Russian thistle, one of the plants that produces the tumbleweed, was generally regarded as a weed by farmers but could be drawn on for fodder, as the Hendersons and others found during the dust bowl years and other times when feed crops failed.

10. Elkhart, Kansas, is about twenty miles north of the Henderson farm and is the closest location offering banking and many comparable services.

11. The state school lands were tracts that were originally removed from settlement to be used to support the public schools.

12. John Muir, *Stickeen: The Story of a Dog* (Boston: Houghton-Mifflin, 1909).

13. Isaiah 41:6–7, KJV.

14. Ephesians 4:3, KJV.

15. Matthew 20:12, KJV.

16. Caroline was primarily offended by the evangelist's attitude, but she also used his mistaken references to the *Titanic* here and similar factual errors in the following to emphasize the level of his general ignorance.

17. Christopher Morley, *The Haunted Bookshop* (New York: Doubleday, Page & Co., 1919).

18. Ole Rölvaag, *Giants in the Earth: A Saga of the Prairies* (New York: Harper & Bros., 1927); Knut Hamsun, *Growth of the Soil* (New York: Modern Library, 1921). Henderson would later incorporate ideas from *Giants in the Earth* into her Master's thesis.

19. Carl Sandburg, *Abraham Lincoln: The Prairie Years.* (New York: Harcourt, Brace & Co., 1928).

Chapter 3: Clouded Horizons, 1930–1933

1. Unidentified University of Kansas faculty note on "The Day When the Well Runs Dry," March 1931.

2. Evelyn Harris File; *New York Times*, August 5, 1934; see also Henderson to Rose Alden, December 12, 1932 (later in this chapter).

3. Unidentified reference. Probably Joseph Klausner, author of the later book, *The Messianic Idea in Israel: from its beginning to the completion of the Mishnah* (New York: Macmillan, 1955).

4. Stephen Vincent Benet, *John Brown's Body* (Garden City, N.Y: Doubleday, Doran & Co., 1928).

5. Isaac Watts, "When I Survey the Wondrous Cross," *Hymns of Praise* (St. Louis, Mo.: Christian Board of Publication, 1921).

6. Rupert Brooke, "The Great Lover," in *The Collected Poems of Rupert Brooke* (New York: Dodd, Mead, 1928).

7. Ecclesiastes 5:19, KJV.

8. Unidentified source.

9. An oft-repeated phrase signaling President Herbert Hoover's effort to assure the American people that the Depression would be a short-term phenomena. See Caroline's concern about this matter in her December 15, 1931, letter to Rose Alden (see page 103); see also Watkins, *The Great Depression*, 64.

10. Citations were not available for these publications.

11. Probably a faculty member at Mount Holyoke.

12. Shakespeare, *King Richard III*, act 1, scene 1, line 1.

13. William Charles Beebe (1877–1962), a naturalist who headed scientific explorations in the Americas and elsewhere, wrote several books of popular science.

14. Sir Walter Scott, *The Heart of Midlothian* (New York: P. F. Collier, 1900).

15. Unidentified Henderson correspondent.

16. This phrase is the one that Henderson assumed jeopardized publica-

tion of these letters; see Henderson to Rose Alden, December 12, 1932 (see page 119).

17. Unidentified source.

18. Explanations for the Depression included charges that families were hoarding money and other resources; see Helen M. Burns, "Banking," in Graham and Wander, *Franklin D. Roosevelt*, 20–22.

19. Christina Rossetti, "Up-hill," *Macmillan's Magazine*, February 1861.

20. Such actions ultimately led to the elimination of telephone service to most of rural Texas County. The Hendersons did not gain telephone service again for at least twenty years.

21. The grasshopper invasion reached such levels in 1937 that farmers spread 175 tons of poison in adjacent Beaver County, Oklahoma; Bonnifield, *The Dust Bowl*, 84–85.

22. Percy Bysshe Shelley, "Rosalind and Helen," lines 66–67.

23. John Masefield, "On Growing Old," in *Enslaved* (New York: Macmillan, 1920).

24. Unidentified reference.

25. In August 1932, the Iowa Farmer's Union had launched a statewide protest and "farmer's holiday"—blocking roads, dumping milk, and organizing other actions across the state under the slogan, "Stay at Home—Buy Nothing—Sell Nothing." Watkins, *The Great Depression*, 118.

26. William Wordsworth, "Lines Written a Few Miles Above Tintern Abbey," line 32.

27. Pearl S. Buck, *The Good Earth* (New York: John Day Co., 1932).

28. In November 1933 Secretary of the Interior Harold Ickes vetoed a proposal to build dams in the Oklahoma Panhandle, arguing that the government should move people out of the area, letting it revert to public domain. See Worster, *Dust Bowl*, 42.

29. Probably John Muir, *The Story of My Boyhood and Youth* (Boston: Houghton, Mifflin, 1913); see also Fred Smith, *Boyhood of A Naturalist* (London: Blackie & Son, 1901).

30. Joseph Husband, *America at Work* (Boston: Houghton, Mifflin, 1915).

31. E. Stanley Jones, *The Christ of the Indian Road* (New York: Abingdon Press, 1925).

32. Pearl S. Buck, *Sons* (New York: John Day Co., 1931); Buck, *The Good Earth*.

Chapter 4: Dust to Eat, 1935–1937

1. Undated and unnamed clipping, probably from the *Wichita Eagle*, ca. 1936, Grandstaff Collection.

2. Graham and Wander, *Franklin D. Roosevelt*, passim; see especially 1–5, 65–66, 76–79.

3. Oklahoma Department of Commerce Web site, "Demographic Forum, C: City Population Estimates, Historical Census Population—City by County, 1890–1990." Available at: *http://www.odoc.state.ok.us/osdc.htm.*

4. Undated and unnamed clipping, probably from the *Wichita Eagle*, ca. 1936, Grandstaff Collection.

5. William Vaughn Moody, "Gloucester Moors," *Gloucester Moors & Other Poems* (Boston: Houghton, Mifflin, 1910).

6. Ecclesiastes 12:5, KJV.

7. See Bonnifield, *The Dust Bowl*, 132–35.

8. *Listing* refers to the use of a lister plow, which throws the earth to both sides of a furrow and permits greater moisture retention in the soil. This technique was especially helpful when combined with contour plowing, which followed the lay of the land rather than straight lines.

9. See I Kings 17:8–16, KJV.

10. William Cowper, "The Solitude of Alexander Selkirk," lines 1–2.

11. Prussic acid, better known as hydrogen cyanide, is an extremely poisonous compound.

12. See Bonnifield, *The Dust Bowl*, 132–35; Worster, *Dust Bowl*, 133–37.

13. Shakespeare, Sonnet 94, lines 9–10.

14. Caroline is probably referring to the soil erosion program of the Soil Conservation Service. The Soil Erosion service had been created under provisions of the NIRA and placed under the Department of the Interior. In March 1935, its management was transferred to the Department of Agriculture and its duties were combined with those of the Soil Conservation Services. See National Archives and Records Administration Web site, "General Records of the Soil Erosion Service and the Soil Conservation Service, 1915–77." *www.nara.gov/guide/rg114.html#114.2.*

15. Henry A. Wallace was secretary of agriculture and Rexford Tugwell served as head of the Resettlement Administration.

16. Alfred Lord Tennyson, "Ulysses," lines 62–69: "It may be that the gulfs will wash us down; / It may be we shall touch the Happy Isles, / And see the great Achilles, whom we knew. / Though much is taken, much abides; and though / We are not now that strength which in old days / Moved earth and heaven; that which we are, we are; — / One equal temper of heroic hearts, / Made weak by time and fate, but stong in will / To strive, to seek, to find, and not to yield."

17. Dust devils are small heat-produced spirals of dust that spin across the prairies even when prevailing winds in the region are relatively still.

18. Other sources noted declines in manners, personal cleanliness, and other related standards reflecting social deterioration; see Bonnifield, *The Dust Bowl*, 75, 191.

19. Caroline's reference to the Rehabilitation Service is unclear. She could be referring to efforts of the Resettlement Administration, which tried both

to reform land use practices and to help those who suffered from land exhaustion and other problems. However, she could also be referring to varied efforts supervised by the Soil Conservation Services.

20. Alexis Carrel, *Man, the Unknown* (New York: Harper & Bros., 1925).

21. U.S. Secretary of State Cordell Hull (1933–1944) implemented President Roosevelt's Good Neighbor Policy to improve ties with Latin America. Here Caroline is probably referring to plans for the Inter-American Conference for the Maintenance of Peace, which was held in Buenos Aires, Argentina, in 1936. Hull's vision for international cooperation was ultimately fulfilled in the creation of the United Nations. See Francis L. Loewenheim, "Cordell Hull," and John Edward Wilz, "Good Neighbor Policy," both in Graham and Wander, *Franklin D. Roosevelt*, 191–94.

22. Edgar Lee Masters (1869–1950), unidentified poem.

23. Robert Frost, "Good-by and Keep Cold," line 29: "Something has to be left to God."

Chapter 5: Slow and Partial Recovery, 1938–1951

1. Undated and unnamed clipping, probably from the *Wichita Eagle*, ca. 1936, Grandstaff Collection.

2. Virginia Woolf, *The Years* (New York: Oxford University Press, Inc., 1931).

3. William "Uncle Bill" Baker was county agent for Cimarron County; see Worster, *Dust Bowl*, 101.

4. John Milton, *Paradise Lost*, book 1, line 108.

5. Dr. John Ise was professor of economics at the University of Kansas.

6. Nora Waln, *Reaching for the Stars* (Boston: Little, Brown & Co., 1939).

7. John Steinbeck, *The Grapes of Wrath* (New York: Viking Press, 1939).

8. The U.S.S.R. had signed a non-aggression pact with Nazi Germany on August 23, 1939; that event convinced many people, Caroline included, of Russia's evil intentions. It also proved to be the beginning of the end of widespread support for Communism among Americans such as Jaffe. However, Jaffe was not yet willing to abandon his faith in Communism.

9. Arthur Hugh Clough, "Say not the struggle naught availeth," line 9.

10. Isaiah 61:3, KJV.

11. The family depicted in John Steinbeck's *Grapes of Wrath.*

12. See Thomas Hardy, "The Breaking of Nations," lines 1–4.

13. Jaffe had been arrested August 17, 1940, and released on bail in December. Caroline apparently had either just been informed of those events or refers to some related development, adding to her and Jaffe's concerns.

14. Jaffe and three others had been charged with criminal syndicalism. Oklahoma's law against criminal syndicalism had been passed amid

post–World War I hysteria and prohibited any organization or activity that sought to bring about political or economic change by force.

15. A phrase from President Roosevelt's second inaugural address that gained widespread use, referring to the need of people suffering from the Depression. See Graham and Wander, *Franklin D. Roosevelt*, 202.

16. Caroline had just received word that an Oklahoma County Court had convicted Jaffe of criminal syndicalism for which he received a five thousand dollar fine and a ten-year sentence in the state penitentiary. Jaffe remained free on appeal until February 1943, when the Oklahoma Court of Criminal Appeals overturned his conviction. The court ruled that Jaffe and the others arrested with him had not been shown to advocate violence and that membership in an organization was not adequate to establish guilt under the law. See Jaffe, *Oklahoma Odyssey*, 154–55.

17. Bob Woods had been arrested with Jaffe and was sentenced to ten years in prison in October 1940.

18. Unidentified reference.

19. Jaffe had requested Caroline's review of a draft of his dust bowl novel, *Full Is the Earth*. She sent eight pages of criticism. The draft of the novel, which was never published, can be found in the Jaffe Collection.

20. Under the wartime gasoline rationing system in use at the time, an A card entitled one to three gallons of gasoline per week.

21. "V. mail" refers to a system employed by the military during the Second World War to maintain mail contact between service personnel and their families while reducing the volume of the mail. This was accomplished by V-mail, which used pre-printed envelopes/sheets that could be photographed and transferred to microfilm for shipping. First employed by British forces, V-mail was adopted by the U.S. Post Office in June 1942. See the Smithsonian National Postal Museum Web site, "V-mail: Learn More about It." Available at: *www.si.edu/postal/learnmore/vmail.html*.

22. This somewhat ambiguous statement appears to be Caroline's effort to make the statements of the day about the contributions of diverse people even more inclusive; thus, she added "no religion" to embrace the efforts of those like Jaffe who were not identified with particular religious traditions or even denied any religious claims.

23. Edgar Lee Masters, unidentified reference.

24. Bernard Devoto, *The Year of Decision, 1846* (Boston: Little, Brown and Co., 1943); Caroline especially enjoyed Devoto's regular column in *Harper's*.

25. Probably the librarian at Mount Holyoke College, where Alden donated the letters she received from Caroline.

26. President Franklin D. Roosevelt died April 12, 1945.

27. James Branch Cabell, *Beyond Life* (New York: R. M. McBride & Co., 1921).

28. A. B. Guthrie, *The Way West* (New York: W. Sloane & Associates, 1949).

29. Eleanor and her family completed a move to Arizona in 1949.

30. The Hendersons maintained a long relationship with the family of Willard Grable. Cecil is his son, and Ann is Cecil's wife.

31. Caroline frequently used scraps of paper for her correspondence as she pursued ever more stringent economics. Letters were written on the backs of greeting cards, advertisements, and even wallpaper.

32. "Bind weed dope" is regional terminology for a poison used to control bind weed.

33. Unidentified reference.

34. Walt Whitman, *Leaves of Grass*, lines 1283–1285.

35. A. S. "Mike" Monroney served in the U.S. Senate from Oklahoma from 1951–1969; despite his concerns about the Optima Dam, construction finally began in 1966 and was completed 12 years later.

36. Probably John O. Knott, *Behind Closed Doors* (New York: Authors & Publishers Corp., 1927).

37. The University of Oklahoma separated black students from whites with a wooden railing from 1948 to 1950. See Gibson, *Oklahoma: A History of Five Centuries*, 403.

38. W. Somerset Maugham, *Of Human Bondage* (New York: Doubleday, Doran, 1932).

39. Probably either Ira Wolfert, *American Guerilla in the Phillippines* (New York: Simon & Schuster, 1945), or Douglas Smith, *American Guerilla Fighting Behind Enemy Lines*, (New York: Bobbs-Merrill, 1943); H. Rider Haggard, *She*, (New York: Longmans, Green, 1887).

40. The Yarbrough school was the public school located closest to the Hendersons.

41. This is probably Lillian Hart (Mrs. Ross Hart), one of Caroline's enduring friends in the community.

42. Harry L. Wilson, *Ruggles of Red Gap*, (Garden City, N.Y.: Doubleday, 1915.

43. George Orwell, *1984* (New York: New American Library, 1949).

44. Johnston Murray served as Oklahoma governor from 1955 to 1959. The bill mentioned here would have permitted cooperative groups to offer phone service as they did grain elevators and other services in rural areas.

Chapter 6: *When Hope Has Gone, 1952–1966*

1. Grandstaff interview.

2. Eli Jaffe, interview with author, Norman, Oklahoma, March 8, 1996; Eli Jaffe to author, February 1, 1996.

3. Walter Van Tilburg Clark, *The Oxbow Incident* (Random House, 1940).

4. In "emergency maize crop," Caroline probably refers to a crop planted

after an earlier crop failed. The term could also describe a crop grown to be held for an emergency, but that does not appear to be the meaning here.

5. J. Frank Dobie, noted author of a number of books on the American west, e.g., J. Frank Dobie, *Apache Gold and Yacqui Silver* (Bramhall House, 1949).

6. *Time*, March 10, 1952, p. 27.

7. Albert N. Williams, *The Water and the Power* (Duell, Sloan, & Pearce, 1951).

8. This contract was for additional cloud seeding efforts to stimulate rain.

9. Puffer was a bird, possibly a nighthawk, who had broken its wing, leaving a bone protruding.

10. Irrigation project near Lees Ferry, Arizona.

11. "Dust out of here" is an example of Caroline's rare use of provincialisms.

12. This is probably Mrs. Ward, one of Caroline's long-time friends from the early years in Texas County.

13. For a description of the bronze tablet, see Henderson to Evelyn Harris, June 21, 1932 (see page 113); William Thomas Hardy, "Afterwards," line 4. The line actually reads: "He was a man who used to notice such things."

14. Joseph McCarthy, U.S. Senator from Wisconsin, 1946–1957, was a leading anti-Communist spokesman.

15. Here Caroline probably refers to Jaffe's effort to write a play about a 1930s labor organizer. That play and other unpublished writings are in the Jaffe Collection.

16. Walter Lippmann (1889–1974) was a leading political commentator with regular articles in major periodicals.

17. Robert Louis Stevenson, *Virginibus Puerisque* (C. Kegan Paul, 1881), chapter 4: "El Dorado," last sentence.

18. Acts 26:19, KJV.

19. *Brown vs. Board of Education*, 347 U.S. 483 (1954). This decision required the integration of public schools.

20. This probably refers to problems with static electricity that may result from drought and wind.

21. This is probably the 1953 film, *Martin Luther*, directed by Irving Pichel.

22. Matthew 16:24, KJV; Kathryn Hulme, *The Nun's Story* (Boston: Little, Brown & Co., 1956); A. J. Cronin, *The Keys of the Kingdom*: (Boston: Little, Brown & Co., 1969).

23. The Clearwater Dam was completed in 1972 on the Clearwater River near Ahsahka, Idaho. The "Wichita Mountain give away" refers to efforts by the army to acquire some of the Wichita Mountain Wildlife Refuge near Lawton, Oklahoma, in order to expand the adjacent Fort Sill. The effort

was successful a few years later. See Fort Sill, Morris Swett Technical Library, Vertical File Collection, U.S. 25 A186C61.

24. Barry M. Goldwater, 1964 Republican presidential nominee, served as U.S. Senator from Arizona 1953–1965 and 1969–1987. The Eisenhower resolution became the basis for the "Eisenhower doctrine" committing the U.S. to protecting the Middle East from Communist aggression.

25. This refers to Caroline's first contact with an agent from Selected Investments, which would lead to the loss of most of their investment. A pyramid scheme, Selected Investments flourished and appeared to offer real opportunities for investors through much of the 1950s. Selected investment files, *The Daily Oklahoman Archives.*

26. April 7, 1957, was Caroline's eightieth birthday. The people she mentions seem to be a collection of her friends from Mount Holyoke, former neighbors, and kin.

27. Matthew 10:29, KJV.

28. Probably Porter tomatoes.

29. Eleanor's husband, August Grandstaff, had died earlier that year.

30. Texas County's annual Pioneer Celebrations began in 1933 and have continued since, although the range of activities was reduced significantly during the Second World War. Usually, a parade, old-timers reunions, a rodeo, and similar events mark the chosen date.

31. This refers to unidentified writing by Bernard DeVoto, one of Caroline's favorite writers. She read all of his books and regularly commented on his "Easy Chair" columns in *Harper's Magazine.*

32. *Time,* September 17, 1959.

33. Admiral Hyman G. Rickover (1900–1986) was a noted critic of U.S. schools. His book *Education and Freedom* (Dutton, 1959) identifies many of the concerns he addressed in various forums.

34. This refers to a Rabbi Plotkin, otherwise unidentified.

35. Lewis Browne, *This Believing World* (New York: Macmillan, 1933).

36. Mr. McNee could be either Nile or Rae McNee, who lived nearby; John Foreman lived just north of the Hendersons. Hooker is a nearby town.

37. Unidentified source.

38. Peter Hurd (1904–1984) was an American artist noted for his landscapes of the Southwest.

39. I. J. and Arthur Strothman both lived in the Four Corners area, as did Jim Jordan, who maintained a business there from the 1930s until the 1960s.

40. Probably, Charles Neider, "Man Against Nature," *Harper's,* 1954.

41. Alan Moorehead, *No Room in the Ark* (New York: Harper Collins Publishers, 1960).

42. Probably Roger T. Peterson, *Wild America* (Boston: Houghton-Mifflin, 1955).

43. The arrangement here described provided for the man identified only

as Lee to work the farm and maintain its property in return for a percentage of the income.

44. This is probably Cecil and Ann Hart.

45. Rabindranath Tagore, unidentified reference.

Epilogue: Lover of the Soil

1. Henderson, "The Love of the Soil," 2–6.

2. See Henderson to Rose Alden, May 29, 1939 (see page 174).

3. "The Last Poem," October 22, 1930; "A Lonesome World," March 26, 1931; and, "The Things Not Seen," April 23, 1931 (not included herein).

Bibliography

Archives and Interviews

Alden, Rose. Alumni Files. Mount Holyoke College Archives and Special
    Collections. Mount Holyoke College. South Hadley, Mass.
The Daily Oklahoman Archives. Oklahoma Christian University. Oklahoma
    City, Oklahoma.
Fort Sill, Oklahoma. Morris Swett Technical Library. Vertical File Collection.
Grandstaff, Eleanor. Grandstaff Collection, 1908–1965. Amherstberg, Ontario.
Grandstaff, Eleanor. Interview by author. Amherstberg, Ontario, December
    29, 1997.
Harris, Evelyn. File. Betterton Library Vertical Files, Betterton, Maryland.
Henderson, Caroline A. Papers, 1908–1967. Manuscript Number MS 0547.
    LD 7096.6 1901 Boa. Mount Holyoke College Archives and Special
    Collections. South Hadley, Mass.
Jaffe, Eli. Jaffe Collection. The Western History Collection. The University
    of Oklahoma. Norman, Okla.

Books

Andryszewski, Tricia. *The Dust Bowl: Disaster on the Plains.* Brookfield,
    Conn.: Millbrook Press, 1993.
Argow, Keith A. *Our National Grasslands: Dustland to Grassland. American
    Forests,* January 1962. [Reprinted by the U.S. Forest Service for official
    use, n.d.].
Bennett, Hugh Hammond. *Soil Conservation.* New York: McGraw-Hill,
    1939.
Bonnifield, Paul. *The Dust Bowl: Men, Dirt and Depression.* Albuquerque:
    University of New Mexico Press, 1979.
Chandler, Lester V. *America's Greatest Depression, 1929–1941.* New York:
    Harper and Row, 1970.
Conrad, David Eugene. *The Forgotten Farmers: The Story of Sharecroppers in
    the New Deal.* Urbana: University of Illinois Press, 1965.
Cunningham, Agnes "Sis," and Gordon Friesen. *Red Dust and Broadsides: A*

Joint Autobiography. Edited by Ronald D. Cohen. Amherst: University of Massachusetts Press, 1999.

Dana, Richard Henry. *Two Years Before the Mast.* New York: The World Publishing Co., 1946.

Drake, Laurence, Leonard A. Solomon, and Harry Birdwell. *History of Conservation in Oklahoma.* Oklahoma Association of Conservation Districts, privately printed [1979?].

Dyck, Mary Knackstedt. *Waiting on the Bounty: The Dust Bowl Diary of Mary Knackstedt Dyck.* Edited by Pamela Riney-Kehrberg. Iowa City: University of Iowa Press, 1999.

Faulkner, Edward H. *Plowman's Folly.* Norman: University of Oklahoma Press, 1943.

Ganzel, Bill. *Dust Bowl Descent.* Lincoln: University of Nebraska Press, 1984.

Gibson, Arrell. *Oklahoma: A History of Five Centuries.* Norman, Okla.: Harlow Publishing Corporation, 1965.

Graham, Otis L., Jr., and Meghan Robinson Wander. *Franklin D. Roosevelt, His Life and Times: An Encyclopedic View.* Old Tappan, N.J.: Macmillan Publishing Co., 1985.

Green, George D. "Great Depression." In *Franklin D. Roosevelt: His Life and Times; An Encyclopedic View,* edited by Otis L. Graham Jr. and Meghan Robinson Wander, 162–66. G. K. Hall, 1985.

Hargraves, Mary W. M. *Dry Farming in the Northern Great Plains, 1900–1925.* Cambridge: Harvard University Press, 1957.

Harris, Evelyn A. *The Barter Lady: A Woman Farmer Sees It Through.* Garden City, N.Y.: Doubleday-Doran, 1934.

The History of Plymouth and Woodbury Counties [Iowa]. N.p., A. Warner and Co., n.d.

Hoig, Stan. "The Rail Line That Opened the Unassigned Lands." In *Railroads in Oklahoma,* edited by Donovan L. Hofsommer, 19–30. Oklahoma City, Okla.: Oklahoma Historical Society, 1977.

Hudson, Lois Phillips. *Reapers of the Dust: A Prairie Chronicle.* St. Paul: Minnesota Historical Society Press, 1984.

Hurt, R. Douglas. *The Dust Bowl: An Agricultural and Social History.* Chicago: Nelson-Hall, 1981.

Husband, Joseph. *America at Work.* Boston: Houghton, Mifflin, 1915.

Jacks, Graham Vernon, and Robert Orr Whyte. *Vanishing Lands: A World Survey of Soil Erosion.* New York: Doubleday, Doran, 1939.

Jaffe, Eli. *Oklahoma Odyssey.* Hyde Park, N.Y.: Eli Jaffe, 1933.

Johnson, Vance. *Heaven's Tableland: The Dust Bowl Story.* New York: Farrar, Straus, 1947.

Jones, E. Stanley. *The Christ of the Indian Road.* New York: Abingdon Press, 1925.

Kraenzel, Carl Frederick. *The Great Plains.* Norman: The University of Oklahoma Press, 1969.

Kramer, Dale. *The Wild Jackasses: The American Farmer in Revolt.* New York: Hastings House, 1956.

Lauber, Patricia. *Dust Bowl: The Story of Man on the Great Plains.* New York: Coward-McCann, 1958.

Lord, Russell. *Behold Our Land.* Boston: Houghton Mifflin, 1938.

Low, Ann Marie. *Dust Bowl Diary.* Lincoln: University of Nebraska Press, 1984.

Malin, James. *The Grassland of North America: Prolegomena to Its History.* Lawrence, Kans.: James Malin, 1947.

McWilliams, Carey. *Ill Fares the Land: Migrants and Migratory Labor in the United States.* Boston: Little, Brown, 1942.

Mitchell, Broadus. *Depression Decade: From New Era Through New Deal, 1929–1941.* New York: Rinehart, 1947.

Morgan, Anne Hodges, and Rennard Strickland. *Oklahoma Memories.* Norman: The University of Oklahoma Press, 1981.

Osburn, Fairfield. *Our Plundered Planet.* Boston: Little, Brown, 1948.

Parks, William Robert. *Soil Conservation Districts in Action.* Ames: Iowa State College Press, 1952.

Rainey, George. *No Man's Land.* Enid, Okla.: George Rainey, 1937.

Riney-Kehrberg, Pamela. *Rooted in Dust: Surviving Drought and Depression in Southwestern Kansas.* Lawrence: University Press of Kansas, 1994.

Rister, Carl Coke. *No Man's Land.* Norman: University of Oklahoma Press, 1948.

Robinson, David. *The Unitarians and the Universalists.* Westport, Conn.: Greenwood Press, 1985.

Rosenberg, Norman J., ed. *North American Droughts.* Boulder, Colo.: Westview Press, 1978.

Saloutos, Theodore, and John D. Hicks. *Agricultural Discontent in the Middle West, 1900–1939.* Madison: University of Wisconsin Press, 1951.

Sears, Paul B. *Deserts on the March.* Norman: University of Oklahoma Press, 1935.

Shannon, David, ed. *The Great Depression.* Englewood Cliffs, N.J.: Prentice-Hall, 1960.

Shover, John L. *Cornbelt Rebellion: The Farmers' Holiday Association.* Urbana: University of Illinois Press, 1956.

Smith, Henry Nash. *Virgin Land.* Cambridge: Harvard University Press, 1970.

Steinbeck, John. *The Grapes of Wrath.* New York: Viking Press, 1939.

Svobida, Lawrence. *An Empire of Dust.* Caldwell, Idaho: Caxton Printers, 1940.

———. *Farming the Dust Bowl.* Topeka: University Press of Kansas, 1996.

Tannehill, Ivan Ray. *Drought: Its Causes and Effects.* Princeton, N.J.: Princeton University Press, 1947.

Texhoma Genealogical and Historical Society, comp. and ed. *Panhandle Pioneers.* 4 vols. Texhoma, Okla: The Texhoma Times, 1970.

Vestal, Stanley. *Short Grass Country.* New York: Duell, Sloan & Pearce, 1941.

Warrick, Richard A. *Drought on the Great Plains: A Case Study on Climate and Society in the USA.* Worcester, Mass.: Clark University, Center for Technology, Environment, and Development, 1980.

Watkins, T. H. *The Great Depression.* Boston: Little, Brown, 1993.

Weaver, J. E., and F. W. Albertson. *Grasslands of the Great Plains.* Lincoln, Nebr.: Johnsen Publishing, 1956.

Webb, David D. "The Thomas Amendment: A Rural Oklahoma Response to the Great Depression." In *Rural Oklahoma,* edited by Donald E. Green, 101–12. Oklahoma City: Oklahoma Historical Society, 1977.

Wecter, Dixon. *The Age of the Great Depression, 1929–1941.* New York: Macmillan, 1948.

Worster, Donald. *Dust Bowl: The Southern Plains in the 1930s.* New York: Oxford University Press, 1979.

Wunder, John R., Frances W. Kaye, and Vernon Carstensen, eds. *Americans View Their Dust Bowl Experience.* Niwot, Colo.: University Press of Colorado, 1999.

Articles

Baird, W. David. "Agriculture in the Oklahoma Panhandle, 1898–1942." *The Chronicles of Oklahoma* 72 (Summer 1994): 116–37.

Davenport, W. "Land Where Our Children Die." *Collier's* 100 (September 18, 1937): 12–13.

Dorman, Robert L. "The Tragical Agrarianism of Alfalfa Bill Murray: The Sage of Tishomingo." *The Chronicles of Oklahoma* 66 (Fall 1988): 240–67.

Floyd, Fred. "The Struggle for Railroads in the Oklahoma Panhandle." *The Chronicles of Oklahoma* 54 (Winter 1976–1977): 489–518.

Fossey, W. Richard. "'Talking Dust Bowl Blues': A Study of Oklahoma's Cultural Identity During the Great Depression." *The Chronicles of Oklahoma* 55 (Spring 1977): 12–33.

Henderson, Caroline A. "A Little Turkey Talk." *Practical Farmer,* February 13, 1912.

———. "Bubbles." *Ladies' World,* ca. Spring 1914.

———. "Bringing in the Sheaves." *Atlantic Monthly* 148 (November 1931): 576–80.

———. "Dust to Eat" (July 16, 1935). Edited by Virginia C. Purdy. *The Chronicles of Oklahoma* 58 (Winter 1980–1981): 440–52.

———. Four untitled pieces. *Practical Farmer,* February 8 and 15, April 19, June 14, 1913.

———. "Letters from the Dust Bowl." *Atlantic Monthly* 157 (May 1936): 540–51. Reprinted in Anne Hodges Morgan and Rennard Strickland,

Oklahoma Memories, 224–44. Norman: The University of Oklahoma Press, 1981; and in John Wunder, Frances W. Kaye, and Vernon Carstenson, *Americans View their Dust Bowl*, 93–112. Niwot, Colo.: University Press of Colorado, 1999, 93–112.

———. "Letters from the Dust Bowl." *Reader's Digest* (September 1936): 19–21.

———. "Our Homestead," *Ladies' World,* February 1914, 14–15, 28.

———. "Our Own Letter from the Dust Bowl." *American Chamber of Commerce Journal* (January 1937): 14–15, 45.

———. "Relaxation." *Ladies' World*, ca. Spring 1914.

———. "Spring in the Dust Bowl." *Atlantic Monthly* 159 (June 1937): 715–17.

———. "The Love of the Soil as a Motivating Force in Literature Relating to the Early Development of the Middle West." Master's thesis, University of Kansas, 1935.

———. "The Woman Who Raised Her Hand." *Christian Register,* November 15, 1927, 720–21.

———. "Turkeys for Profit." *Practical Farmer,* April 13, 1912.

———. "What I Read Last Year." *Practical Farmer,* May 4, 1912.

Henderson, Caroline, and Evelyn Harris, "Letters of Two Women Farmers I." *Atlantic Monthly* 152 (August 1933): 236–45.

———. "Letters of Two Women Farmers II." *Atlantic Monthly* 152 (September 1933): 349–56.

Langham, Wright H., Richard L. Foster, and Harley A. Daniel. "The Amount of Dust in the Air at Plant Height During Wind Storms at Goodwell, Oklahoma, in 1936–1937." *Journal of the American Society of Agronomy* 30 (February 1938): 139–44.

Lookingbill, Brad. "'A God-forsaken Place': Folk Eschatology and the Dust Bowl." *Great Plains Quarterly* 14 (Fall 1994): 273–86.

———. "Likely Stories: Historians and the Dust Bowl Moment." Paper presented at the annual meeting of the Mid America Historical Association, Stillwater, Okla., September 1997.

———. "Dusty Apocalypse and Socialist Salvation: A Study of Woody Guthrie's Dust Bowl Imagery." *The Chronicles of Oklahoma* 72 (Winter 1994–1995): 396–413.

Malin, James. "Dust Storms: Part One, 1850–1860." *Kansas Historical Quarterly* 14 (May 1946): 129–44.

———. "Dust Storms: Part Two, 1861–1880." *Kansas Historical Quarterly* 14 (August 1946): 265–96.

———. "Dust Storms: Part Three, 1881–1900—Concluded." *Kansas Historical Quarterly* 14 (November 1946): 391–413.

McDean, Harry C. "Dust Bowl Historiography." *Great Plains Quarterly* 6 (Spring 1986): 117–26.

Petersen, Peter L. "A New Oslo on the Plains." *Panhandle Plains Historical Review,* 1976.

Pratt, William C. "Rethinking the Farm Revolt of the 1930s." *Great Plains Quarterly* 8 (Summer 1988): 131–44.

Purdy, Virginia C. "Dust To Eat." *The Chronicles of Oklahoma* 58 (Winter 1980–1981): 440–52.

Saloutos, Theodore. "The New Deal and Farm Policy in the Great Plains." *Agricultural History* 43 (July 1969): 345–55.

Schwieder, Dorothy and Deborah Fink. "Plains Women: Rural Life in the 1930s." *Great Plains Quarterly* 8 (Spring 1988): 79–88.

Ware, James. "The Sooner N.R.A.: New Deal Recovery in Oklahoma." *The Chronicles of Oklahoma* 54 (Fall 1976): 339–51.

Webb, Walter Prescott. "The American West: Perpetual Mirage." *Harper's Magazine* 214 (May 1957): 37–38.

Weisiger, Marsha L. "The Reception of *The Grapes of Wrath* in Oklahoma: A Reappraisal." *The Chronicles of Oklahoma* 70 (Winter 1992–1993): 394–415.

Worster, Donald. "The Dirty Thirties: A Study in Agricultural Capitalism." *Great Plains Quarterly* 6 (Spring 1986): 107–16.

Government Documents

Clark, Everett R. *A Preliminary Report of the Growth and Effectiveness of Windbreaks in the High Plains Area of Oklahoma.* Panhandle [Oklahoma] Agricultural Experiment Station Bulletin, No. 55. Goodwell, Okla.: Panhandle [Oklahoma] Agricultural Experiment Station, 1934.

Daniel, Harley A. *Calculated Net Income Resulting from Level Terraces on Richfield Silt Loam Soil and Suggested Lines of Defense Against Wind Erosion.* Panhandle [Oklahoma] Agricultural Experiment Station Bulletin, No. 58. Goodwell, Okla.: Panhandle Agricultural Experiment Station, 1935.

Langham, Wright H. *Fertility Losses from High Plains Soils Due to Wind Erosion.* Panhandle [Oklahoma] Agricultural Experiment Station Bulletin, No. 63. Goodwell, Okla.: Panhandle Agricultural Experiment Station, 1937.

U.S. Congress. House. *The Future of the Great Plains.* The Report of the Great Plains Committee to the House of Representatives. 75th Cong., 1st sess., 1937. S. Doc. 144.

U.S. Department of Agriculture. Agricultural Adjustment Administration. *Agricultural Adjustment: A Report of Administration of the Agricultural Adjustment Act May 1933 to February 1934.* Washington, D.C.: GPO, 1934.

————. Agricultural Adjustment Administration. *Agricultural Adjustment in 1934.* Washington, D.C.: GPO, 1935.

————. Bureau of Agricultural Economics. "Land Acquisition Plan: Tri-State Land Utilization and Land Conservation Project, Part I." Project Symbol: LU-NM-38-21. Kiowa Grasslands Office, Clayton, New Mexico. Prepared March 23, 1938.

Web Sites

National Archives and Records Administration Web site, "General Records of the Soil Erosion Service and the Soil Conservation Service, 1915–77." Online. Available at: *www.nara.gov/guide/rg114.html#114.2.* January 3, 2001.

Oklahoma Department of Commerce Web site, "Demographic Forum, C: City Population Estimates, Historical Census Population—City by County, 1890–1990." Online. Available at: *http://www.odoc.state.ok.us/osdc.htm.* January 1, 2001.

Smithsonian National Postal Museum Web site, "V-mail: Learn More about It." Online. Available at: *www.si.edu/postal/learnmore/vmail.html.* January 6, 2001.

Index

Accounting, 194, 196–97, 227, 230, 234

Aging: challenges summarized, 21–22; concerns expressed, 167; social isolation, 27; standard of living, 26; Ulysses allusion, 154, 253n.16

Agricultural Adjustment Act (AAA), 138, 143, 144–45, 153, 158

Alden, Mrs.: letters to, 58–60, 77–79, 105–106, 121–24, 249n.5

Alden, Rose: background, 31–32; collecting Caroline's letters, 186; as donor of reading materials, 8; *Ladies' World* writings not acknowledged to, 12; letters to, 33–44, 45–50, 60–62, 72–74, 75–77, 85–87, 91–92, 95–96, 103–105, 119–21, 124–25, 163, 169–70, 174–75, 182–84, 186, 221–23, 249n.5; Mount Holyoke collection, 52; not saving some letters, 63–64

American Chamber of Commerce Journal: "Our Own Letter from the Dust Bowl," 159–62

American dream, 143–44

American Red Cross, 81, 82, 111–12

America at Work, 124

Anti-hoarding, 108

April, 74

Art: views on, 234

Atlantic Monthly: "Bringing in the Sheaves," 17, 96–100, 103; first article, 17; "Letters from the Dust Bowl," 137, 147–57; letters suggested, 121; "Letters of Two Women Farmers" (I and II), 17–18, 93–94, 106–19; Rose sending stories from, 75; "Spring in the Dust Bowl," 163–66

Automobiles, 208–209

"Backgrounds: Another Letter from Our Homestead Lady," 68–69

Baker, William ("Uncle Bill"), 171, 254n.3

Bankers, 108

Beaver county, 11

Beebe, William, 107, 251n.13

Behind Closed Doors, 199

Beyond Life, 189

Bible: daily reading of, 45; and standards for life, 69; Will's interest in, 6, 37

Biography, 68–69

Birthday celebration, 221–22, 258n.26

Blister beetles: and crop destruction, 58

Boa, Mrs. (mother), 77, 105; visits, 73, 76, 92, 95

Boa, Robert (father), 4–5; death of, 45–46

Boa, Susan (Susie) (sister), 5, 34, 59, 77; health, 105; newspaper article with, 167; reading materials, 73

"Bringing in the Sheaves," 17, 96–100

Broomcorn farming: described, 246n.24, 249n.7; harvesting, 55–56; overproduction, 78; prices, 39; pulling, 86; rain at harvest, 48; threshing, 55–56

Brown, John, 95

Browne, Alice, 38, 249n.9
Browne, Lewis, 229
Brown v. Board of Education (1954), 215, 257n.19
Buffalo grass, 71, 78
Bumper crops: of 1919–26, 14; post-war, 24

Cabell, James Branch, 189
Carlyle, Thomas, 69
Carrel, Alexis, 158
Cather, Willa, 206
Cattle raising: calving, 177, 202–203, 222, 234; dairy prices, 78; Depression era, 117, 145–46; drought, 115, 150; and dust storms, 19, 148; feed programs, 151; frontier, 10; hailstorm, 110; herd of 1947, 86; as income source, 7; lack of grass, 214; meat prices, 203; names for cows, 78; native grasses, 152, 174; in 1950, 197; scattered grazing, 166; selling off, 190, 231; shipped to pasture, 148, 153–54; success, 185; water, 102; after Will's accident, 160; winter storms, 220, 221, 229
Century Magazine, 48, 249n.18
Cereals, 84–85
Charities, 28, 111, 120, 228
Cherry trees, 216, 225
Chicago's Columbian Exposition (1893), 208
Chicken raising: Depression era, 156; early success, 38–39, 48, 57, 58; Eleanor as young helper, 59; feed for, 224, 226; henhouse toppled, 189; overview, 7; permanent chicken-house, 71; prices low, 43, 123; starting out, 36; winter storm, 219–20
Christianity: hope of heaven as motive, 85
Christian Leader, 103
Christian Register: letter published in, 64, 87–90
Christ of the Indian Road, 125

Christmas: sad memories, 172
Citizenship, 75
Citizens' petition, 113
Civilian Conservation Corps (CCC), 138, 185
Civil Works Administration (CWA), 138, 144
Clearwater Dam, 218, 257n.23
Cold weather, 121–22, 193; blizzards, 182, 219–20, 222, 224–25, 227, 228; in cabin, 42; dread of, 116; dust storms, 207; houses, 122; in 1950s, 207, 208, 209; without electricity, 199
Colorado village experience, 21, 241
Communist Party (U.S.): Caroline's views observed, 23. *See also* Jaffe, Eli
Conservation plans, 166
Contour farming, 149, 151, 152; heavy rains, 161; need for rain, 157, 160, 216–17; results, 155, 163
Cooperative movements, 175
Corn: harvesting, 55; later dominance, 249n.7
Cornerstone, 151, 162
Cotton, 211
Cottonwoods, 67–68
Country Gentleman, 94, 121
County relief administration, 144
Cousin from Canada, 73, 77, 85
Cow chips, for fuel, 49, 118, 249n.19
Cow peas, 46, 70, 115
Credit, 113
Criminal syndicalism charge, 23, 179, 254–55nn.14,16
Crop failures: Depression era, 146, 153; in 1940s, 189; overview, 9
Crop reduction programs. *See* Wheat acreage reduction program
Cutworms, 122

Dairy: Depression era, 110; early years, 39–40, 55, 58, 70–71
Dana, Richard Henry, Jr., 66
Dawson, Lieutenant, 85
"Day When the Well Runs Dry, The," 7, 100–103

Debt, 113, 118

Democracy, 80

Department of Agriculture, 166

Devoto, Bernard, 32, 186, 226, 255n.24, 258n.31

Dickens, Charles, 47

Dictators, 176, 179

Dignity, human, 19

Dinosaur pit, 150, 159

Disappointment, 67

Dobie, J. Frank, 208, 209

Domestic duties: sharing, 6–7, 44

Donations to causes, 28

Droughts: Depression era, 18, 115, 117, 122, 124, 141, 147, 148, 149, 150–51, 157, 158, 164, 169; as divine punishment, 142; and hot winds, 53; longing for rain, 146–47; New Deal, 138; of 1909, 37–38; of 1911, 42–43; of 1912–13, 12, 50, 58; of 1916, 78; of 1918, 85; of 1950s, 24, 217; Webb perspective, 10

Ducks, 171

Dust Bowl, 3, 23

Dust bowl: challenge to quality of life, 242; conditions in late 1940s, 189; end of, 24; farmers' contribution, 141; farmlands described, 141–42; map, 139; recovery and "comeback," 171–72; in 1951, 200; in 1954–55, 214; in 1956, 216–17; resuming in 1952, 205, 207, 210–11, 212

"Dust bowl moment," 3–4

Dust devils, 154, 253n.17

Dust to eat, 19, 140, 141

"Dust to Eat," 137, 140–47

Dust pneumonia, 19, 148

Dust storms: abandonment of farms, 148; Caroline's descriptions of, 137; cattle raising, 148; conservation to reduce, 138; Depression era, 123, 124–25; driving in, 123; eating during, 55; effects indoors, 140–41, 147, 154; emotional toll, 19–20, 154; erosion control, 148–49; farming, 160; first experience, 54–55; help-lessness and frustration, 164; illness, 148; jack rabbits, 165; in 1938, 169; overview, 18–19; painting house, 154; spring, 164–66; terrifying cloud, 171; visibility, 19, 140, 147, 164, 235; worst in 1937, 164

Education: Caroline's views of summarized, 16, 17; doubts about her use of, 242; Master's degree (Caroline), 17; nature of, 79–80; neighbors' views of summarized, 16–17; overview, 5

Egg money, 7, 39, 78, 123, 183, 197, 201, 234

Eleanor Henderson. *See* Grandstaff, (Sarah) Eleanor Henderson

Elections, 47, 119–20

Electricity: bills, 235; breakdowns, 210, 219, 220; economies with, 26–27, 208, 230; electric blanket, 225; electrification, 195; static, 216; storms, 229; stove, 230

Elkhart flour mill, 151–52

Emerson, Ralph Waldo, 65

Erosion control, 148–49, 152; experiments, 157; handicap, 165; native grass pastures, 174; report, 153; results, 155

Eva, Okla.: map, 6

Evangelists, 15, 88–89, 251n.16

Expenses, farm, 194, 196–97

Failure, sense of, 21–22, 205

Family, importance of, 28

Farmers: crop reduction, 143; expenses, 153; "suitcase," 151; survival during Depression, 118

Farmers' movement, 118, 252n.25

Farm help, 181, 182, 184

Farming, changes, 4

Farm women, 75

Federal Emergency Relief Administration (FERA), 138, 144

Feterita, 78

First World War: antiwar sentiments, 81; entering the war, 84; knitting for soldiers, 81; nephew from Canada, 73, 77, 85; optimism and failure, 83; people's contribution, 81–82, 84; prices, 13; soldiers returning from, 87; unity theme, 81, 82, 84; writings, 13

Flour millers, 151–52

Flowers, 233, 236, 237; dust conditions, 141, 157; as extravagance, 80; hollyhocks, 201; larkspurs, 210; in 1950s, 213, 223; rose catalog, 200; spring, 222–23; tamarix, 232; window boxes, 107

Foreclosures, 155–56

Foreign policy, 162, 218–19; 258n.24

Fort Sill, 218

Friendships, 122

Frost, Robert, 166

Fullness of life, 9

Garden, 36, 86; dust storms, 211; failures, 58; hailstorm, 110; ploughing, 194; significance of, 7; successes, 57, 185, 187; variety in, 46–47, 334

Gilbert, Mabel, 47, 249n.10

Goldwater, Barry, 218, 258n.24

Government, 125; aid, 157; aid criticisms rebutted, 144–46

Grandstaff, August: illness and death, 24–25, 224; marriage, 139; work, 178

Grandstaff, David Eugene, 24, 190, 224, 228, 232, 235, 236, 237

Grandstaff, (Sarah) Eleanor Henderson: accomplishments, 22; announcement of parents' deaths, 239–40; Arizona, 183, 190; asthma, 183; birth, 11, 53; child, 190; childhood, 48–49, 68, 76, 77, 79; correspondence with, 23–24, 28–29; education, 15–16; expecting child, 168, 187, 188–89; function of letters to, 205; harvesting, 96, 99, 152; health issues, 188, 216, 217; high school, 15–16; home purchase, 169–70; infancy, 39, 40, 41; Iowa farmhouse, 163; and Eli Jaffe, 181;

letters to, 187, 191–98, 200–204, 207–13, 216–17, 218–21, 223–28, 229–30, 231–39; marriage, 139, 158–59; Master's degree in literature, 206; medical training, 16, 104, 105, 114, 122, 123, 124, 139; professional success, 175, 178; research, 170; responsibility for Robert, 170; at the University of Kansas, 91, 104

Grapes of Wrath, The, 176, 179

Grasshoppers, 46, 58, 111

Gray hair, 48, 73

Great American Desert, 10

Great Depression: "Bringing in the Sheaves" article, 17; conditions, 106–107; documenting impact, 93; effects of, 117; farmers' survival, 118; financial disaster, 109; letters on effects of, 17–18; politicians, 102, 104, 251n.9; prices, 18; prices falling, 103–104, 106–107; reasons for staying, 149–50; social deterioration, 155, 253n.18; wheat donations for relief work, 111–12; work projects, 144

Great Plains: aridity, 10; history and changes, 4; literature, 17, 206; settlement, 140

"Greetings from 'Our Homestead Lady'," 65–66

Grevstad, Dagny, 43, 246–47n.32

Grevstad, Nicolay A., 246–47n.32

Hale, Edward Everett, 75

Hand-mill for grains, 56, 84–85

Hardy, Thomas, 179

Hardy, William Thomas, 213

Harris, Evelyn, 17–18

Harvesting: *Atlantic Monthly* description, 96–99; away from home, 115, 116; with baby, 40; broomcorn, 55–56; corn, 55; Depression era, 115; early years, 52; help offered, 238–39, 258–59n.43; hired help, 170; machinery repairs, 211; wet season, 185

Hatchery, 156

Health issues: abdominal tumor, 206, 239; anxiety, 167, 178, 191, 221, 222, 226, 230, 231; arthritis, 185; asthma, 167, 178, 237, 238; brain hemorrhage, 189–90; chronic cough, 163; cough, 237; deafness, 236; early illness, 76; eye problems, 188, 191, 237; falls, 189; flu, 178; general deterioration, 167; heart problems, 178; hernia, 182, 185, 188; hip broken, 231; muscle complaints, 191; overview, 22; teeth, 163; tonsils, 180; Will's hope of relief while in Arizona, 214; winter weather, 199; worn down, 175; wrist problems, 188, 230

Heaven's Tableland, 3

Hell: depicted, 88–89

Henderson, Caroline Agnes Boa: background, 4–5; child's birth, 11, 53; death, 29, 240; diptheria, 5, 33; high school remembered, 226; life summarized, 3; marriage, 34, 35, 51, 246n.28

Henderson, Wilhelmine Eugene (Will): accidents, 160, 173; background, 6; death, 29, 240; early description, 34; handyman skills, 7; later relationship with Caroline, 28; meeting Caroline, 5; optimism, 25, 60; thesis dedicated to, 9

History: importance of, 68

Hitler, Adolf, 172

Hoarding, 108, 252n.18

Hobos/tramps, 117, 120

Homeschooling, 13–15

Homestead: expansion of, 11–12; opening, 35–36; patent arriving, 69; "proving up", 59, 63, 249–50n.23

Homesteading: beginning of Caroline's, 5; deciding to stay, 43, 70; moving into house, 51; settlement of Oklahoma Panhandle, 10

Homestead Lady, 11–14

"Homestead Lady's Scribbling Pad, The," 63, 79–85

Hoover, Herbert, 102, 104, 119, 251n.9

Hope, as symbol, 113

Hopkins, Professor, 96

Horse collars, 223

Horses, 36, 114–15, 121, 178

House: additions to, 52; described, 14; improvements to, 38

Hull, Cordell, 162, 254n.21

Humanities, value of, 233

Human rights, 199

Humus, 165

Husband, Joseph, 124

Ickes, Harold, 123, 252n.28

Income tax, 213–14, 227, 228, 234

Indians, 60–61, 72–73, 218; attitudes to, 28

Iowa farmers' movement, 118, 252n.25

Iowa farm home: bequeathing of, 184; income from, 26; inheritance of, 168; repairs to, 163

Irrigation, 161–62, 211

Ise, John, 173, 254n.5

Jack rabbits, 165

Jaffe, Eli: an associate of ejected from Communist Party, 202; beaten severely, 23; book manuscript, 182, 255n.19; Caroline's description of, 169; children, 198–99, 214, 215; comparison of Caroline and Willa Cather, 206; criminal syndicalism charge, 23, 179, 254–55nn.14, 16; giving up Communist views, 227; journalistic success, 173; letters to, 170–74, 184–85, 186–87, 188–90, 198–200, 213–16, 217–18, 228–29, 231; military training, 182, 184; overview, 22–23, 168; trial, 179–81, 254n.13; writing career, 199

January, 74

Jeffersonian vision: Caroline's view of, 5, 9; destruction of, 4, 137; doubts about, 242; love of the land, 9; promise of, 5, 20; quality of life, 20, 242; spirit fulfilled, 242

Johnson, Professor, 96

Johnson, Vance, 3

Kafir (Kafir corn), 249n.7

Keys of the Kingdom, 218

Kohler electric motor, 173, 194–95, 198, 199

Kulaks, 177, 199

Ladies' World magazine: "Backgrounds: Another Letter from Our Homestead Lady," 68–69; critical reflections, 13; demise of, 63; first article, 12; first letter to, 12, 50–51; "Greetings from 'Our Homestead Lady'," 65–66; "The Homestead Lady's Scribbling Pad," 63, 79–85; limits of personal responsibility, 25; "Our Homestead," 51–58; "Our Homestead Lady," 69–71; "Our Homestead Lady's Calendar of Everyday Thoughts," 63, 74, 75; publication in not acknowledged to Rose Alden, 12; reader response, 12; "Relaxation," 66–68; significance of articles, 64; types of columns, 63

Lamb, Charles, 8, 45

Land, abandoned, 165, 241; increasing acreage, 14

Land, love of: educated settlers', 16; interests and writings, 4; in Master's thesis, 20; mutual commitment to, 8–11; pagan, 119; unforgiving land, 241

Laundry. *See* Washing

Laws of the universe, 166

Letters: joy from, 65–66

"Letters from the Dust Bowl," 137, 147–57

"Letters of Two Women Farmers" (I and II), 17–18, 93–94, 106–19

Liberal arts tradition, 4

Liberal Center (Unitarian), 173

Lincoln, Abraham, 75

Lindbergh, Charles, 180

Lippman, Walter, 215

Listing, 145, 149, 253n.8; basin-type, 162

Long, Stephen, 10

Loss, sense of: defeat, 241; letters to Eleanor, 24; loss of hope mourned, 223, 226; measurement of success, 242–43; observed, 20, 21–22

"Love of the Soil as a Motivating Force in Literature Relating to the Early Development of the Middle West, The": described, 20; discussed, 8–9, 241–42; writers examined in, 20. *See also* Master's thesis

Luther, Martin, 217

McCarthy, Joseph, 214, 257n.14

Machinery: harvesting, 96, 97; overview, 22; pick-up, 234; purchasing, 14; repairs and expenses, 172, 211, 212, 225, 226; worn out, 178, 233

McLaren, Grissell, 38, 158, 249n.8

Maize crop: "emergency," 207, 256–57n.4

Maize-heading, 55

Man, the Unknown, 158

Man Against Nature, 235

Manchester Guardian, 176, 177

Maps: Eva, Okla., 6; dust bowl, 139

Married life, 34, 35, 51, 246n.28

Masters, Edgar Lee, 162, 185

Master's degree in literature, 17, 95

Master's thesis: ambivalence about land expressed in, 241–42; discussed, 8–9; "Giants of the Earth," 91, 251n.18; personal insights, 20. *See also* "Love of the Soil as a Motivating Force in Literature Relating to the Early Development of the Middle West, The"

Mendohlson, Jack, 27

Mental furnishings, 74

Milo maize, 165

Monroney, A. S. ("Mike"), 198, 256n.35

Montessori, Maria, 67

Moral character, 144

Mordt, Anders L., 247n.32

Mordt, Dagny Grevstad. *See* Grevstad, Dagny

Mount Holyoke College: Henderson Collection, 32; reunions, 41, 175
Muir, John, 80, 124
Murdock, Victor, 32, 186

Native grasses, 141, 152, 172; pastures, 174
Nature, love of, 119
Nelson, J. H., 17
New Deal: criticisms of, 144–45; role of, 138. *See also* individual programs
New Mexico: dust storms, 165
Nice, Margaret Morse, 159
No Man's Land, 10–11
Normalcy, 119–20
"No Room at the Ark," 235
Nun's Story, The, 218

Of Human Bondage, 200
Oil fields, 61–62
Oklahoma Territory, 11
O'Leary, R. D., 17, 93
Optimism, 147, 157, 183
Organic Act (1890), 11
Orwell, George, 202
"Our Homestead," 51–58
"Our Homestead Lady," 69–71
"Our Homestead Lady's Calendar of Everyday Thoughts," 63, 74, 75
"Our Own Letter from the Dust Bowl," 159–62
Out-migration, 139, 146, 148; erosion control, 165; reasons for staying, 149–50; recovery discussions, 161–62
Overproduction, 99

Panhandle: drought conditions, 10; region described, 10–11; settlement, 10–11
Panhandle College, 176
Parity prices, 125
Patriotism, 80, 85
Peabody, Francis, 16
Peace, 162, 185, 187, 190
Peanuts, 46, 115
Pearl Harbor, 181

Peasants, 97, 179; Kulaks, 177, 199
Pets, 123, 208, 210, 231, 235
Pictures, references to, 60
Pie-melon (rhubarb), 57, 249n.21
Pigs, 193
Pilot training, 183
Pioneer Day celebration, 225, 258n.30
Pioneer experience, 4; fascination of, 9; meaning of dreams, 21; writers, 20
Poetry, 45, 96; interest in, 8; "Souls," 72
Ponca Reservation, 60–61
Population decline: Depression era, 139, 148, 151; dust storms, 19; educated people, 16; mid-century, 27; onset, 11; social isolation, 14
Poverty: in Chicago, 107–108; Depression era, 120; regimentation of, 145
Practical Farmer: payments from, 48; "What I Read Last Year," 44–45; writing for, 13, 31
Prairie Acre, 114, 213
Prices: broomcorn farming, 39; dairy, 78; Depression era, 113, 154; exchange values, 143; farmers' holiday plan, 118; First World War, 13; Great Depression, 18, 93, 94, 247n.37; in 1913, 50; parity, 125; Second World War, 167; wheat, 99–100, 103–104, 111, 115
Production, controlled, 143
Prussic acid, 150, 253n.11
Public library, 60
Public opinion, 80
Public Works Administration (PWA), 138
Putney, Robert (nephew): in Chicago, 181, 188; at Christmas, 172; described, 168; and music, 173–74; studies, 170, 171; war time, 183, 185, 187, 188; working on farm, 191, 192; worrying about, 200

Quality of life: details of daily comforts, 21; Jeffersonian vision denied, 20, 242

Race relations, 215–16; overview, 28
Racial issues, 199
Railroads: arrival of, 49, 57; No Man's
    Land, 11; memories of early, 208;
    wheat donations, 111, 112
Rain making, 209
Reaching for the Stars, 174
Reading, 44–45, 47; books as birthday
    gifts, 44, 80; broadening perspec-
    tive, 68–69; dog story, 80; early
    days, 36–37; evenings for, 7–8; fic-
    tion, 44; periodicals, 45, 73; poetry,
    45; public library, 60; sources, 8;
    Will's later, 200. *See also* individual
    titles; "What I Read Last Year"
Recovery, agricultural, 118, 167, 171;
    economic, 156; improvements,
    174–75
Red Cross, 81, 82; and wheat dona-
    tions, 111–12
Regimentation idea, 145
Rehabilitation Service, 157, 253–54n.19
"Relaxation," 66–68
Relief programs: country administra-
    tion, 144; Oklahoman's wish to
    avoid, 150
Religion: Caroline's views, 242–43;
    Christian principles, 125; conflicts
    over, 15; universal principles, 229;
    Will's early, 6. *See also* "Woman
    Who Raised Her Hand, The"
Repossession, of farm land, 146
Restful thoughts, 68
Retirement, 25–26, 238; financial self-
    limitations, 26–27; means for, 200;
    security for old age, 118
Revival meetings, 15, 88–89, 251n.16
Revival preachers, 142
Rollers, 19. *See also* Dust storms
Roosevelt, Eleanor, 228
Roosevelt, Franklin D., 119, 120, 186
Rossetti, Christina, 109
Ruggles of Red Gap, 201
Running water, 186, 190
Rural Electrification Authority, 195,
    196
Russian thistle: on abandoned land,

71, 155; as cattle feed, 123, 145, 174;
    described, 250n.9; and dust
    storms, 149

St. Louis, 117
Schutt, Miriam, 43
Scott, Sir Walter, 107
Seagulls, 161
Second World War: farming boom,
    24; Hitler before, 172, 174; isola-
    tion from, 183; prelude to, 173;
    prices, 167; rationing, 183, 255n.20;
    shortages, 183; as waste, 186
Seed supplies, 165
Segregation, 215–16
Selected Investments, 219, 258n.25
Self-reliance, 150
Self-respect, loss of, 19, 110, 137; work
    projects, 144
Settlers, transitory, 69–70
Sewing, 49, 51, 52
Shelley, Percy Bysshe, 112
Silo maize, 52
Simple living, 74
Social distance from neighbors, 14–17
Socialism, 120, 177
Social isolation: Christmas visits, 49;
    later years, 27; in neighborhood,
    59; trips to town, 49; wartime, 184
Social Security, 219, 234
Soil Conservation Districts, 138
Soil Conservation Service (SCS), 138,
    152, 163, 253n.14
Southern plains, harsh conditions, 10
Soviet Union (former USSR):
    Caroline's views of possibly cen-
    sored, 121, 251–52n.16; foreign pol-
    icy, 177, 190, 218–19; human rights,
    199; non-aggression pact with
    Germany, 176, 265n.8
Spanish settlement, 10
Spiritual leaders, 217
Spiritual needs, 27
"Spring in the Dust Bowl," 138,
    163–66
Stable: construction of, 52
Stamps, 192, 208

Statehood, 11

State school lands, 79, 250n.11

Stevenson, Robert Louis, 215

Stoicism, 59–60

Suitcase farmers, 151

Supreme Court, 153

Tariffs, protective, 145

Taxes, 113, 118

Taxpayers' leagues, 113

Telephone service, 84, 86, 110–11, 252n.20

Terrace farming: machines for, 151; rain destroying, 161; results, 166

Texas county, 11; dust storms, 19; later population levels, 27; population decline, 139

Texhoma, 123

This Believing World, 228–29

Thomas, Norman, 119, 120

Thoreau, Henry David, 47

Threshing, 49; alone, 76–77, 78; broomcorn, 55–56; machinery breakdown, 225

Tolstoy, Leo, 217–18

Topsoil, 165

Tractor sales, 156

Transportation problem, 111–12

Travel: in Arizona, 214; with child, 59; for a Christmas tree, 159; Colorado, 104, 181; Kansas City, 169–70; Lawrence, Kan., 91–92; Mesa Verde Park, 176; New Mexico, 104, 178; in 1910, 53–54; unable to leave the farm, 195–96; visit with mother, 70; visit with mother and sister, 61, 250n.26; Yellowstone, 178–79

Travel books, 69

Tree planting, 107

Turkey raising: articles about, 13; early amusement, 39; early success, 43, 46, 48, 57; Eleanor as young helper, 59; fair start, 39, 55; importance of income, 7; reasons for discontinuing, 13

Typhoid fever, 120

Unearned income, 144

Unitarian church: account of Lawrence founding, 103; dust bowl affects Caroline's beliefs, 27–28; ethical problem, 87–90; Hendersons' belief in, 15, 91; later years, 27; literate qualities, 15; publications of, 8, 173; searching questions, 173

United Brethren church, 87–90

University of Kansas (KU): Caroline's studies, 93; Eleanor accepted, 91–92; Prairie Acre, 114

V-mail, 184, 255n.21

Wallace, Henry A., 3, 22, 153, 253n.15; "Dust to Eat," 137, 140–47

Wanderers, 117, 120

Washing, 196, 197

Washing machine, 178

Wastefulness, 74, 82, 118

Watch repaired, 232

Water and the Power, The, 209

Water pump, 100–103, 109

Water supply, 78–79, 229; irrigation, 162; stock ponds, 142

Way West, The, 193–94

Webb, Walter Prescott, 10

Wells: drilling, 52, 57; for irrigation, 162; selling pipe from, 155. *See also* "Day When the Well Runs Dry, The"

Wellton-Mohawk project, 211

"What I Read Last Year," 44–45

Wheat: crop failures, series of, 141; crop of 1926, 140; crop of 1952, 212, 213; crop recovery, 184; cutworms, 122; Depression era, 115–16, 116–17; donations for relief work, 111–12; failure to plant, 160; first article on, 17; hailstorm, 110; harvest and prices, 116–17; in 1940s, 187, 190; in 1950s, 24, 199, 200, 201–202, 215, 225; overexpansion, 14; precarious condition of, 152; prices, 99–100, 103–104, 111,

115; prospects for 1936, 154–55; ten-year average, 187; yield, 115
Wheat acreage reduction program, 123, 138, 143
Wichita Mountain Wildlife Refuge, 218, 257–58n.23
Wild America, 237
Wind erosion, 141
Windmill, 52, 100–103, 109, 225, 229
Winds of doctrine, 142
Windy conditions, 106
Winter feed, 249n.7; Depression era, 117, 122, 152, 165; exhausted, 182; in 1950s, 212
Winter storms: cattle affected, 86–87; sleet over Christmas, 41–42; snow, 56–57
Witch hunts, 181
"Woman Who Raised Her Hand, The" 64, 87–90

Women: Caroline analyzing pioneers, 20; conquest of frontier, 20, 21; educated, 16, 47
Wood, Robert (Bob), 181, 202, 255n.17
Work: attitudes toward, 100; projects, 144, 153; workday, 7
Works Project Administration (WPA), 138
World wars. *See* First World War; Second World War
Worry, burden of, 25. *See also* Health issues, anxiety
Worster, Donald, 3
Writings: career overview, 3; on First World War, 13; last article, 23; readers' response, 22; status as writer, 22, 23; talent recognized, 137

Yucca plant (soapweed), 70, 145, 166